This book offers an in-depth look at the discourse underpinning Western corporate reporting. It provides a much-needed reminder to environmental reporting researchers that they need to consider the philosophical roots of what they are investigating. While a fascinating read, the book provides a sad indictment of the state of most environmental reporting which presents the natural world as separate, and therefore not something for which it has any responsibility. While environmental reporting has come a long way and is becoming almost commonplace, the study presented in this book suggests that corporate entities are still fundamentally antagonistic towards the natural world.

— *Carol Tilt, University of South Australia, Australia*

Corporate Environmental Reporting

This book explores corporate environmental discourse by examining a sample of corporate environmental reports through the lens of environmental philosophy. Findings include the predominant use of a dualistic approach towards nature, which highlights the perceived 'separateness' of companies from the natural world. Also explored are the corporate articulations of interconnectivity and transcendence, two philosophical approaches that are also in common use in western culture. The expression of these themes reveals the discursive underpinnings of a harmful relationship with nature. Exploring the ways in which discourse informs corporate relationships with nature allows for an in-depth 'diagnosis' of current environmental problems.

The history of environmental philosophy demonstrates how some powerful philosophical approaches have shaped the western relationship with nature over time, and continue to do so through corporate environmental reporting. *Corporate Environmental Reporting: The Western Approach to Nature* demonstrates how corporate reporting is used to reduce the perception of the corporate responsibility, and contributes to the erosion of broader cultural restraints against the harmful treatment of nature. As such, discourse is integral to the survival of the world which we – and other members of our biotic community – are utterly reliant on. It shows the latest state of knowledge on the topic and will be of interest both to students at an advanced level, academics and reflective practitioners. It will be of interest to researchers, academics, and students in the fields of accounting, management, environmental philosophy and sustainable management.

Dr Leanne J Morrison is a lecturer at the RMIT School of Accounting, Melbourne, Australia.

Routledge Studies in Accounting

For a full list of titles in this series, please visit https://www.routledge.com/
Routledge-Studies-in-Accounting/book-series/SE0715

Corporate Environmental Reporting
The Western Approach to Nature

Leanne J Morrison

Taylor & Francis Group

LONDON AND NEW YORK

First published 2020 by Routledge

2 Park Square, Milton Park, Abingdon, Oxon, OX14 4RN

605 Third Avenue, New York, NY 10017

Routledge is an imprint of the Taylor & Francis Group, an informa business

First issued in paperback 2020

Library of Congress Cataloging-in-Publication Data
A catalog record for this title has been requested

ISBN: 978-1-138-33721-3 (hbk)
ISBN: 978-0-367-78545-1 (pbk)

Typeset in Sabon
by codeMantra

Contents

List of Figures

List of Tables

Preface

I was inspired to write this book after reading Carolyne Merchant's seminal work on the ways Western culture's attitude towards nature has changed over time. I read Merchant prior to starting my PhD, and turned up to my first meeting with my supervisors inspired by her ideas, but thinking it was a long way from corporate environmental reporting. I had just completed a research project which examined the different ethical approaches of stakeholders, but I hadn't quite pinned down my PhD topic. I knew I wanted to research something about corporate environmental reporting, but I didn't know what. I was afraid that I might have to abandon my philosophical training; that accounting was too far removed from philosophy, and that I was lucky enough to have been able to publish in this niche, but there was little chance of an academic career if I kept writing in the obscure space between accounting and philosophy.

I mentioned Merchant as a throwaway comment – our supervisory meetings often covered vast terrain; conversations in multiple directions, which may or may not be directly related to my PhD, but somehow connected, like a spiderweb or a set of tangled roots. Fortunately, my supervisors had enough trust in my creativity and intellect and recognised that Merchant had inspired me. I was over the moon when one of my supervisors jumped in with "that's great, go with that."

Before I got to this point, though, I had experienced the research baptism by fire otherwise known as the Honours Dissertation. It was a steep learning curve, to say the least. Part of the way through this process, I questioned whether I was capable of completion and considered giving up and returning to work as an accountant. At that time, I was living on the edge of the Tasmanian Wilderness, in the beautiful Huon Valley. Distraught at the idea of giving up, I took a walk over the hills in my backyard and sat on a large rock in the forest that overlooked the valley. There I had an epiphany. I felt how the rock beneath me supported my body; how the trees were providing the air for me to breathe. The birdsong was soothing; the fresh air cooled my skin. I had a profound realisation of how I was a part of an enormous and ancient natural process; a process I was deeply in love with. I realised that this was my purpose – that this beautiful natural world that supported me was my inspiration, the reason I was pushing myself through these challenges.

Since then, when I am faced with a decision or a challenge, I remember that moment and question myself – what are you doing this for? Will this help your cause? The rock and the trees and birds were present for me, can I be present for them?

One of the most pressing threats to the natural world to which I have dedicated this book is corporate environmental impact. My goal with this book, as with my life's work, is to challenge the processes which cause this impact. This book takes the thread which Carolyne Merchant used and weaves its way through a history of western environmental philosophies. There are many ways we can think about nature, and most of us switch between outlooks – none of us are purely transcendent, dualist, or interconnected in our thinking, but each of these philosophical approaches shapes our actions in different ways. Extending this understanding to corporate environmental impact, we can examine how corporate actions are also shaped by philosophies. In fact, before we even start to examine *what* companies should be reporting, it is imperative to examine how they are relating to nature – are they communicating in a way which shapes their actions towards exploitation? protection? community? Examining the philosophical underpinnings of companies – those entities which have grown to dominate our social and natural worlds in the race for profit – is an integral step in changing that relationship. As more and more people are realising, companies need to turn the volume down on profit and dial up the community and natural values that will be imperative if we are to live through the current series of social and environmental changes. If humans are to be a part of the Earth's future, we need to examine our role and make some radical changes. I hope this book contributes to those changes.

Acknowledgements

While it may be only my name on the cover of this book, it has not been a task undertaken alone. Many people have contributed to this work – more than I list here.

With heartfelt thanks, I acknowledge the invaluable encouragement of Associate Professor Trevor Wilmshurst and Dr Sonia Shimeld.

My darling husband Gordon Morrison has demonstrated super-human levels of patience, support and flowers. Without you, this book could not have been written. You are my left arm and the sparkle in my blood cells.

I deeply appreciate the support and affection of my wonderful daughters Wanda, Laela and Una. I feel honoured to be able to watch you emerge into three fabulous human beings whose creative minds make such unique and valuable contributions to the world.

Dr Lauren McGrow has likewise been the source of invaluable love, inspiration and feedback, which I treasure more with each passing year.

My friends and colleagues at the University of Tasmania, RMIT University and the Centre for Social and Environmental Accounting Research have also provided me with a beautiful community in which to write this book. I thank everyone in these communities for their intellectual rigour, inspiring conversations and enthusiastic support.

I also acknowledge the Mouheneenner, Nuenonne, Lyluequonny people of the Palawa Nations, and the people of the Woi wurrung and Boon wurrung language groups of the Kulin Nations, on whose unceded lands this book was written. I respectfully acknowledge their Ancestors and Elders past, present and future.

This research was supported by an Australian Postgraduate Award Scholarship.

1 Western Environmental Discourse and the Corporate Report

In this period of crisis, time taken for the development of theory seems luxury indeed. But if we do not understand the development and the defects in the western story of reason and nature, we may remain trapped within it or settle for one of its new versions.

(Plumwood, 1993, p. 196)

Introduction

By articulating the relationship between the corporation and the natural world, corporate environmental reporting implicitly draws from cultural attitudes towards nature. Since this relationship has been blamed in large part for the current environmental crisis, it is imperative that we closely examine the values with which it is informed. In order to explore these underpinning values in this book, I examine the corporate relationship with nature through the lens of western environmental philosophy.

The way people and organisations communicate about the natural world can be called cultural discourse. Such discourse is made up of spoken word, written text, but also by images, custom, traditions and actions. Even such disparate artefacts as architecture, magazine covers and art can be included in a culture's discourse. When we consider the roles of such discourse, it becomes clear that it not only *reflects* the way those within that culture think and behave, but it also *shapes* our thoughts and behaviour. Consider for a moment the ways nature is discussed in popular culture in Australia; quite often as the subject of economic debate (for example, the Murray Darling Basin being degraded for the economic benefit of cotton growers, or natural habitat being erased for mining companies). This not only reflects the way Australians value nature, but also perpetuates certain ideals.

If we compare how nature is reflected in the popular culture of Australia with how it is represented in another culture, say, Malaysia, we might notice some differences. This difference would then tell us that discourses change from culture to culture. Or perhaps we might compare how nature is reflected in the popular culture of Australia in 2018 with that of 1918. We would likely notice some differences there, too.

If discourses differ between cultures, and over time, then they are malleable, and might be used to understand the values and attitudes of different eras or cultures. This book does exactly that. In this book, I will examine western culture's approach to nature, over time, and in particular, in the contemporary era.

Cultural discourse about nature reflects and informs how cultures interact with and consider the natural world. These discourses also inform such texts as the corporate environmental report. By articulating the relationship between the corporation and the natural world, corporate environmental reporting implicitly draws from cultural attitudes towards nature in its discourse. Because the natural world is currently experiencing the unprecedented pressure of human activity (predominantly from humans living in western cultures), and because much of this pressure stems from corporate activity, this book explores the discourse of corporate environmental reporting in an attempt to unravel some of the ways companies communicate about nature, and what this might convey about the corporate relationship with nature.

One way of understanding the different discourses about nature is to examine their historical use. Throughout the history of western culture, one particular body of discourse provides an in-depth exploration of the human-nature relationship: environmental philosophy. In order to explore the underpinning philosophies which guide the relationship between humans and nature, this book examines the corporate relationship with nature through the lens of western environmental philosophy. In doing so, it highlights the dynamics inherent in the corporate relationship with nature. The analysis presented in this book will test corporate relations to nature and consider the implications. In doing so, it opens up the field for what environmental philosopher Val Plumwood, in 1993, described as "new, less destructive guiding stories" (1993, p. 196), which she argued are necessary in the construction of healthy relationships between western culture and the natural world. As no resolution has been reached since Plumwood first proposed these "guiding stories," the relevance of her call to action persists, 26 years later (Adams & Belasco, 2015; Dryzek, 2013; Mathews, 2014). The guiding intent of this book reflects what Plumwood articulates – to explore the discourse which guides our western relationship with nature in order to provide insight into current conditions.

This book is an acknowledgement of the profound dependence of human existence on the wellbeing of our natural environment. While much of this book might be interpreted as a critique of western approaches to nature, I also link back to a past in which western culture acknowledged its interdependence with, and respect of, nature. This profound sense of interconnectivity is evident in multiple early sources, including in Giambattista della Porta's scientific volumes written in the fourteenth century, in which he articulated that "...the parts of this huge world... are knit together... so that when one part suffers, the rest also suffer with it, even so the parts and members of this huge creature the World... are linked in one common bond" (as cited in Merchant, 1989, p. 104). This quote reminds us that human (and corporate) actions are connected via a complex network of relationships to the wellbeing of not just other humans, but to all "the parts and members" sharing life on this planet. As such, this book is informed by a deep love of nature, and a concern for the effects western culture has had on its welfare.

Keeping these intentions in mind, this first chapter introduces the reader to some of the issues that inform the writing of this book. It does so by first explicating the aims and motivations for writing this book, then outlining the book will proceed to unravel the problem of the corporate relationship with nature, chapter by chapter. This explication will present some background to the topic. In doing so, I will explain the problem, the reasoning for the approaches adopted in this book and the justifications for undertaking the research which underpins the writing of this book.

Background

That the natural world is currently experiencing significant distress is a view which is shared by much of the scientific community (IPCC, 2013; Mitchell, Lowe, Wood, & Vellinga, 2006; Oreskes, 2004; Raupach, McMichael, Finnigan, Manderson, & Walker, 2012; Steffen, Grinevald, Crutzen, & McNeill, 2011). This is also the view of the wider community, where concern for the environment has been growing (Bradley, Reser, Glendon, & Ellul, 2014; Reser, Bradley, Glendon, Ellul, & Callaghan, 2012), and negative attention is being increasingly directed towards large corporations. In an attempt to answer these concerns, 92% of large corporations now publicly report on their environmental interactions (KPMG, 2015).

Despite the changes evident in corporate discourse however, damage to the environment continues to grow. Evidence of this damage includes the increase in carbon (and equivalents) emissions (IPCC, 2013), increasing rates of flora and fauna extinctions (Steffen et al., 2011), reductions in natural habitat (Attfield, 1991), increasing air, water and terrestrial pollution (Gregory, 2009) and the continued consumption of fossil fuels, which is attributed to the increase in average global temperatures (IPCC, 2013; Steffen et al., 2011). The apparent disconnection between the environmental discourse and its outcomes indicates the possibility of a subversive problem embedded in the discourse. Consequently, I undertake an in-depth exploration of corporate discourses and the philosophies which underpin them in order to identify any potential underlying problems.

What Is the Problem?

While there are many causes for the current distress of the natural environment such as overpopulation and consumerism (Crutzen & Stoermer, 2000; Steffen et al., 2011), in this book I focus on corporate impacts. In aggregate, the corporate world controls a large proportion of the world's economy and natural resources (CorpWatch, 2001; Vitali, Glattfelder, & Battiston, 2011) and is therefore perceived to be responsible for much of today's environmental damage (de Vries, Terwel, Ellemers, & Daamen, 2015; Nyilasy, Gangadharbatla, & Paladino, 2014; Spence, 2009). In light of these factors, the corporate relationship with nature requires careful examination. Consequently, I aim to explore how environmental discourse informs the corporate relationship with nature.

One lens through which to explore the corporate relationship with the natural world is that of western environmental philosophy. *Western environmental philosophy is the lens adopted in this book since the West is responsible for a large proportion of environmental damage*, despite supporting only a minority of the world's population (Figuero & Mills, 2001; Milstein, Thomas, & Hoffmann, 2018). This situation suggests an argument that the current damaged condition of the natural environment can be attributed to western culture's interaction with the environment (Kheel, 2008; Merchant, 1989). Since discourse articulates cultural values, it therefore presents a germane example to analyse cultural attitudes towards the natural world.

Implicitly drawing from western attitudes towards nature, corporate environmental reporting articulates the relationship between the corporation and the natural world (Kathyayini, Tilt, & Lester, 2012). In order to unravel the problem of the discrepancy between cultural discourse and contemporary environmental conditions, it is useful to closely examine the values which inform corporate environmental reporting. In this book, I aim to illuminate how the underpinning philosophical approaches have shaped organisational environmental reporting, and in doing so I pose a twofold question:

> How is western environmental philosophy communicated through corporate environmental reporting; and what does this convey about the corporate relationship with nature?

In responding to these questions, I have taken a critical approach. Critical approaches are those which aim to deconstruct dominant paradigms such as positivist and enlightenment thought (Agger, 1991). These dominant paradigms are a source of power for cultural institutions such as capitalism (Spence, 2009), patriarchy (Irigaray, 2004) and other institutions which implicitly dominate the cultural landscape (Archel, Husillos, & Spence, 2011; Plumwood, 1993) which actively shape the way we approach the world (Horkheimer, 1982). In this book, it is the dominant approaches which shape the way people (and organisations) approach the natural world which is the focus.

I also adopt an interdisciplinary approach. Such an approach reflects the perspective of Thompson Klein (2010), who illustrates that rather than juxtaposing and comparing the perspectives of multiple disciplines, interdisciplinarity integrates the ideas and perceptions of multiple disciplines in order to create research which is neither one discipline or another, but *both* (or in this case, *a few*). In this book a broad, or wide interdisciplinarity is adopted; this means that the disciplines which are used in this book are not those that are normally considered complementary, or easily combined. Combinations of philosophy, accounting and history have not heretofore been integrated in the extant literature in the manner demonstrated in this book. In what Thompson Klein (2010, p. 20) establishes as an authentic interdisciplinarity, this book uses "the concepts and insights of one discipline [to] contribute to the problems and theories of another."

Outline of Book

The first of these multiple disciplines to be discussed in this book is that of philosophy. The next chapter (Chapter 2) will introduce the concepts of western environmental philosophy from a historical point of view. Chapter 2 introduces the three primary philosophical themes which will be used in the analysis of the corporate environmental reports: dualism, transcendence and interconnectivity. The historical passages of these philosophical themes will be traced back to the pre-Socratic era of Ancient Greece, and their vestiges detected in the dominant institutions of contemporary western culture. The chapter will discuss the ways these philosophical themes have informed the western relationship with nature over time, and the way they continue to do so.

Next, in Chapter 3, some corporate reporting background will be charted. Chapter 3 will explore some of the key influences of corporate environmental reporting, including accounting, sustainable development and critical theory. While corporate environmental reporting represents the potential to address the changes required for environmental wellbeing, this chapter explores whether it may have failed in this charge. Some of the philosophies which underpin corporate reporting by constructing barriers to change will also be highlighted in the chapter. The critical underpinnings of this research are also outlined in Chapter 3.

The methods which are to be used in identifying and analysing the underpinning philosophical values implicit in corporate environmental reporting will be outlined in Chapter 4. Critical discourse analysis will be introduced and discussed in terms of the exploration of corporate environmental discourse in this book. The choice of texts which will undergo such analysis will also be explained. In charting the ways I explore these fundamental issues, Chapter 4 will also provide a discussion of the approaches underpinning these choices.

Chapters 5 and 6 will then consider what was found in the reports. First, Chapter 5 will provide an introductory account of the case study companies; exploring how and to what degree each company has expressed particular environmental philosophies. Chapter 6 will then extend these findings to explore some of the commonly used discursive mechanisms expressed in the environmental reports and interviews. This layer of results will explore how western environmental philosophy is communicated through corporate environmental reporting.

Chapter 7 will provide an analysis of what the findings mean in terms of the problems which I seek to explore in this book. It will articulate how western environmental philosophy is communicated through corporate environmental reporting, and what this conveys about the corporate relationship to nature.

Chapter 8 concludes the book by discussing the major findings and contributions of the research, outlining some of the limitations and making some suggestions for further research which could extend the research which informs this book.

Summary

By way of introduction, this chapter began with a discussion of the motivations which provided the impetus for this book. The observation that there could be a dissimilitude between the shared cultural discourse and actual environmental outcomes indicated that there could be more going on than is ostensible. In seeking to look deeper into the environmental discourse, the contemporary corporate environmental report provides an ideal location for such an investigation. Similarly, western environmental philosophy is a fitting lens through which to observe these practices. From these beginnings, a twofold question was proposed, which will govern the direction of this book:

> How is western environmental philosophy communicated through corporate environmental reporting; and what does this convey about the corporate relationship with nature?

This question is twofold in that it first asks *how* western environmental philosophy is expressed through corporate environmental reporting, and also asks what this means to the corporate relationship with the natural world. To answer this twofold question, a mapping of the path which this book undertakes has been presented in this chapter. From providing interdisciplinary backgrounds of philosophy, history, accounting, corporate reporting and critical theory, to the critical discourse analysis, dual layers of results, analysis and conclusion, this chapter has mapped the overarching narrative which this book will follow. The following chapters will flesh out this narrative, beginning with a contemplation of western environmental philosophy and its cultural impact over time.

References

Adams, D. H., & Belasco, J. (2015). The Mythic Roots of Western Culture's Alienation from Nature. *Tapestry Institute Occasional Papers, 1*(3).

Agger, B. (1991). Critical Theory, Poststructuralism, Postmodernism: Their Sociological Relevance. *Annual Review of Sociology, 17*, 105–131.

Archel, P., Husillos, J., & Spence, C. (2011). The Institutionalisation of Unaccountability: Loading the Dice of Corporate Social Responsibility discourse. *Accounting, Organizations and Society, 36*(6), 327–343.

Attfield, R. (1991). *The Ethics of Environmental Concern* (2nd ed.). Athens: The University of Georgia Press.

Bradley, G., Reser, J., Glendon, A., & Ellul, M. (2014). Distress and Coping in Response to Climate Change. In K. Kaniasty, K. A. Moore, S. Howard, & P. Buchwald (Eds.), *Stress and Anxiety: Applications to Social and Environmental Threats, Psychological Wellbeing, Occupational Challenges, and Developmental Psychology* (pp. 33–42). Berlin: Logos.

CorpWatch. (2001). *Corporate Globalization.* Retrieved from San Francisco: www.corpwatch.org

Crutzen, P., & Stoermer, E. (2000). The Anthropocene. *Global Change Newsletter, 41.*

de Vries, G., Terwel, B., Ellemers, N., & Daamen, D. (2015). Sustainability or Profitability? How Communicated Motives for Environmental Policy Affect Public Perceptions of Corporate Greenwashing. *Corporate Social Responsibility and Environmental Management, 22*(3), 142–154.

Dryzek, J. (2013). *The Politics of the Earth: Environmental Discourses* (3rd ed.). Oxford: Oxford University Press.

Figuero, R., & Mills, C. (2001). Environmental Justice. In D. Jamieson (Ed.), *A Companion to Environmental Philosophy* (pp. 426–438). Cambridge, MA: Blackwell Publishing.

Gregory, M. R. (2009). Environmental Implications of Plastic Debris in Marine Settings—Entanglement, Ingestion, Smothering, Hangers-On, Hitch-Hiking and Alien Invasions. *Philosophical Transactions: Biological Sciences, 364*(1526), 2013–2025. doi:10.2307/40485979

Horkheimer, M. (1982). *Critical Theory.* New York: Seabury Press.

IPCC. (2013). *Climate Change 2013: The Physical Science Basis.* Cambridge: IPCC.

Irigaray, L. (2004). The Power of Discourse and the Subordination of the Feminine. In J. Rivkin & M. Ryan (Eds.), *Literary Theory: An Anthology* (2nd ed., pp. 795–811). Cambridge, MA: Blackwell Publishing.

Kathyayini, K., Tilt, C. A., & Lester, L. H. (2012). Corporate Governance and Environmental Reporting: An Australian Study. *Corporate Governance, 12*(2), 143–163.

Kheel, M. (2008). *Nature Ethics.* London: Rowman & Littlefield.

KPMG. (2015). *Currents of Change; The KPMG Survey on Corporate Responsibility Reporting 2015*. Netherlands: KPMG.

Mathews, F. (2014). Environmental Philosophy. In N. Trakakis & G. Oppy (Eds.), *A History of Australasian Philosophy* (pp. 543–591). Dordrecht: Springer.

Merchant, C. (1989). *The Death of Nature: Women, Ecology, and the Scientific Revolution*. New York: Harper & Row.

Milstein, T., Thomas, M., & Hoffmann, J. (2018). Dams and Flows: Immersing in Western Meaning Systems in Search of Ecocultural Reflexivity. *Environmental Communication*, 1–14. doi:10.1080/17524032.2018.1423626

Mitchell, J., Lowe, J., Wood, R., & Vellinga, M. (2006). Extreme Events Due to Human-Induced Climate Change. *Philosophical Transactions of the Royal Society, 364*, 2117–2133.

Nyilasy, G., Gangadharbatla, H., & Paladino, A. (2014). Perceived Greenwashing: The Interactive Effects of Green Advertising and Corporate Environmental Performance on Consumer Reactions. *Journal of Business Ethics, 125*(4), 693–707.

Oreskes, N. (2004). The Scientific Consensus on Climate Change. *Science, 306*(5702), 1686. doi:10.1126/science.1103618

Plumwood, V. (1993). *Feminism and the Mastery of Nature*. London: Routledge.

Raupach, M., McMichael, A., Finnigan, J., Manderson, L., & Walker, B. (2012). *Negotiating Our Future: Living Scenarios for Australia to 2050*. ACT: Australian Academy of Science.

Reser, J., Bradley, G., Glendon, A., Ellul, M., & Callaghan, R. (2012). *Public Risk Perceptions, Understandings and Responses to Climate Change and Natural Disasters in Australia and Great Britain*. Retrieved from Brisbane, Australia.

Spence, C. (2009). Social Accounting's Emancipatory Potential: A Gramscian Critique. *Critical Perspectives on Accounting, 20*, 205–227.

Steffen, W., Grinevald, J., Crutzen, P., & McNeill, J. (2011). The Anthropocene: Conceptual and Historical Perspectives. *Philosophical Transactions of the Royal Society, 369*, 842–867.

Thompson Klein, J. (2010). A Taxonomy of Interdisciplinarity. In R. Frodeman (Ed.), *The Oxford Handbook of Interdisciplinarity* (pp. 15–30). Oxford: Oxford University Press.

Vitali, S., Glattfelder, J., & Battiston, S. (2011). The Network of Global Corporate Control. *PLoS One, 6*(10), e25995.

2   Western Environmental Philosophy

The Impacts of Western Environmental Philosophy

Philosophy explains and influences the shared values of cultures and provides a way to interpret the forces that guide cultural perspectives. This chapter examines some of the philosophies which underpin western relationships with nature, and by reflection, contemporary corporate environmental reporting. A historical approach is taken to explore the impacts of various environmental philosophies which have guided the relationship between western culture and the natural world through time. First, the argument that philosophy informs the way the world is understood is explored through the concept of social construction. Next, a historical overview of how the various environmental philosophies emerged is discussed. In the process of this discussion, three main themes will be highlighted which will then be explored in depth: dualism, transcendence and interconnectivity. The intersection between these themes and contemporary environmental issues is of particular interest, as is the way these themes are woven into not only our cultural understanding of nature, but the corporate relationship with the natural world. This corporate view will be explored in more depth in the following chapter.

Exploring the philosophical underpinnings of the western, and in particular corporate, relationship with the natural world is an important aspect which is fundamentally implicated in the current distress of the natural environment. This distress represents the culmination of a pernicious relationship with the natural world over a long period of time. Current understandings of the state of the natural environment include accounts of unprecedented temperature increases in the atmosphere and oceans on a global scale (IPCC, 2013). These changes are predicted to have and in many cases have already had, such wide-ranging effects as changing the timing of migratory patterns, seasonal changes, increased occurrence of extreme weather incidents (Walther et al., 2002), social inequity, food security issues and the capacity of the planet to sustain life (Raupach et al., 2012). As such, the relationship between nature and corporate reporting is an important narrative to critique.

Many of these changes to the natural environment have been attributed at least in part to the impact of human behaviour (Mitchell, Lowe, Wood, & Vellinga, 2006; Steffen, Grinevald, Crutzen, & McNeill, 2011). It is widely accepted in the scientific literature that human behaviour has adversely effected biogeochemical cycles and terrestrial water cycles and is responsible for the spike in greenhouse gas emissions which has led to profound and dangerous changes in the global climate (Baskin, 2015; Giddens, 2008; Oreskes, 2004). These trends have led to the designation of the title 'Anthropocene' to describe a geological era of extensive human impact on the rest of the natural world, from the first Industrial Revolution onwards (Steffen et al., 2011).

Despite only one-fifth of the world's population living in western countries, it is the West which has been responsible for a substantial proportion of environmental damage (Figuero & Mills, 2001). This is in large part due to the changes which have taken place since the British Industrial Revolution of the eighteenth century (Hawkins et al., 2017; Steffen et al., 2011). Much of the global political discussion around environmental protection has focused on slowing the rate of 'development' in emerging economies, rather than imposing reduced growth on already industrialised nations (Gonzalez, 2001). This aspect of distributive environmental injustice is addressed in this book by critiquing western approaches to the natural environment. This approach repudiates the reinforcement of the somewhat imperialist myths that have underpinned a focus away from the western contribution to these problems (Bullard, 2015; Gonzalez, 2001; Jackson, 2017).

Consequently, there is a strong argument that the current environmental conditions are directly linked – at least in part – to the history of western culture's interaction with the environment (Kheel, 2008; Mathews, 2014; Merchant, 1989). In order to explore this interaction, this book adopts the view that a fundamental method of expressing cultural values is through discourse. The philosophies which inform this discourse then become an important aspect to explore.

Corporate environmental reporting sits at the intersection between western environmental philosophy and commercial operations. Implicitly drawing from a history of western attitudes towards nature in its discourse, corporate environmental reporting aims to communicate the environmental implications of corporate activities (Kathyayini, Tilt, & Lester, 2012). However, such reporting has also been critiqued for its tendency to mask, and even contribute to, environmental damage (Cooper & Senkl, 2016; Milne, Tregidga, & Walton, 2009; Spence, 2009). In order to contribute to the debates surrounding corporate environmental reporting, it is important to investigate the processes underpinning current practice. This book aims to illuminate the role of western environmental philosophy in shaping the organisational response as disclosed in the environmental reports.

This chapter responds to these problems by first discussing the notion of social construction and the role it plays in western approaches to the natural world. This discussion leads to a review of a history of western environmental philosophy, following some key themes which can be traced from Ancient Greece through to the current day. These themes will help to underscore many of the current tensions within environmental philosophy and will subsequently be used to analyse the discourse of corporate environmental reporting.

The Role of Social Construction

What we understand as reality is actually conceived through a filter of shared social understanding (Berger & Luckman, 1966; Mercadal, 2014). This shared social understanding is an agreement which has been built over time, through multiple social institutions and practices, and informs the dominant paradigms within cultures. Often, these dominant paradigms are founded on assumptions which are taken for granted, and thus left unquestioned (Foucault, 1972; Hickey, 2005).

It is through these dominant paradigms that we understand the natural world and our relationship to it. Since environmental philosophy explores the notion of how we relate to the environment, it provides a road map with which to explore the multiple ways in which western culture has interacted with the environment over time. In this way, social constructionism is a useful tool to introduce the multiplicity of ways in which corporations might communicate about the environment, each of which may be underpinned with a particular set of values. By highlighting the changing nature of western relationships with the natural world, the socially constructed and malleable nature of our contemporary views towards these issues is illuminated, as Tarnas articulates:

> ...only by recalling the deeper sources of our present world and worldview can we hope to gain the self-understanding necessary for dealing with our current dilemmas.
>
> (Tarnas, 1996, p. xi)

Social construction is based on the observation that the dominant reality is a result of the combination of multiple social agreements about how the world operates, informing the ways we engage with the world (Banerjee, 2003). Much of what is generally considered as knowledge, or 'truth,' has been constructed through the mechanisms of culture and society (Berger & Luckman, 1966; Mercadal, 2014). These social agreements are maintained in social practices such as discourse, legislation, the media and traditions, culminating in what is broadly understood as culture.

Merchant (1989) has demonstrated how the changing of narratives about the environment reflect changes in cultural values and perceptions. Through a longitudinal study of representations of nature from the early Middle Ages through to the consequences of the scientific and industrial revolutions, Merchant establishes that the western relationship with the natural world has been shaped by social and cultural values over time. This book takes a similar approach, focusing on the relationships between humans and the rest of the natural world through the lens of western environmental philosophy. Looking through this lens at contemporary corporate environmental reporting will highlight the role of environmental philosophies in the production of these reports.

Although what is considered the concept of 'nature,' or 'the environment' today has undergone many changes over time, western discourse understands these terms as that which is not human (Plumwood, 1991). As this chapter articulates, a view of nature which excludes humans is itself problematic and associated with western views which have been reinforced over time. However, within environmental philosophy, humans are increasingly embraced as a part of nature (Mathews, 1994). Rather than attempting to provide a concise definition of these terms here, this chapter discusses some of the more prominent ways the natural world has been understood in western culture. In this way, an understanding will slowly unfold which renders such definitions as socially constructed and contrived. From this rendering, some key themes will be discerned and utilised in understanding the current corporate relationship with nature.

Western Culture

Exploring the ways in which the concept of nature has been constructed over time highlights the relevance of a historical perspective. In order to discover the ways in which the social construction of nature has changed, the scope of this historical perspective has been limited to western thought. While it is acknowledged that other conceptions are likely to present a more integrated relationship with nature (Mathews, 2006), western culture is considered the source of the paradigm at the heart of the current environmental condition, and therefore it is this paradigm that most requires critique and deconstruction (Plumwood, 1993; Shafer, 2006).

Jenks (2005) describes culture as an accumulation of customs, values, language and beliefs. He suggests that the intangible aspects of a culture characterise and distinguish particular groups from other groups. He proposes that although the concept of culture is difficult to singularly define, cultures can be comprehended through analysis of traditions of thought and ideological foundations. This book explores the thought and ideological foundations of a broad category of culture known as western culture. Western culture is the focus of this book due to its relationship with not only a significant proportion of environmental damage (Hay, 2002), but also with corporate practices and reporting (Birkin & Polesie, 2012; Klein, 2015).

In this book, the West refers to that part of global culture which is often distinguished as 'Anglo-American.' Although this distinction contains within it a multitude of variations, it can be recognised as a culture which has its origins in Ancient Greece, but has travelled to Northern Europe and the UK, and is characterised by colonial forces throughout much of the world, including Australia, Canada, New Zealand and the US (Said, 1993). Key characteristics of contemporary western culture include the preference towards modern capitalism, patriarchy, and a predominantly Christian population (Austin, 2005). In this book, western culture refers to a set of cultural norms which are founded in these themes. While not unproblematic in itself, and defying these generalisations at its edges, the concept of western culture or the West is a useful tool when analysing the flow of a particular set of cultural values through time (Said, 1993).

A History

The history presented in this book is shaped by what Haraway (2004) has called an amodern history. According to Haraway, an amodern history is vividly present in each moment, rather than something relegated to the past which has little effect on current events and attitudes. She argues that a multi-layered present is built on histories which are always at hand, reflected in social conventions, beliefs and practice. This view is shared by Foucault et al. (2003), who proposed the idea of a genealogical history. Accordingly, this book draws from Haraway (2004) and Foucault (1972, 2003) to provide an amodern historical view of western environmental philosophies, from which to reflect on contemporary corporate reporting.

Similarly, Guldi and Armitage (2014) call for the analysis of long-term history as a method for understanding the ways in which "multiple pasts" have engendered present conditions (p. i). They argue that by looking further into history, more informed decisions can be made about the present, and encourage other historians to contextualise current events by looking at what has been coined in historical disciplines as the longue durée. They discuss how this approach is integral to the analysis of the history of human interactions with the environment, particularly in light of current climate change issues. As such, a history ranging from the Pre-Socratic era to contemporary times provides the long durée for this book.

Following previous studies in environmental thought (Hadot, 2006; Merchant, 1989), a historical perspective is taken in this book in order to expose a variety of philosophical themes which have dominated the cultural discourse at different periods, and which still influence contemporary western attitudes towards the natural world.

Western Environmental Philosophies

The affluence, practices and ideology of western culture have been widely blamed for the current state of the environment (Figuero & Mills, 2001; Merchant, 2006). In particular, the business practices of the West have attracted a large amount of animosity regarding environmental damage (Birkin & Polesie, 2012; Hawken, 1993). Tracing the patterns of thought and philosophy which have led to this situation sheds light on current practice.

Mathews (2006) dismantles the contemporary dominant paradigm, which she argues has created and maintains contemporary western culture's harmful worldviews towards nature. She proposes that in western societies, there is an underlying ontology of mastery and control of the world for human needs. She establishes that the attempt to control the natural world is founded on a materialist approach which denies the intrinsic value of nature. Lacking intrinsic value, the environment is valued only in correlation with its capacity to contribute to the welfare of humans. Mathews argues that the onset of this materialistic view of nature prepared the way for the inherently exploitative approaches to the natural world which are evident in western culture today.

Traditionally, ethics considers the moral relationships between people and attempts to theorise felicitous relations in order to articulate normative ethical systems. As mentioned, environmental philosophy can be traced back to earliest recorded history, however the schools of thought which today constitute the bulk of western environmental ethics began to flourish in the 1960s and 1970s (Brennan & Lo, 2011; Fox, 1990; Hay, 2002). To inform an understanding of corporate environmental discourse, some of the fundamental principles which contemporary environmental philosophies attempt to engage with are outlined below.

Intrinsic and Instrumental Values

An underlying theme in contemporary environmental ethics is the notion of value. In traditional ethics, only humans are considered intrinsically valuable (Brennan & Lo, 2011). This view has been reinforced by institutions within western culture such as Christianity, Enlightenment thought and neoliberal economics. In line with the ideologies of these institutions, non-human members of our biotic community are considered only instrumentally valuable, that is, they are only valuable by virtue of what they can contribute to human wellbeing. This principle was exemplified in the eighteenth century by Kant, who disapproved of animal cruelty only because of its potential to foster cruelty between human subjects (Kant, 2001/1786). This perspective has been shifted only slightly in more recent times, to include human-like beings into the net of moral consideration. For instance, Singer (1990/1975) calls for the inclusion of all sentient beings into the web of moral consideration on the grounds that since they are capable of suffering, they exhibit an interest in their own wellbeing. This view is reflected in the growing popularity of animal liberation groups since the 1960s and 1970s. One of the key differences between Kantian principles and Singer's approach is whether animals should be valued for their own sake (their intrinsic value), or for the value they can provide humans (their instrumental value).

More recently, the criterion of sentience has been superseded in environmental philosophy by the concept of biocentrism. Biocentrism holds that since many members of the biotic community exhibit evidence that indicates an interest in survival and wellbeing, the net of moral consideration should be cast over a much broader population. However, conspicuous arguments against this approach include the grounds against protecting the wellbeing of living elements such as viruses (Brennan & Lo, 2011). Despite these obvious limitations, biocentrism does raise questions about where the limits to moral consideration should lie.

Ecofeminism

Environmental ethicists call the bias towards allowing only humans intrinsic value *anthropocentric*. Plumwood (1991) argues that the division drawn between the human and non-human worlds indicates a deep underlying dualism which is reflected in many relationships of domination and hierarchy. In a nuanced reflection on western views about the environment, Plumwood (1991) elucidates some underlying patterns. She argues that these patterns value an oppositional rationalism, which reinforces the domination of 'the other,' including nature and women. These values are inherently guided by a western masculine logic. Plumwood calls this bias towards the masculine perspective androcentricism.

To counter the andro- and anthropocentricism which underpin western thought, Plumwood (1991) draws attention towards the relationships *between* members of the biotic community. Alongside a focus on relationships, she calls for a richer understanding of the emotionality and particularity of environmental ethics. This indicates a step away from the historical tendency to formulate universal and abstract understandings of relationships which is evident in earlier, more patriarchal western ethical frameworks.

Deep Ecology

Deep ecology is another philosophical system which addresses the issue of the perception of a hierarchical relationship between humans and the environment. Rather than focusing on particularities, as Plumwood's account of ecofeminism calls for, deep ecology expounds a way to incorporate the natural environment into the sense of self (Naess, 1973). First articulated in 1973, deep ecology builds on the potential for a sense of oneness with the natural world. Deep ecology considers that the distinction of individuals, separated from nature by not only our rationality, but also by what is traditionally considered the boundaries of our physical body, is nothing but a socially constructed illusion. Drawing from the metaphysics of Spinoza, who expressed the (at the time blasphemous) idea that God *is* everything, and from quantum physics, which diminishes the distinctions we have traditionally used to identify separate objects, deep ecologists reframe conceptions of individuality (Mathews, 1991). Through the lens of deep ecology, each person is part of a larger system which includes our immediate environment and extends to include larger ecosystems until eventually, the global and even universal system is considered our 'Self' (Mathews, 1991; Naess, 1973).

Aristotelian Ethics

Ecofeminism and deep ecology can both be traced back to aspects of Aristotelian thought which reflect the context of the moral agents. This approach contradicts with other philosophical systems which reduce ethical considerations (and context) to principles which can be applied universally. Aristotle's virtue ethics account for the particularities of each moral decision by taking into consideration the virtues or characteristics of agents, along with the circumstances and wider contexts (Ackrill, 1981; Nussbaum, 1988).

Aristotle's conception of nature is also conducive to a conception of nature as a living system which is common to ecofeminism (Plumwood, 1993) and deep ecology (Mathews, 2001); his understanding of the intimate relationship between form and matter demonstrates an underlying egalitarianism which repudiates earlier (and later) biases away from the physical world.

Environmental philosophies which stem from Aristotelian thought fit neatly into contemporary conceptions of nature as a living system, and also concur with a move away from anthropocentricism (Fox, 2000). Deep ecology and ecofeminism are both considered radical environmental ethical systems, due to their critique of modern western thought and anthropocentricism. As such, they both call for radical changes in the ways humans relate to the world around (and within) us.

Fundamental Issues in Western Environmental Philosophy

In this book, I identify some of the dominant themes evident in western environmental philosophy in order to ascertain how they are communicated in contemporary corporate environmental reporting, and what this means for the corporate relationship with nature. To identify some of the philosophical themes which inform the western approach to nature, an exploration of some historical issues is useful. Fundamental issues embedded within western approaches to nature centre around the concept of duality (Plumwood, 1993). Dualism is reflected in the valorisation of a transcendent world at the expense of embodied experience, but also in the valorisation of human rationality over intuition or emotionality, of discrete objects over interconnectivity and of the western world over other cultures (Plumwood, 1991).

At a fundamental level, dualism is expressed as an ontology of discrete objects (Birkin, 1996). This ontology reflects not only the separation of humans from our environment, but between objects within this environment. Many contemporary environmental philosophies such as ecofeminism and deep ecology juxtapose the ontology of discrete objects against a focus on the relationships, or the interconnectedness between things (Mathews, 1994).

Immanence

In contrast to the metaphorical separation integral to dualism, interconnectivity is a concept which is widely drawn from in contemporary environmental philosophy (Hay, 2002; Mathews, 1991; Naess, 1973). Focussing on the interconnected nature of the physical world, contemporary environmental philosophies such as deep ecology (Mathews, 2001; Naess, 1973) and ecofeminism (Plumwood, 1991) attempt to foster reconnections between the human experience and the natural world. While these approaches differ subtly, a common thread between them is the move away from the valorisation of the human experience at the expense of the rest of the natural world.

In the move to highlight the intrinsic value of the natural world, the concept of immanence has been introduced into philosophical debate. Immanence is a term used to describe the view that nature is sacred and divine in and of itself (Crosby, 2003). This corresponds with the view that nature is intrinsically valuable, in that there is no external source of evaluation. As such, the idea that there is a power beyond nature is rejected by the view of the immanence within nature (Crosby, 2003).

Interconnectivity

Immanence describes one aspect of an interconnected approach to the natural world. Interconnectivity combines concepts of the relationships between objects, the place of humans as part of nature, the value of the particular and intrinsic value.

The tension between interconnectivity and an ontology of discrete objects provides a backdrop for the multiplicity of western approaches

towards the natural world. The tension between these two ways of per-
ceiving the world unfolds early in philosophical history, illustrated by
the different perspectives of Heraclitus, Plato and Aristotle.

The philosophies of Ancient Greece planted seeds from which many of
the West's current attitudes have grown. One of the earliest philosophers
of whom written records still exist is Heraclitus (circ. 585–475 BCE),
who constructed many of the intellectual foundations upon which later
philosophers built (Hadot, 2006). His philosophies reveal a perception
of the workings of nature which reflect what we recognise today as interconnectivity. His approach incorporates growth and decay, birth and
death, in a dynamic continuous cycle which focuses on the processes
within nature, rather than the discrete objects involved.

As such, he describes day and night as two interconnected aspects of
the 24-hour cycle, rather than as two distinct phenomena. Echoing this
argument, he describes life and death as two elements of the same event:

> They do not comprehend how a thing agrees at variance with itself;
> it is an attunement turning back on itself, like that of the bow and
> the lyre. The name of the bow is life; its work is death.
> (Heraclitus, as cited in Kahn & Heraclitus, 1979, p. 65)

The principle underpinning this argument is a reduction of the distinctions between things; the melding of opposites which represent different
aspects of the same phenomenon. In this way, Heraclitus focuses on the
relationships between things, rather than on distinctions. This perspective is an important departure from the ontology of discrete objects.

A well-known Heraclitian proverb claims that a person "cannot step
twice into the same river" (as cited in Kenny, 2010, p. 17). Using an
ontology of discrete objects, a river can be identified as water, a place or
perhaps a name. Through the lens of interconnectivity however, a river
is constantly changing; its path, its banks and its name may change over
time. The river's most essential ingredient may be water, but even this
is constantly subject to change; it might flood or dry to a trickle, have
different qualities in the changing seasons. From a molecular level, the
individual water particles are in constant motion. Accordingly, what we
might distinguish as the river itself is also in flux – never quite the same
from one moment to the next. This proverb then points to the incessant
flow which constitutes the natural world. By focusing on these inherent
qualities, an ontology of discrete objects becomes less compelling. Despite this, an ontology of discrete objects is still a dominant paradigm
informing western approaches to nature.

Another Heraclitian proverb: "phusis kruptesthai philei" is commonly
translated as "nature loves to hide" (as cited in Kahn & Heraclitus, 1979,
p. 33). The impact of this proverb has been traced through history to reveal how this culturally accepted interpretation has informed the western

approach to nature (Hadot, 2006). Most telling, though, is an alternative translation which is more in keeping with Heraclitus' other fragments: "the essence of a thing that is born is to die" (Hadot, 2006, p. 7).

This alternative translation reveals how ideas about nature are socially constructed, since the common translation (nature loves to hide) aligns with western cultural views of nature. Hadot (2006) explores how interpretations of this fragment have been influenced by and also influence western attitudes towards nature throughout the ages. He argues that the idea that nature is hiding influenced the path of the scientific revolution and is still inherent in the ontology of scientifically revealing the hidden laws of nature. This also concurs with the view in western thought that nature is passive, with secrets available for humans to expose and exploit (Plumwood, 2009). These interpretations provide powerful examples of the inherent dominance embedded in the western approach to nature, implicitly shared through ostensible discourse (Merchant, 1989).

Heraclitian thought was a profound influence in Plato's (429–347 BCE) philosophies, particularly the concept of the world as a constant process. This influence can be gauged by the following passage, in which Plato replicates Heraclitus' notion of constant flux:

> …a man is called the same from childhood to old age. He is called the same despite the fact that he does not have the same hair and flesh and bones and blood and all the body, but he loses them and is always becoming new. And similarly for the soul: his dispositions and habits, opinions, desires, pleasures, pains fears, none of these remains the same, but some are coming-to-be, others are lost.
>
> (as cited in Kahn & Heraclitus, 1979, p. 167)

A fundamental difference, though, is that Plato interpreted constant flux as unknowable, and therefore not real. From this premise, Plato developed his theory of forms, in which an abstract world of forms is inhabited by the perfect and original version of all things. In Plato's conception, because this abstract world never changes, it is only this world of forms which is knowable, and therefore truly real (Ackrill, 1981). The concept of Plato's forms has resonated through the times, with the underlying notion that the temporal world is an illusory and inferior imitation of another transcendent world. Both dualism and transcendence can trace their foundations back to different aspects of Plato's philosophies, including his theory of forms.

Plato's student Aristotle provided some eloquent rebuttals of the concept of forms (Ackrill, 1981). For Aristotle, the physical substance of a thing and its form are two interconnected characteristics – much like the colour and shape of an object (Ackrill, 1981). Unlike Plato, Aristotle did not agree that the form of a living thing was separate from the thing itself, but rather, represented its capacity for life. From this perspective,

Aristotle's conception of what is most real is a composite of form and matter, with any other transcendent understanding stemming first from the physical world. This approach contradicts the concepts underpinning dualism and materialism, and as such coincides with the essence of contemporary philosophies such as ecofeminism and deep ecology (Mathews, 1991).

An important aspect of the way nature was considered in Ancient Greece involves the distinction between nature and art. For the early Greeks, this distinction was crucial, since nature was an organic manifestation of divinity, and therefore created by no one (including any God), whereas art is a created object (created by something external to it). As demonstrated by Mesomedes, an Ancient Greek poet, nature is the origin of all things in itself:

> Principle and origin of all things
> Ancient Mother of the world,
> Night, darkness and silence.
>
> (as cited in Hadot, 2006, p. 27)

Until the Enlightenment, western thought was considered relatively organic (Hamilton, 2002; Hay, 2002). In the art and literature which constitute the discourse of this time, nature is depicted as a benevolent mother (Merchant, 1989). Depicting nature as a mother in this sense highlighted the dependent qualities of the human to nature relationship (Dodson Gray, 1981), but also paved the way for the misogyny which would later be introduced into the discourse about nature (Kheel, 2008).

Throughout the Renaissance, the comprehension of the Earth as a person provided a powerful restraining ethic (Merchant, 1989); however, during this time, changes were being promoted by those seeking to exploit nature as a resource. As early as the first century CE, mining was considered a serious trespass against the personhood of the Earth. Merchant (1989) cites Pliny the Elder (CE 23–79) who warned that earthquakes were the response of the Earth to being violated by the act of mining:

> For it is upon her surface, in fact, that she has presented us with these substances, equally with the cereals, bounteous and ever ready, as she is, in supplying us with all things for our benefit! It is what is concealed from our view, what is sunk far beneath her surface, object, in fact, of no rapid formation, that urge us to our ruin, that send us to the very depths of hell...when will be the end of thus exhausting the earth, and to what point will avarice finally penetrate!
>
> (Pliny, as cited in Merchant, 1989, p. 30)

Merchant (1989) demonstrates that as the practice of mining became more prevalent, the benign personification of nature as a loving mother was transformed into a wicked stepmother archetype, who maliciously conceals metal stores from her dependent children (humans). This stance of nature against humans reflected the establishment of a dualistic approach to the natural world.

Dualism

The distinction between humans and nature was further amplified as Christianity colonised western thought. Under Christianity, the source of life was shifted from the Earth itself, to an exterior source – God (Merchant, 1989). Merchant (1989) argues that under this new perspective, God was seen as the ruler and creator of the Earth, and of all natural environments. This provided a major shift in perspective: the Earth was no longer sacred in and of itself, and became sacred only through its status as a product of an external god. A consequence of this shift was the weakening of the normative restrictions on harming nature.

In the creation narratives of the Bible, God gave the power to Adam to name all of the plants and animals and advised that the Earth was to be used at Adam's discretion for the benefit of humans (Dobel, 2001; White, 1967). This powerful narrative placed humans at the top of a hierarchy; creating a rift between humans and the rest of the natural world (Dodson Gray, 1981), however this was a gradual shift, with older perspectives of the natural world as intrinsically valuable still holding sway throughout the Renaissance (Merchant, 1989). It wasn't until the Enlightenment that the schism between humans and the devalued natural world gained dominance in western thought, giving foothold to dualism through Cartesian philosophy and the scientific rationality of Newtonian thought (Banerjee, 2003; Bristow, 2011).

Enlightenment Thought

Through the narratives of Christianity, Cartesian philosophy and Newtonian science, a worldview was established that allowed the level of environmental exploitation which elicited the Industrial Revolution of England in the eighteenth century and which has been directly implicated in current environmental impairment (Birkin & Polesie, 2012; Merchant, 1989, 2006).

The perception that humans are separate from the natural environment was escalated by Descartes when he philosophically disconnected the object of observation with the act of observation (Belova, 2006; Descartes, 1901/1641). Descartes systematically doubted the existence of everything, until at last he arrived at one thing that could not be doubted: the fact that he was doubting. This led him to conclude that his own reason (his capacity to doubt) was the only thing that could be said to definitely exist (Bristow, 2011), effectively repudiating the existence (not to mention the value) of the natural world.

Since the existence of the natural world cannot be proved in Descartes' argument, our connection to it is tenuous. In what is known as the Cartesian split, the only part of the world that I can be sure actually exists is my own rational mind. This notion that the temporal world is entirely illusory further eroded the normative restrictions which discourage humans from harming it (Merchant, 1989).

Cartesian philosophy was influential in the development of other systems of thought, including Newton's scientific theories (Mathews, 1991). By his time, the idea of an external source of life had become well established, and Newton's scientific methodology strengthened the validity of this idea further. By creating a mechanical view of nature, Newtonian science expanded the split between people and the physical world, further diminishing the normative restraints against exploiting the environment (Hay, 2002; Mathews, 1991). This materialist conception of nature as without intrinsic value removed the grounds to treat the natural environment with respect in and of itself (Mathews, 2006). With the perception of nature as a conglomeration of insensible and unrelated parts came the erosion of a normative ethical framework which would hinder exploitation (Merchant, 1989).

The universe according to Newton's conception was constructed from a collection of disparate objects. By conceptualising a universe made in this way, the logical connections which link objects within a system are diminished. By diminishing these links, an ontology of discrete objects which is central to dualistic principles was cemented into the western worldview (Mathews, 1991). Enlightenment thinkers such as Newton and Descartes helped to liberate (enlighten) those in western culture from the superstitions and religious power structures of the Middle Ages, but also moved it closer towards the materialist culture of Modernity (d'Entreves, 2014). The division between 'mind' and 'matter,' and the increasing mechanisation of the West's conception of nature changed the perception of people's place in nature profoundly.

In response to Cartesian and Newtonian narratives, the distinctions between humans and the rest of the natural world were anchored into the western worldview. The hierarchy between humans and the natural environment was magnified and the gap was amplified into what is now known as dualism. Western thought maintains a myriad of other dualisms, such as the masculine/feminine, reason/emotion, mind/body and human/nature dualities. Plumwood (1991) reflects that these dualities have been particularly stressed in the rationalist tradition, and further reinforce an oppositional framework in which each dualism represents the pattern of dominance which permeates western thought. As such, discourse which expresses dualism communicates a domineering and potentially exploitative attitude towards the natural world.

Hamilton (2002) asserts that the relationship between instrumental rationality and intuition can also be considered through a dualistic lens. He claims that historically, humans have related to the natural world through intuition, yet since the scientific and industrial revolutions of the Enlightenment, intuition has been diminished and is now considered trivial. He claims that instrumental reason has been the basis for economics since that time, contributing to the decline of a dynamic relationship between humans and nature.

Hamilton (2002) demonstrates that neoliberal economics was an expression of Enlightenment thinking which has privileged instrumental rationality at the expense of the natural environment. He illustrates that such economics is a direct result of an impersonal rationality where the value of actions can be calculated in purely monetary or numerical terms. In parallel with Newton's machine-like conception of the world, economics presents the world as a calculator.

Modernism

Modernism was founded on many of the conceptualisations of Enlightenment thought, magnifying them to distortion. For instance, Hamilton (2002) describes modern (or neoliberal) economics through its focus on individuality, objectivity and instrumental reason. He explains that modern economics views people as individuals focused on maximising their wealth, exclusive of any emotional or relational context – principles which are hostile to the natural environment.

Arendt describes Modernity variously as an age of mass society; of bureaucratic administration and anonymous labour; of elite domination and manipulation of public opinion; and of homogeny and conformity (d'Entreves, 2014). These institutions are affiliated with accounting and the modern corporation. In relation to environmental philosophy, Arendt discusses Modernity in terms of the effort to escape the restrictions of physicality and temporality of Earthly life through the application of science and technology. This effort is witnessed through the narrative of space exploration and colonisation; through the attempt to recreate and manipulate life artificially, to extend our life spans (d'Entreves, 2014) and through the construction of 'virtual' spaces and communities.

Foucault (1970) similarly notes the epistemological differences between what he calls the 'epistemes' of the classical and modern eras. He points towards the changing perspective of humans at the beginning of the Modern era, to see themselves as transcendent from the world (Best & Kellner, 1991). These themes exemplify an attempt to transcend and diminish the natural environment, and have informed much of the contemporary approach towards nature within western culture.

Transcendence

Latour (2016a, 2016b) concurs with Arendt in terms of the transcendent basis of Modernism, in particular of Modernist views of nature. He explores the link between the first image of the Earth seen from space and how this profoundly changed perceptions towards the natural world. This image itself, now so familiar, was the first to portray nature from such a distance – from a transcendent height. Latour argues that the image of the Earth from space has little relation to what we consider our natural environment from the vantage point of the Earth itself.

Dodson Gray (1981) links the transcendent worldview with the underpinning principles of Christianity, calling attention to the hierarchical structures inherent within this religion. She explores the 'Man-Above' concept, demonstrating how Christianity is guided by an ontological structure where God is transcendent and above men, who are considered above women and children, who are themselves placed above animals and plants, with the idea of nature placed at the very bottom of this hierarchical worldview. It is through this metaphorical lens that the Christian tradition has historically viewed physical reality. Dodson Gray explains that this worldview is indicated in the religious texts, with the following example from the Christian Bible (Psalm 8:3–8):

> When I consider thy heavens, the work of thy fingers,
>   the moon and the stars, which thou hast ordained;
> what is man, that thou art mindful of him?
>   and the son of man, that thou visitest him?
> For thou hast made him little lower than the angels,
>   and hast crowned him with glory and honour.
> Thou madest him to have dominion over the works of thy hands;
>   thou hast put all things under his feet,
> all sheep and oxen,
>   yea, and the beasts of the field,
> the fowl of the air, and the fish of the sea,
>   and whatsoever passeth through the paths of the seas.

While many people in contemporary western culture would consider themselves secular as individuals, western cultural practices still reflect a Christian past, through legislation which enforces Christian values, to the worldviews which still profoundly influence the way we interpret the world, and in particular the way we interact with nature (Dobel, 2001; Dodson Gray, 1981; Merchant, 1989).

Christianity cemented the transcendent worldview into western culture, however the seed was planted well before the introduction of this theology. In Ancient Greece, Platonian thought introduced dualistic principles, however these principles are also inherent in a transcendent worldview. Plato's cave allegory is a classic example of how concepts of transcendence are implicitly woven into his philosophies.

In the cave allegory Plato explains that all people are trapped in a metaphorical cave, and what they perceive as reality is nothing more than moving shadows projected onto a wall from the light of a fire. One of the people – the philosopher – escapes from the cave and as he leaves, realises that his version of reality had heretofore been nothing but illusion, and that 'true' reality only exists outside of the cave. He goes to the mouth of the cave, sees that the 'real' source of light is the sun, a million times brighter than the fire in the cave. The philosopher re-enters the cave to share his newfound wisdom about the 'true' reality of the world, only to be put to death (Latour, 2004). Traditional interpretations of this myth hold that the sunlight represents reason (Brennan, 2006), and that the cave, along with its illusory projections represents the natural world (Bourdeau, 2004).

In some senses this myth reflects a dualistic view, but it also sets up a set of transcendent principles which convey the natural world as less 'real' than human reason – a transcendent value. This archetype is also evident in many religious beliefs – Christianity views a transcendent heaven, or a transcendent God as superior to Earth, as does Islam; Buddhism urges its devotees to strive for a transcendent nirvana, and many new age spiritualities valorise a transcendent spiritual plane, or the 'soul' over physical reality (Dodson Gray, 1981; Meyer, 1999; Plumwood, 1993). Contemporary western culture and corporate values adhere to this pattern through the valorisation of reason, profit and capital at the expense of the physical world (Bourdeau, 2004; Bourdieu, 1986).

While the transcendent worldview has been a steadfast counterpart of western culture for millennia, this view was somewhat reconstructed in the nineteenth century. At this time, 'transcendentalism' emerged in opposition to the dominant values of the Enlightenment (Nash, 1973; Hay, 2002). At that time, environmental philosophers such as Emerson, Thoreau and Muir began to express a new appreciation of the natural environment, which they perceived as being threatened by the continual pioneering of the American wilderness. This appreciation was embedded in, and stemmed directly from, a Christian understanding of the natural world. In 1836, Emerson declared that "nature is the symbol of spirit...the world is emblematic..." (as cited in Nash, 1973). While this approach is more sympathetic to nature than other versions of transcendence, it is still based on the view that the physical world is a reflection (a symbol, or emblem) of a transcendent god, rather than having an inherent value in and of itself. As such, transcendentalism can be seen as an attempt, with varying degrees of success, to overcome the metaphysical barriers of Christianity's devalorisation of nature.

Summary

Three themes which emerge from this literature review are interconnectivity, dualism and transcendence. Ranging from the pre-Socratic era to contemporary times, these three approaches have been woven into the fabric of western culture. The historical view which was taken in this chapter has followed this thread in a nonlinear pattern, reflecting Haraway's amodern view of the role of history (2004), and Foucault's genealogy (Foucault, 1972; Kendall & Wickham, 1999), both of which see the present as a reflection of past events; that the relationship between the present and the past is a constantly negotiated now. As such, evidence of these philosophical themes in the corporate environmental report will help to explain corporate relationship with the natural world.

This chapter has outlined the profound impact of history through a social constructionist view. The relationship between philosophy and the treatment of the natural world has been demonstrated through the multiple lenses of interconnectivity, dualism and transcendence. Being themselves the product of cultural influence, these philosophical approaches are both socially constructed and constructing. As such, they do not represent the only way to view the natural world and are not always complete and distinct categories. For instance, the themes at time overlap and can be viewed from multiple angles. The perspective provided in this chapter, while informed by a historical review, is also informed by the researcher's interpretation of western history.

Interconnectivity's branches connect ecofeminism, deep ecology and immanence with Ancient Greek philosophers such as Heraclitus and Aristotle, while the roots of contemporary dualism and transcendence have been traced to Platonian thought, and reflected in powerful western institutions such as Christianity, Newtonian science and Cartesian philosophy (Abram, 1996). The beginnings of the philosophical separation of humans and nature are detected in the philosophies of Ancient Greece and have continued to be woven through western philosophies and world views throughout the ages (Wiman, 1990). These traditions in thought have allowed for the erosion of normative restraints which would counter the favouring of economic benefit over the wellbeing of the natural environment (Kheel, 2008; Warren, 1998).

This chapter has provided a background for contemporary philosophical approaches to the natural world, and consequently, for the corporate relationship with nature. The next chapter will instead focus on the more pragmatic relationships between the contemporary corporate world and nature, particularly through accounting and corporate reporting.

References

Abram, D. (1996). *The Spell of the Sensuous: Perception and Language in a More-than-Human World*. New York: Vintage Books.

Ackrill, J. L. (1981). *Aristotle the Philosopher*. Oxford: Clarendon Press.

Austin, J. (2005). *Culture and Identity* (2nd ed.). Frenchs Forest, NSW: Pearson.

Banerjee, S. B. (2003). Who Sustains Whose Development? Sustainable Development and the Reinvention of Nature. *Organization Studies, 24*(1), 143–180.

Baskin, J. (2015). Paradigm Dressed as Epoch: The Ideology of the Anthropocene. *Environmental Values, 24*(1), 9–29.

Belova, O. (2006). The Event of Seeing: A Phenomenological Perspective on Visual Sense-Making. *Culture and Organization, 12*(2), 93–107.

Berger, P., & Luckman, T. (1966). *The Social Construction of Reality: A Treatise in the Sociology of Knowledge.* New York: First Anchor.

Best, S., & Kellner, D. (1991). Foucault and the Critique of Modernity. In *Postmodern Theory: Critical Interrogations* (pp. 34–75). London: Macmillan Education.

Birkin, F. (1996). The Ecological Accountant: From the Cogito to Thinking Like a Mountain. *Critical Perspectives on Accounting, 7*(3), 231–257.

Birkin, F., & Polesie, T. (2012). *Intrinsic Sustainable Development: Epistemes, Science, Business and Sustainability.* Singapore: World Scientific Publishing Company.

Bourdeau, P. (2004). The Man – Nature Relationship and Environmental Ethics. *Journal of Environmental Radioactivity, 72*(1), 9–15.

Bourdieu, P. (1986). The Forms of Capital. In I. Szeman & T. Kaposy (Eds.), *Cultural Theory: An Anthology* (pp. 81–93). Oxford: Wiley-Blackwell.

Brennan, A. (2006). Review of Bruno Latour, Politics of Nature. *Environmental Ethics, 28*(2), 221–224.

Brennan, A., & Lo, Y. (2011). *Environmental Ethics.* Retrieved November, from http://plato.stanford.edu/entries/ethics-environmental/

Bristow, W. (2011). *Enlightenment.* Retrieved April 30, from http://plato.stanford.edu/entries/enlightenment/

Bullard, R. (2015). Environmental Racism and the Environmental Justice Movement. In M. A. Cahn & R. O'Brien (Eds.), *Thinking about the Environment: Readings on Politics, Property and the Physical World* (pp. 196–204). London: Routledge.

Cooper, C., & Senkl, D. (2016). An(Other) Truth: A Feminist Perspective on KPMG's True Value. *Sustainability Accounting, Management and Policy Journal, 7*(4), 494–516.

Crosby, D. A. (2003). Transcendence and Immanence in a Religion of Nature. *American Journal of Theology and Philosophy, 24*(3), 245–259.

d'Entreves, M. P. (2014). *Hannah Arendt.* Stanford University. Retrieved December 1, from http://plato.stanford.edu/archives/sum2014/entries/arendt/

Descartes, R. (1901/1641). *Meditations on First Philosophy.* Dayton, OH: Wright State University, 2005.

Dobel, P. (2001). The Judeo-Christian Stewardship Attitude to Nature. In L. Pojman (ed.), *Environmental Ethics: Readings in Theory and Application* (3rd ed., pp. 24–28). Belmont, CA: Wadsworth.

Dodson Gray, E. (1981). *Green Paradise Lost.* Wellesley, MA: Roundtable Press.

Figuero, R., & Mills, C. (2001). Environmental Justice. In D. Jamieson (Ed.), *A Companion to Environmental Philosophy* (pp. 426–438). Cambridge, MA: Blackwell Publishing.

Foucault, M. (1970). *The Order of Things: An Archeology of the Human Sciences.* London: Tavistock Publications.

Foucault, M. (1972). *The Archaeology of Knowledge.* New York: World of Man, Pantheon Books.

Foucault, M., Rabinow, P., & Rose, N. S. (2003). *The Essential Foucault: Selections from the Essential Works of Foucault, 1954–1984.* New York: New Press.

Fox, W. (1990). *Toward a Transpersonal Ecology.* Boston, MA: Shambhala.

Fox, W. (2000). Deep Ecology and Virtue Ethics. *Philosophy Now, 26*(April/May), 21–23.

Giddens, A. (2008). *The Politics of Climate Change: National Responses to the Challenge of Global Warming.* London: Policy Network.

Gonzalez, C. G. (2001). Beyond Eco-Imperialism: An Environmental Justice Critique of Free Trade. *Denver University Law Review, 78,* 979.

Guldi, J., & Armitage, D. (2014). *The History Manifesto.* Cambridge: Cambridge University Press.

Hadot, P. (2006). *The Veil of Isis: An Essay on the History of the Idea of Nature.* Cambridge, MA: The Belknap Press of Harvard University Press.

Hamilton, C. (2002). Dualism and Sustainability. *Ecological Economics, 42*(1–2), 89–99.

Haraway, D. J. (2004). *The Haraway Reader,* New York: Routledge.

Hawken, P. (1993). *The Ecology of Commerce: A Declaration of Sustainability.* New York: HarperBusiness.

Hawkins, E., Ortega, P., Suckling, E., Schurer, A., Hegerl, G., Jones, P., Joshi, M., Osborn, T. J., Masson-Delmotte, V., Mignot, J., Thorne, P., & Oldenborgh, G. J. (2017). Estimating Changes in Global Temperature since the Preindustrial Period. *Bulletin of the American Meteorological Society, 98*(9), 1841–1856.

Hay, P. (2002). *Main Currents in Western Environmental Thought.* Coogee: University of New South Wales Press.

Hickey, A. (2005). Applying Deconstruction: Establishing a Critical Viewpoint. In J. Austin (Ed.), *Culture and Identity.* Frenches Forest, NSW: Pearson.

IPCC. (2013). *Climate Change 2013: The Physical Science Basis.* Cambridge: IPCC.

Jackson, S. (2017). Enduring and Persistent Injustices in Water Access in Australia. In A. Lukasiewicz, S. Dovers, L. Robin, J. McKay, S. Schilizzi, & S. Graham (Eds.), *Natural Resources and Environmental Justice: Australian Perspectives* (pp. 121–132). Clayton South: CSIRO Publishing.

Jenks, C. (2005). *Culture.* London: Routledge.

Kahn, C. H., & Heraclitus. (1979). *The Art and Thought of Heraclitus: An Edition of the Fragments with Translation and Commentary.* Cambridge: Cambridge University Press.

Kant, I. (2001/1786). Rational Beings Alone Have Moral Worth. In L. Pojman (Ed.), *Environmental Ethics: Readings in Theory and Application* (3rd ed., pp. 31–32), Belmont, CA: Wadsworth.

Kathyayini, K., Tilt, C. A., & Lester, L. H. (2012). Corporate Governance and Environmental Reporting: An Australian Study. *Corporate Governance, 12*(2), 143–163.

Kendall, G., & Wickham, G. (1999). *Using Foucault's Methods. Introducing Qualitative Methods.* London: Sage.

Kenny, A. (2010). *A New History of Western Philosophy.* Oxford: Oxford University Press.

Kheel, M. (2008). *Nature Ethics.* London: Rowman & Littlefield.

Klein, N. (2015). *This Changes Everything: Capitalism vs The Climate.* New York: Simon & Schuster.

Latour, B. (2004). *Politics of Nature.* Cambridge, MA: Harvard University Press.

Latour, B. (2016a). Onus Orbis Terrarum: About a Possible Shift in the Definition of Sovereignty. *Millennium – Journal of International Studies, 44*(3), 305–320.

Latour, B. (2016b). *Reset Modernity.* Lecture: University of Tasmania.

Mathews, F. (1991). *The Ecological Self.* London: Routledge.

Mathews, F. (1994). Relating to Nature. *The Trumpeter, 11*(4), 159–166.

Mathews, F. (2001). Deep Ecology. In D. Jamieson (Ed.), *A Companion to Environmental Philosophy* (pp. 218–232). Cambridge, MA: Blackwell.

Mathews, F. (2006). Beyond Modernity and Tradition: A Third Way for Development. *Ethics and the Environment, 11*(2), 85–113.

Mathews, F. (2014). Environmental Philosophy. In N. Trakakis & G. Oppy (Eds.), *A History of Australasian Philosophy* (pp. 543–591). Dordrecht: Springer.

Mercadal, T. (2014). *Social Constructionism.* Hackensack, NJ: Salem Press.

Merchant, C. (1989). *The Death of Nature: Women, Ecology, and the Scientific Revolution.* New York: Harper & Row.

Merchant, C. (2006). The Scientific Revolution and the Death of Nature. *Isis, 97*(3), 513–533.

Meyer, J. M. (1999). Interpreting Nature and Politics in the History of Western Thought: The Environmentalist Challenge. *Environmental Politics, 8*(2), 1–23.

Milne, M. J., Tregidga, H., & Walton, S. (2009). Words Not Actions! The Ideological Role of Sustainable Development Reporting. *Accounting, Auditing & Accountability Journal, 22*(8), 1211–1257.

Mitchell, J., Lowe, J., Wood, R., & Vellinga, M. (2006). Extreme Events Due to Human-Induced Climate Change. *Philosophical Transactions of the Royal Society, 364,* 2117–2133.

Naess, A. (1973). The Shallow and the Deep, Long-Range Ecology Movement. A Summary. *Inquiry, 16*(1–4), 95–100.

Nash, R. (1973). *Wilderness and the American Mind.* New Haven: Yale University Press.

Nussbaum, M. C. (1988). Non-Relative Virtues: An Aristotelian Approach. *Midwest Studies in Philosophy, 13*(1), 32–53.

Oreskes, N. (2004). The Scientific Consensus on Climate Change. *Science, 306*(5702), 1686.

Plumwood, V. (1991). Nature, Self, and Gender: Feminism, Environmental Philosophy, and the Critique of Rationalism. *Hypatia, 6*(1), 3–27.

Plumwood, V. (1993). *Feminism and the Mastery of Nature.* London: Routledge.

Plumwood, V. (2009). Nature in the Active Voice. *Australian Humanities Review, 46,* 113–129.

Raupach, M., McMichael, A., Finnigan, J., Manderson, L., & Walker, B. (2012). *Negotiating Our Future: Living Scenarios for Australia to 2050.* ACT: Australian Academy of Science.

Said, E. W. (1993). *Culture and Imperialism.* London: Chatto & Windus.

Shafer, W. (2006). Social Paradigms and Attitudes toward Environmental Accountability. *Journal of Business Ethics, 65*(2), 121–147.

Singer, P. (1990/1975). *Animal Liberation: A New Ethics for Our Treatment of Animals* (2nd ed.). New York: Avon Books.

Spence, C. (2009). Social Accounting's Emancipatory Potential: A Gramscian Critique. *Critical Perspectives on Accounting, 20*, 205–227.

Steffen, W., Grinevald, J., Crutzen, P., & McNeill, J. (2011). The Anthropocene: Conceptual and Historical Perspectives. *Philosophical Transactions of the Royal Society, 369*, 842–867.

Tarnas, R. (1996). *The Passion of the Western Mind: Understanding the Ideas that Have Shaped Our World View.* London: Random House.

Walther, G.-R., Post, E., Convey, P., Menzel, A., Parmesan, C., Beebee, T. J. C., Fromentin, J.-M., Hoegh-Guldberg, O., & Bairlein, F. (2002). Ecological Responses to Recent Climate Change. *Nature, 416*(6879), 389–395.

Warren, K. J. (1998). The Legacy of Carolyn Merchant's The Death of Nature. *Organization & Environment, 11*(2), 186–188.

White, L. (1967). The Historical Roots of our Ecological Crisis. *Science, 155*, 1203–1207.

Wiman, I. M. B. (1990). Expecting the Unexpected: Some Ancient Roots to Current Perceptions of Nature. *AMBIO, 19*(2), 62–69.

3   Corporate Reporting

Introduction

Corporate environmental reporting sits at the junction of western environmental philosophy, cultural discourse and the environmental impact of corporations. By articulating the relationship between the corporation and the natural world, corporate environmental reporting implicitly draws from western attitudes towards nature in its discourse. The previous chapter identified philosophies that have impacted the western cultural approach to the natural world. This will provide some useful tools to unpack the contemporary corporate relationship with nature. Chapter 3 now explores corporate environmental reporting, in particular where philosophy and corporate reporting intersect. Since corporate environmental reporting is a branch of accounting, in that it *gives an account* of the corporate relationship with the natural world, this chapter will first explore some of the issues within accounting itself. Specifically, the ways in which discourse and accounting intertwine to socially construct particular perceptions which have been adopted as part of wider western worldviews. This chapter also explores the area of *sustainability reporting*, as this is primarily the space out of which environmental reporting has emerged. Some of the problems inherent in both sustainability and environmental reporting will be discussed here.

To begin this discussion, the value neutrality of accounting is first deconstructed. This deconstruction will allow for a deeper problematisation of the institution of accounting, in particular the environmental reporting practices which have emerged from it. Such problematisation includes the role that philosophy can play in understanding these practices.

Social Construction through Accounting

The idea that an exploration into the history of the West's relationship with the natural world is able to shed light on the practice of contemporary environmental reporting is fundamentally based on the view that

environmental reporting is itself a social construction. Social constructionism can be explained as the idea that cultural and social norms are
constructed through multiple social practices. It has been argued that
all social practices express and reinforce social values. Social practices
include the ways in which individuals interact with each other and the
world around them, but also includes the ways in which institutions interact with broader society.

One such social practice is accounting. Conventional perspectives
present accounting as a collection of objective facts, and therefore outside of the scope of cultural influence. This objective view of accounting is maintained by accountants through a positivist approach which
has traditionally discouraged critical questioning. Such an approach explains accounting through the lens of wealth maximisation and assumes
that decision-makers are exclusively self-interested wealth maximisers.
Challenging this view is the position that any human-made institution
is necessarily social, and informed by social values. Such an argument
holds that accounting cannot therefore be a value-neutral act.

This book concurs with the views of Ruth Hines (1988) and other accounting researchers who recognise the role of accounting in the construction and perpetuation of shared cultural understanding. Such an
approach implicates accounting in the creation and maintenance of social values, particularly through the bias towards economic calculations
and an avoidance of subjectivity. Critical accounting researchers such as
Hopwood (1987) argue that the economic perspective is made real by
accounting. Hopwood outlines that one of the consequences of this social
construction is that a style of management has been constructed which
distances the organisation from physical and temporal realities such as
the work process, the natural world and the community. Values which
are more easily measured (such as monetary values) are included in the
accounting equation, and thus afforded visibility. In contrast, other values
which are less easily measured (such as social or environmental wellbeing)
are excluded, and therefore silenced. Underpinning this view, Gray (2010)
draws attention to the complex interrelationships that are involved in
any true account of sustainability. He juxtaposes this against the relative
simplicity of accounting's quantitative bias towards objectivity and measurement. In this way, accounting has become an instrument for the construction and perpetuation of the privileging of economic benefit over the
wellbeing of people and the rest of the natural world (Broadbent, 2007).

Accounting's ability to construct such a mechanism is based in part
through the illusion of objectivity, which draws from a masculine
rationality[1] (Broadbent, 1998; Young & Williams, 2010). This theme
is expanded by Young (2015), who challenges the underpinning masculine perspective of not only accounting practice, but also accounting
research. She points out that objectivity, abstraction, neutrality, autonomy and efficiency are valorised through accounting. Further to these

qualities, Oakes and Hammond (1995) argue that economic rationalisation, which is in turn based on values such as self-interest and wealth
maximisation, do not take into account other motivations such as the
maintenance of social relationships, a quality often aligned to the concept of the feminine.

Also drawing from a feminist perspective, Cooper and Senkl (2016)
argue that accounting is implicitly informed by a phallocentric position
which silences the perspective of 'the other.' 'The other' is a term frequently used in feminist literature which reflects the idea that there are
others who are disadvantaged by the privileging of a dominant perspective. In terms of accounting, Cooper and Senkl establish the dominant
perspective as phallocentric, and 'the other' as social and environmental
values. They establish that the phallocentric perspective of traditional
accounting is informed by the urge to control. By perpetuating the profit
motive, such traditions aim to silence and diminish the importance of
social and environmental values.

As part of her wider project, Young (2010) challenges some of the
underpinning assumptions upon which accounting is based. She draws
attention to the value judgements involved in categorising business activities into traditional accounting groupings such as assets, liabilities,
revenues, expenses and owners' equity. In doing so, she argues that in
the process of placing events into these categories, possible overlaps are
disregarded, and many events are excluded from the accounting equation, such as the effects of pollution, or the qualities of employees. The
result of this process is that value judgements become embedded into the
accounting system, valorising financial objects and disregarding other
perspectives which place more value on environmental and social wellbeing. These value judgements are cemented into the accounting worldview by the perspective that accounting gives a 'true and fair view,' and
is a neutral conduit for objective information.

This notion has been explored by others, including Ruth Hines, in her
seminal work which critiques the conception of organisational boundaries (1988). In her critique, Hines demonstrates that what is commonly
understood as an organisation has been constructed through an implied
social agreement. The role of accountants in composing and maintaining the illusion that organisations are based on objective understanding is illuminated. Hines points towards the sources of these illusions,
but further to this, she falls short of examining the foundations of such
constructions.

Critical accounting research projects such as those outlined above dismantle the notion that accounting is somehow outside of the network
of socially constructed and constructing institutions. In doing so, they
critique the notion that accounting is necessarily objective and value
neutral. The next step is to explore how this sense of objectivity affects the practice of accounting. Joseph (2012) argues that by 'tethering'

accounting to the goal of objectivity, the potential roles accounting might play – for instance, in sustainability reporting – are limited. He argues that for accounting to genuinely encompass social and environmental reporting, its bias towards objectivity and measurement must give way.

Through its bias towards objectivity, measurement, masculine rationality and self-interest and wealth maximisation, accounting embeds and perpetuates these values. As such, the discourse of accounting shapes not only organisational practice, but also broader social understanding.

Accounting as Discourse

Accounting is often described as the language of business. To give an account of something is to tell a story about it, based on the experiences and underpinning ideologies of the teller (Broadbent, 1998). An account may be a narrative told numerically, literally or some other form of expression that has a shared meaning.

Language, according to Wittgenstein (1953/2010), has at its core a shared meaning understood by others. Shared understanding is created over time through the social experience. As such, Wittgenstein grounds language in the lived experience of people. Language forms part of what we understand as communication and overlaps with other forms of communication, such as visual mediums, facial and body expressions and what Wittgenstein calls language games. Language games acknowledge the complex ways in which language is used, for instance, the shared understanding of sarcasm, shared ideology and different forms of conversation.

To give an account of something is to provide a description of events; in other words, to tell its story. Traditionally, the account of business has been expressed not only through the language of calculations, numbers and monetary symbols, but is also apparent in reports to management, CEO statements, media commentary and accounting standards. More recently, accounts of business also include narratives read through traditional and social media, commentary by external stakeholders such as environmental and grass roots organisations with different perspectives and priorities, individual conversations, advertising, observation, online discussion lists and sponsorship (Buhr, 2007; Dey, 2007; Georgakopoulos & Thomson, 2008). This list is far from exhaustive but goes some way to demonstrating that the broader narrative of business is not exclusive to what is produced by financial accounting, or even by business itself.

Cooper and Puxty (1994) illustrate how the language of business is made up of a web of texts, each one informed by the context from which it emerges. Each organisational report is informed by prior reports within the organisation, the industry and business. Likewise, it is informed by business attitudes, as well as broader societal expectations.

A single corporate report can only be understood as part of a larger web of understandings, much of which goes unnoticed and without meaningful critique.

One such taken for granted aspect of accounting narratives is the authority of the author. Cooper and Puxty's (1994) deconstruction of the patriarchal position of the author creates a space for reader interaction and analysis, allowing for multiple textual interpretations, rather than one singular authoritative version of a text. They explicate how deconstructing the implicit textual relationships invites a dialogue between reader and text, thus effectively reproducing a different text with each reading.

The intertextuality of accounting discourse is also explored by Shearer and Arrington (1993), who focus on other aspects of the patriarchal nature of accounting. From a feminist perspective, they demonstrate how nature is negated through accounting. Their exploration of these issues stems from a feminist reading of genesis, where Adam was granted authority over Eve as well as all of nature. Feminist literature explores the ways in which concepts of women and nature have become intertwined (see, for example, Haraway, 2004; Merchant, 1989; Plumwood, 1993). Shearer and Arrington continue this theme by exploring the ways in which accounting discourse has devalued or negated both women and nature. They link this patriarchal approach to the natural world with accounting, in which rationality and abstraction is valued over the material. In this way, accounting is used as a tool for harnessing and controlling nature, by way of only assigning value once it has been negated and transformed into a 'resource.' A similar argument is made for women, whose traditional work within the family home and community is not a part of the accounting discourse and as such remains silenced (ideas which are explored further in Neimark, 1992; Waring, 1988).

From these arguments, then, accounting discourse contributes to the western cultural project to dominate and tame the natural world; it creates and sustains the western bias against nature. The annual report in particular has been explored by Tinker and Neimark (1987) and Neimark (1992), who discuss the influence of the annual report on the perception within society that both nature and women should be dominated. They argue that rather than being passive describers of economic events, annual reports play a formative role in legitimising socially constructed perceptions of class, gender and nature. By analysing the discourse of General Motors' annual reports over a period of decades, they demonstrate how the organisation has actively shaped public perception for business purposes. It did so through the use of discourse which intrinsically perpetuated social values; more than this, through historical analysis, they found that in some instances, General Motors instigated particular social values that advanced its financial interests.

The relationship between gender and accounting is a theme picked up again by Oakes and Hammond (1995), who examine the underpinning bias towards a masculine perspective as communicated through the discourse of accounting. They illustrate how this bias is expressed through the assumption that decision-makers are informed by a competitive self-interested rationality often associated with neoliberal economics. The bias towards self-interest is seen by Oakes and Hammond as a manifestation of the separation between self and others which is a defining feature of western culture. By introducing feminist theory into the accounting literature, they attempt to dismantle the hegemony of the western, masculine perspective.

Other accounting researchers such as Walters-York (1996) have illustrated the impact of traditional western discourse on accounting through an analysis of the language used in accounting. Walters-York outlines that accounting typically biases positivist language, which she describes as language "stripped of its poetic character" (p. 47). She traces the historical bias towards positivist language to Plato, who claimed that meaning was best expressed through the use of verifiable and objective facts – that is, positivist language. Aristotle on the other hand, favoured the use of poetic and metaphorical language to communicate meaning. Metaphorical language held sway in western traditions until the Enlightenment, when scientific and philosophical enquiry attempted to create universal meanings which supress conflicting ambiguities. Positivist language still remains deeply embedded in the way meaning is legitimised and communicated in everyday western life. Its valorisation is also evident in accounting practice and research.

Young (2013) continues this exploration in an analysis of how metaphor is utilised in accounting discourse. Drawing from Lakoff and Johnson's foundational text which established the role of metaphor in human cognition (1980), Young illustrates how metaphors reveal the perceptions underpinning our understanding of organisations. The ways in which metaphor structures perceptions of the organisation is exemplified in the common metaphor of the organisation as a machine. By considering organisations as machine-like, Young argues that the efficiency, inputs and outputs of the organisation become the focal point of our perception, and thus our expectations. This perception silences understandings of the organisation that take into account other aspects such as conflict, power and relationships.

Metaphors such as the organisation as a container – with an interior delineated by a boundary (Hines, 1988), and an exterior (with externalities) – are constructed through social practice which maintains cultural perceptions about organisations (Young & Williams, 2010). The ways in which metaphor structures our thinking remain largely unquestioned, yet inform much of our decision-making and understanding of the world. As such, it is vitally important that research which questions the use of metaphor is undertaken, in order to expand our capacity to critically engage with the discourse of accounting and business.

Hopwood (1987) also critiques accounting's façade of neutrality, by demonstrating how such a façade has constructed the modern organisation, maintaining this construction for particular ends. He proposes that rather than being a passive mechanism as it is commonly understood, accounting aids in the construction of particular economic and social realities. In part, this is accomplished through the utilisation of an economic rationalisation founded in the positivist language of post-Enlightenment western thought.

Arrington and Francis (1993) argue that through promoting these values, accounting silences the potential for other perspectives to be heard. Accounting's underlying bias towards economic efficiency and capital growth (values associated with neoliberal economics and the post-Enlightenment) has built a practice which is directly implicated in an attitude of dominance towards the natural world. In particular, the discursive nature of the calculations involved in accounting discourse is underpinned by a particular set of values (Miller & Napier, 1993). Calculative texts are commonly considered as purely technical and as such, neutral. Contrary to this commonly held assumption, Miller and Napier (1993) demonstrate how calculative texts (such as accounting) are informed by social practice and contribute to the construction of a social reality which perpetuates post-Enlightenment values.

Post-Enlightenment values have been so thoroughly embedded in many modern institutions that they have formed a hegemony which is often left unquestioned. Tregidga, Milne, and Kearins (2014) describe hegemony as an ideology which has become so dominant that it is considered 'common sense' and is often described as 'natural,' and thus succeeds in being taken for granted. They argue however, that underpinning such hegemony of ideas is a silencing of other perceptions. By illuminating hegemonies, the power structures concealed within are exposed.

As outlined above, accounting practice discursively and metaphorically distances the organisation from the natural world. It does so in part through its attempt to objectively portray business practice in the quantitative language of logical positivism. Thus, accounting is linked to a post-Enlightenment approach to the natural world, in which rationality and abstraction are valued over the material. Within the accounting discourse such paradigms are encoded, structuring the ways in which the physical world can be understood and valued, through the eyes of business.

Accounting and Sustainability Reporting

Traditionally, the information required of an organisation has been almost exclusively financial in nature. This kind of information has been an important mechanism used to manage and control organisational operations. Externally too, the financial duties of organisations have been considered the primary way in which the corporation interacts, benefits and impacts wider society. The fiscal behaviour of corporations has instigated depressions, global financial crises and contributed to the gross domestic product of nations, events which affect wider society and are therefore under tight scrutiny. With each financial crisis, accounting standards have come under pressure to change and adapt to new conditions.

Now with parallel problems in the natural environment which threaten to influence social life in ways at least equally as profound as the financial crises which have occurred in the past, organisations have experienced growing pressure to report on social and environmental issues. Framed this way, the connection between accounting and sustainability reporting may seem like a logical link, however the problems of linking sustainability and accounting have been widely discussed in the accounting literature.

Bebbington and Gray (2001) in particular, examine the problems of allowing sustainability reporting to be controlled by corporate interests, claiming that "it is difficult to imagine anything more guaranteed to put the final nail in humankind's coffin than letting this hijacking go un-contested" (p. 561). Their concern is the role accounting plays in legitimising the possibility that corporate activities can be sustainable with only minor modifications to current practice. According to these authors, in order to be truly sustainable, corporate practices must be questioned deeply. This contestation will likely require a profound transformation, particularly in light of the underlying hegemony of corporate values.

Sustainability and Environmental Reporting

While some organisations were reporting on social and environmental issues prior to the 1990s, these reports primarily focused on human resource issues. This kind of reporting expanded to encompass broader issues throughout the 1990s until the present time. Initially reporting on these issues was largely limited to the supply of additional information within the annual report and tended to be highly variable in both quantity and quality (Deegan & Gordon, 1996). When stand-alone social and environmental reports began to appear, they were produced predominantly by organisations within environmentally sensitive sectors such as the mining and petroleum industries (Deegan & Gordon, 1996).

The practice of sustainability reporting has expanded and according to KPMG, who each year produce a report on the state of sustainability reporting, social and environmental reports are now produced by 92% of the largest companies (by revenue) worldwide (KPMG, 2015). KPMG also found that by 2015, reporting was no longer dominated by environmentally sensitive industries.

Reports which disclose a range of information broader than purely financial are labelled variously, with 43% of the companies surveyed by KPMG (2013) calling their reports 'sustainability,' 25% 'corporate social responsibility,' 14% 'corporate responsibility' and the remainder labelling their reports under other names such as 'sustainable development,' 'corporate citizenship,' 'environmental and social' and 'people, planet, profit' reports. They are also known as integrated, triple bottom line and social reports, depending on their focus. By 2015, 56% of the world's largest companies included such information within their annual financial reports (KPMG, 2015). What all of these reports have in common is that they include non-financial organisational information.

One of the key terms which connect all of these reports is the word 'sustainability.' The underlying meaning of this term has been widely debated. In the accounting literature, Gray (2010) and Bebbington and Gray (2000) argue that since sustainability is a global issue, it is meaningless to claim sustainability at an organisational level. They explain that most sustainability reports do little to address or change global sustainability issues and are more akin to propaganda – constructing a 'dominant discourse' which attempts to influence community perception around sustainability. In this way, organisations continue to operate unchallenged by any meaningful changes that might be required to attain actual sustainability.

Common organisational understandings of the term 'sustainability' are based on the concept of sustainable development, which was most notably defined in the Brundlandt Report as: "development that meets the needs of the present without compromising the ability of future generations to meet their own needs" (WCED, 1987, p. 87). While it is noted that other definitions of sustainability exist, the Brundlandt definition remains the most referred to in the context of organisational sustainability reporting.

The terms 'sustainability' and 'sustainable development' have been critiqued widely, with some strong arguments that there can be no sustainable development within the current accounting and commercial frameworks. The corporate capture of the term 'sustainability' has stripped it of meaningful definition. Sustainability can now refer to anything which is marginally less harmful to the environment than current practice.

Despite efforts to integrate the concept of sustainability into the ontology of business, it seems to have remained outside the realm of normal business operations (Joseph, 2012). Joseph argues that one reason for this is that sustainability and the ontology of business remain fundamentally at odds, and that any reformation must begin with the ideology of the underpinning framework of business – capitalism. This view is shared by others (for example, Greenfield, 2008), who argue that the legally embedded function of public organisations to maximise wealth disallows any meaningful path towards actual sustainability.

Similarly, Lehman (1999) proposes that one of the reasons sustainability reporting perpetuates the status quo of business is that the frameworks upon which it has been constructed are based on approaches which limit the potential for reform and innovation. He argues that while corporations inhabit a privileged position as potential agents of change, they have instead failed to transform the currently pernicious relationship between corporate action and the natural environment. The fault, according to Lehman, lies in the underpinning approaches upon which sustainability reporting models have been developed. These underpinning approaches are based on traditions in accounting which are constructed on procedural liberal foundations. An attempt to standardise sustainability issues is an integral aspect of this foundational premise; a pattern demonstrated by sustainability reporting systems already in use such as the Global Reporting Initiative (GRI). Lehman argues that by continuing to underpin sustainability reporting on a procedural approach, no fundamental changes will be made to business operations. In response, Lehman encourages critical examination of the underlying principles of social and environmental accounting in order to promote public debate.

A central aspect of sustainability reporting is the reporting of the environmental impacts of organisational activities. Gray (2010) argues that the real purpose of environmental reports is to represent how the organisation would like stakeholders to view the issue of environmental sustainability – as something contained and controllable, able to easily coincide along with economic growth. The coincidence of environmental sustainability and economic growth is a view which contradicts the scientific consensus (Hawken, 1993; Oreskes, 2004).

Corporate Environmental Reporting

Concern about environmental damage is not a recent phenomenon. Nor is the response to provide an 'account' in response to these concerns. As early as 1664, reports on the environmental effects of a rapidly industrialising culture were being published (Bruyn, 2001). It has been argued that the publication of such early examples of environmental reports represent a move in western culture to attempt to manage the natural world; moving away from an older world view of humans as a part of nature, to a hierarchical perspective which grants humans the right to manage the rest of the natural world for maximum human benefit (Kheel, 2008; Merchant, 1989). These changes occurred at a time in European history which coincided with the onset of the Industrial Revolution.

As industrialisation advanced, it instituted a world view based on neoliberal economics (Birkin & Polesie, 2011; Hamilton, 2002; Merchant, 2006). Concern for the environment waned as the potential of perpetual economic growth obscured the adverse consequences of treating the environment as a resource provided for the purpose of growing wealth. However, after several centuries, and as the disadvantages of industrialism become apparent, the West is beginning to recognise the need to take corrective action (Birkin & Polesie, 2012). One aspect of this corrective action is the growing response from corporations to report on the impact their commercial decisions have on the natural environment, through environmental reporting.

Corporate environmental reporting provides corporations with a means to communicate their interactions with the natural environment to stakeholders and the wider community. More specifically, it is an instrument used to illustrate the relationship between the company and the natural environment. Although environmental reporting has become an important way to communicate these issues, there remains a high degree of scepticism about these types of reports, as discussed in broader society as well as in the accounting literature. It has been argued that current practices of environmental reporting perpetuate a 'business as usual' approach to environmental management (Lehman, 1999). This argument is supported by others who claim that the procedural and technical focus of corporate sustainability reporting masks an underlying antagonism towards making meaningful changes that could moderate the environmental damage linked to modern corporate activities (Gray, Adams, & Owen, 2014; Shafer, 2006).

Environmental Reporting as Stakeholder Engagement

It is argued that the wellbeing of the natural world is the most pressing issue affecting the global population today (Gray, 2010; IPCC, 2013; Klein, 2015; Mitchell, Lowe, Wood, & Vellinga, 2006; Oreskes, 2004; Reser, Bradley, Glendon, Ellul, & Callaghan, 2012; Steffen, Grinevald, Crutzen, & McNeill, 2011). The business community increasingly responds to stakeholder concerns for environmental health by reporting on the environmental effects of organisational activities (Kolk, 2003; O'Riordan & Fairbrass, 2014). While stakeholder engagement remains a primary objective for organisations to provide sustainability reports, there is a large degree of cynicism both within the academic literature and in the wider community of stakeholders about the authenticity of these reports (Haque, Deegan, & Inglis, 2016; Joseph, 2012; Morrison, Wilmshurst, & Shimeld, 2018).

Cho, Roberts and Patten (2010) maintain this critical view by exploring the corporate attempt to influence stakeholder perceptions in relation to environmental reporting through the manipulation of language. They find that unfavourable outcomes tend to be reported using technical terms, while more straightforward language is used to communicate favourable outcomes. Others have also demonstrated the deceptive aspects of sustainability reporting by organisations, with Livesey (2001) comparing the reports of Royal Dutch Shell with actual events which were drastically different from those reported; Clare, Krogman and Caine (2013) and Spence (2009) who discuss the use of particular language which obfuscates environmental impact and others (Birkin & Polesie, 2011; Gray, 2010; Lehman, 1999) who question the integrity of such reporting.

Stakeholder engagement provides a perspective which attempts to deconstruct the hierarchy of the corporation. Donaldson and Preston (1995) define stakeholders as anyone with legitimate interests in the activities of an organisation. They argue that any reciprocal interests of the organisation in the stakeholder are not as consequential as the stakeholder's own interests; however, Gray et al. (2014) present a definition of a stakeholder as any person who is either influenced by, or can influence the organisation, leading to a more bilateral understanding of stakeholder engagement.

As Gray et al. (2014) explain, stakeholder engagement embraces a systems-based perspective of the organisation. They introduce a deep ecology perspective by expanding the list of potential stakeholders to include non-human life, in a move which promotes the relationship between stakeholder engagement and accountability. In this account of stakeholder engagement, two versions compete – one based on accountability, which grounds the organisation in an ethical relationship with the systems within which it is bound; the second based on what Unerman and Bennett (2004) describe as the organisation prioritising stakeholders with the greatest economic influence. This second account clearly fails to decentralise the organisation from its hierarchy of power.

Unerman and Bennett (2004) identify two issues with implementing stakeholder engagement in an organisational setting. The first issue is how the organisation might identify and connect with stakeholders, particularly when there is a wide range of individuals influenced by the organisation. The second issue is how to determine some kind of consensus of stakeholder expectations. Unerman and Bennett's solution is to use a Habermassian framework which provides procedures for achieving consensus among diverse groups through discourse.

Habermas is a member of the Frankfurt School of critical theorists. The Frankfurt School bases its version of critical theory on Kantian ethics which aim for an individualistic rendering of freedom; an aim which may be compatible with the rationality of business aims, but is not consistent with an environmental ethic which values natural qualities. The method proposed by Unerman and Bennett betrays its Kantian roots by its drive to find a universal and singular solution to stakeholder expectations.

The deep ecology perspective of stakeholder relationships provided by Gray et al. (2014) however, overcomes the limitations of an ethical framework founded on an oppositional logic, and allows for the inclusion of multiple voices. This perspective is closely aligned with accountability, a term which highlights the responsibility of organisations towards others, and acknowledges the impact of organisational decisions on others, but also the impacts others have on the organisation.

Accountability and Transparency

Stakeholders are considered important to the organisation through their ability to influence, or to be influenced by the organisations' activities (Gray, Owen, & Maunders, 1987). The idea that the organisation owes a responsibility to stakeholders gives rise to the theme of accountability; a concept which Gray et al. (2014) regard as central to sustainability reporting. Accountability builds on links between the organisation and its stakeholders, with the goal of allowing stakeholders a more direct voice with which to express interest. From this perspective, Gray et al.'s understanding of accountability attempts to deconstruct the hierarchy of the organisation by empowering stakeholders to influence the organisation, and in turn, opening the organisation up, or answering to, stakeholder interests.

While accountability may lie at the heart of corporate sustainability and environmental reporting, it is a concept which has also been critiqued through the lens of psychoanalysis (Roberts, 2009). Through this perspective, the self-awareness of the organisation creates a self-protective barrier between the organisation and stakeholders. Roberts (2009) argues that this leads to a kind of self-censorship and deception in the reporting process which hinders the purposes of accountability and creates fractures in the relationships between the organisation and its stakeholders.

Similarly, Andrew (2007) critiques the procedural and technical approaches which have usurped the accountability project, demonstrating that these approaches exclude authentic ethical considerations, with organisations relying on accountability measures which promote a distance between the organisation and those to whom it is accountable. Since organisational dialogue with stakeholders is considered an essential element of accountability, barriers to this process are frequently critiqued.

Hopwood (2009) argues that while non-financial reporting may potentially increase transparency, it is equally likely to reduce visibility and construct a barrier between organisations and their stakeholders. He posits that this could occur through the construction of new ways to deflect questioning and increase the monolith of corporate legitimacy. One way to counter this tendency is through the readings of alternative accounts. Alternative accounts are likely to take the form of a document which has been put together for the express purpose of filling the gap left by corporate or organisational sustainability reporting (Adams, 2004; Dey, 2007), including unofficial information which informs stakeholder opinion.

Any text, such as a single organisational environmental report, is bound to other sources of information in an inter-textual web (Cooper & Puxty, 1994; Kristeva, 1986). Part of this web is produced by the organisation itself, in the form of advertising, public relations, websites and social media (Buhr, 2007; Campbell & Beck, 2004; Tregidga, Milne, & Lehman, 2012). Other parts of this intertextual web are received by stakeholders through a wide variety of information sources, including conversations, blogs, online discussion groups (Unerman & Bennett, 2004), media and sponsorships. These alternative accounts provide information which is not provided through the accounts produced by the organisation (Georgakopoulos & Thomson, 2008). These externally produced accounts have been called shadow accounts (Dey, 2007).

While sustainability reporting has the potential to improve transparency between organisations and their stakeholders, many stakeholders retain a degree of cynicism towards the information provided in such reports (Adams, 2004; Crane, Matten, & Moon, 2008; Joseph, 2012). This cynicism may be explained by the various gaps which have been identified in the literature, such as the reporting-performance portrayal gap (Adams, 2004), the assurance expectations gap (Swift & Dando, 2002), the legitimacy gap (Moerman & Van Der Laan, 2005) and the credibility gap (Dando & Swift, 2003). While corporate organisations have been slow to fill this vacuum, pressure groups and non-governmental organisations have not.

Barriers between organisations and their stakeholders have been described in terms of a disparity between organisational reporting and stakeholder perception. These disparities have been explained as a lack of credibility on the part of the organisation (Dando & Swift, 2003); discrepancies between what the organisation claims, and information available from other sources (Adams, 2004), and differences in ethical approaches (Morrison et al., 2018; Rodrigue, 2014). Some of these gaps are discussed below.

Dando and Swift (2003) argue that for organisations and their reports to be perceived as credible, trust must be cultivated. They argue that the trust of stakeholders does not seem to be increasing at the same rate that sustainability reporting is being taken up by organisations. The lack of credibility is also reflected in little trust in assurance providers who assure the accuracy of data provided in the reports. Stakeholders need assurance of more than just data accuracy in order to close the credibility gap between stakeholders and organisations, particularly in the area of sustainability reporting.

Haque et al. (2016) examine the gap between what stakeholders expect, and what is provided in the corporate disclosures of Australian companies, particularly in light of information relating to climate change. The expectation gap which they identify is traced to a lack of proactive stakeholder engagement as well as the preoccupation with wealth-maximisation. They implicate managers' lack of interest in accountability in the failure to adequately report on climate change issues, leading to a widening expectation gap.

In a study based on a single organisation, Adams (2004) revealed a gap between information which was being portrayed by the company and that being provided by external sources. She argues that this gap between the ethical, social and environmental information being portrayed, and actual performance creates a disparity between the organisation and stakeholders' perceptions. Adams (2004) demonstrated that the magnitude of this gap is a measure of the organisation's accountability to stakeholders.

Similarly, Rodrigue (2014) drew on the gap found by Adams (2004), using similar methods to conclude that when the information provided about environmental issues by an organisation differs from that available from other sources, there is a gap in the ethical expectations. Rodrigue (2014) also found that as the gap between the ethical approaches of an organisation and its stakeholders widens, the level of accountability is consequently lowered.

Morrison et al. (2018) also explore the ethical gap between a single case study company and its stakeholders. We found that as the relationship between the stakeholder and company became less direct, the gap between the ethical approaches also widened. Since the company's purpose in producing an environmental report was to communicate with more distant stakeholders, this finding demonstrated that a gap of this nature made the report less valuable; to both the company and its stakeholders.

A Critical Approach

In light of the problems in corporate environmental reporting which have been discussed in this chapter, I adopt a critical approach in this book. A critical approach is a way to find and expose the underpinning meanings attached to social acts. The intention of such an approach is to illuminate the philosophies which inform social conventions (Archel, Husillos, & Spence, 2011). As such, there is great value in the illumination of underpinnings over which a dominant discourse has grown and calcified. This is particularly so in the case of environmental discourses.

The histories of environmental discourses contain implicit meanings which carry with them certain approaches towards the treatment of the natural world. To discursively explore such meanings is to identify another layer of communication which is subtle, yet potentially more powerful than that which is explicitly communicated. In seeking to identify these implicit meanings, this book takes a critical approach which builds from the traditions of critical theory.

Critical theory incorporates theoretical approaches which seek to "liberate human beings from the circumstances that enslave them" (Horkheimer, 1982, p. 244). Critical theory interrogates assumptions which are often taken for granted, but which nevertheless inform the way people understand and interact with the world (Agger, 1991). In particular, it argues against a positivist view of the world which claims value neutrality.

Critical theory grew from a profound dissatisfaction with positivism and capitalism, both of which can be said to stem from Enlightenment thought. Foundational critical theorists were part of the Frankfurt School group of philosophers in the early twentieth century. Initially, this movement grew from a sense of surprise that Marx's predictions about the demise of capitalism did not manifest. In exploring why capitalism did not self-destruct as predicted, the Frankfurt School critical theorists developed the idea of 'false consciousness' which guides people's actions. 'False consciousness' is the mechanism by which people internalise cultural values and norms, which in turn instils a sense of obedience within the social system. In this state, people accept the existing social system as an inevitable and rational outcome of history (Agger, 1991).

Agger (1991) argues that positivist thinking is directly linked to 'false consciousness' through its denial of any underpinning values. He explains how positivism holds that it is possible to reflect an objective reality in the absence of any presuppositions. The Frankfurt School of critical theorists argued that during the Enlightenment, positivism replaced mythology as the dominant ideology guiding western culture. The danger in this is that positivism is a mechanism for perpetuating the status quo, through its inability to reflect on its presuppositions. In this way, positivism perpetuates passivity, since people are taught to uncritically accept the world 'as it is' (that is, as positivism presents the world).

Ideologies such as positivism, Enlightenment thought, capitalism and Modernity are inherently linked. This interrelated group of approaches is broadly the target of Frankfurt School critique (Bohman, 2013). Connecting Enlightenment with the project to dominate the natural world, critical theorists find fault with the western anthropocentric approach towards nature (Horkheimer & Adorno, 1987) as part of a broader critique of Modernism (Habermas, 1987).

Critical thought traces the beginnings of Modernity back to the Enlightenment, when domination of nature was brought about in part through the growth of positivist scientific thought. This way of relating to the environment which diminished the West's enchantment with nature was reflected in a similar disenchantment with the inner lives of people. In order to counter this deadening of the inner (human nature) and outer (natural environment) worlds, critical theorists such as Horkheimer and Adorno advocated a new model for rationality which embraces creativity, intuition and emotion (Brennan & Lo, 2011). The rejection of an anthropocentric and oppositional rationality recognises the possibility of relationships between humans and nature which allow both to flourish. The problematisation of these Enlightenment values within the critical accounting literature has prepared the ground for further analysis of our approach to nature. Accordingly, this book applies the lens of western environmental philosophy to deepen our understanding of the corporate relationship with nature.

Link to Western Environmental Philosophies

By moving away from the rationalist tradition of Enlightenment ideals, critical accounting becomes capable of embracing issues of environmental impact and interaction from a theoretical foundation. As Plumwood (1991) argues, many aspects of Enlightenment thought are averse to nature, due to the underlying basis for assessing value based on the ethical subject's ability to reason, which necessarily excludes much of the rest of the environment of which we are a part. From this basis, Enlightenment philosophers such as Kant assessed that humans alone should be considered as ends in themselves. While Kant's original standard has since been expanded to include other beings, the dichotomy between the rational and emotional is still retained.

To understand the problem that this poses to environmental philosophy, it should be pointed out that the Enlightenment quest for pure reason represents a pursuit to magnify and grant greater importance on the one trait that separates humans from the rest of the natural world. As a consequence of the valorisation of intellectual reason, other traits that humans share with the rest of the natural world become devalued, leading to a dualism between reason and nature. Since human characteristics such as sexuality, emotion and intuition are shared with other members of the biotic community, they become devalued and interpreted as signs of weakness or deficiency. Like critical theorists, environmental philosophers highlight the hierarchical power structure inherent in such ideologies.

Since much of western culture is informed directly from Enlightenment ideologies, it becomes apparent that dualisms which valorise a masculine, abstract and generalising rationality are exceedingly ingrained in western culture in a much greater sense. Plumwood (1991, 1993) argues that the valorisation accorded to this type of rationality is fundamental to the anthropocentrism of western culture. From this perspective, critical theory can help to deconstruct the current hegemonic dualism, but only philosophies which are based on interconnection, relationship and enabling will be capable of building a world view which embraces values not exclusive to humans.

For meaningful change to take place, Plumwood calls for a critique of the anthro- and androcentric world views inherent in western culture. This is the role played by critical theory in the broader sense – deconstructing commonly held assumptions which are seen to be a fundamental cause of environmental harm.

In critical accounting research, the underpinning assumptions which guide traditional (positivist) accounting practice are highlighted and critiqued. This chapter has outlined a number of these critical accounting projects which share an approach, in that the taken for granted underpinnings of accounting are deconstructed for detailed critique.

In common with the Frankfurt School of critical theorists more broadly, critical accounting theorists are driven by a problematisation of the status quo ubiquitous in wider western culture. By deconstructing the rationalities which uphold this status quo, the critical school of thought within accounting research has the potential to become a mechanism for the betterment of natural and human wellbeing. Currently, critical theorists propose that accounting does not serve this purpose, but instead upholds the structures inherent in western society that silences the voices of women, of the readers of accounting texts and of nature.

This book contributes a critical perspective through an exploration of how corporate environmental reporting can be viewed through the lens of western environmental philosophy. Such a critique deconstructs the perception of objectivity in terms of how the corporation reports on these issues and highlights the ways such approaches advance particular values at the expense of others. By asking how the corporation communicates western environmental philosophy, I attempt in this book to deconstruct the corporate relationship with the natural world.

This chapter has provided an outline of the current tensions within the environmental reporting literature. This is juxtaposed against the approaches inherent in western environmental philosophy. Through a comparison of these two bodies of literature, it is apparent that the two disciplines demonstrate parallels. For instance, a review of western environmental philosophy reveals the changing attitudes towards the environment over the course of western history. Likewise, these changes are reflected in the ways in which accounting has communicated the ideals of business. The act of accounting itself represents a kind of fissure between the natural world and human life through the use of abstract calculations (Miller & Napier, 1993) and the underpinning world view of neoclassical economics (Hamilton, 2002). This is a view which is reflected in the notion within environmental philosophy which separates human reason from the rest of the physical world (Plumwood, 1993). While environmental philosophies have developed over the past 50 years to begin to encompass the intrinsic value of the natural world, this approach is lagging in wider western culture, specifically in the practice of accounting for the environment.

Ostensibly, environmental reporting represents a move away from the dualistic approach which separates and devalues nature. While reporting about environmental issues by organisations represents the potential for a sympathetic relationship between organisations and the environments within which they operate, the discussion presented in this chapter demonstrates that the academic and broader communities have not been entirely convinced. In this way, the changes that western environmental philosophy calls for within our cultural institutions have the potential to be answered by corporate environmental reporting, however this potential can only be answered through first analysing the values from which corporate environmental reporting currently draws.

Summary

In summary, this chapter has outlined the ways in which accounting has reflected changes in western environmental philosophy. In doing so, it has highlighted the ways in which accounting – and corporate environmental reporting in particular – constructs barriers which reinforce the dualistic approaches towards the natural world. Dualism in this sense is expressed through other parallel ideologies such as neoliberal economics and post-Enlightenment thought and through mechanisms such as quantitative expression and positivist language.

Common terms such as sustainability and sustainable development were critiqued in this chapter, along with the values which inform contemporary corporate environmental reporting. Alternative approaches, such as feminism, deep ecology and accountability were introduced as alternative lenses through which current corporate practices appear implicitly pernicious.

This chapter has established that while the increasing production of environmental reports represents a potential step towards diminishing the metaphorical distance between organisational understanding and nature, it is yet to realise this capacity. In order to realise this potential, the values which underpin accounting and corporate approaches must first be critiqued and dismantled. This chapter has also outlined the foundations of the critique which this book undertakes. The following chapter next explores how such a critical perspective might be embodied to ask some important questions about how environmental philosophy can inform our understanding of corporate relationship with nature, and how this might help us to reduce the damage that large companies are doing to the natural world.

Note

1 Masculine rationality is described as oppositional, competitive and self-interested. It attempts to appear impartial and objective, but masks an underlying tendency to dominate (Plumwood, 1991).

References

Adams, C. (2004). The Ethical, Social and Environmental Reporting-Performance Portrayal Gap. *Accounting, Auditing & Accountability Journal, 17*(5), 731–757. doi:10.1108109513570410567791

Agger, B. (1991). Critical Theory, Poststructuralism, Postmodernism: Their Sociological Relevance. *Annual Review of Sociology, 17*, 105–131.

Andrew, J. (2007). Prisons, the Profit Motive and Other Challenges to Accountability. *Critical Perspectives on Accounting, 18*(8), 877–904.

Archel, P., Husillos, J., & Spence, C. (2011). The Institutionalisation of Unaccountability: Loading the Dice of Corporate Social Responsibility Discourse. *Accounting, Organizations and Society, 36*(6), 327–343. doi:10.1016/j.aos.2011.06.003

Arrington, E. C., & Francis, J. R. (1993). Accounting as a Human Practice: The Appeal of Other Voices. *Accounting, Organizations and Society, 18*(2–3), 105–106. doi:10.1016/0361-3682(93)90028-5

Bebbington, J., & Gray, R. (2000). Accounts of Sustainable Development: The Construction of Meaning within Environmental Reporting. *Aberdeen Papers in Accountancy, Finance & Management Working Paper No. 00-18.*

Bebbington, J., & Gray, R. (2001). An Account of Sustainability: Failure, Success and a Reconceptualization. *Critical Perspectives on Accounting, 12*(5), 557–588. doi:10.1006/cpac.2000.0450

Birkin, F., & Polesie, T. (2011). An Epistemic Analysis of (Un)Sustainable Business. *Journal of Business Ethics, 103*(2), 239–253. doi:10.1007/s10551-011-0863-4

Birkin, F., & Polesie, T. (2012). *Intrinsic Sustainable Development: Epistemes, Science, Business and Sustainability.* Singapore: World Scientific Publishing Company.

Bohman, J. (2013). Critical Theory. *Stanford Encyclopedia of Philosophy.* Retrieved from http://plato.stanford.edu/archives/spr2013/entries/crtitical-theory/

Brennan, A., & Lo, Y. (2011). Environmental Ethics. *The Stanford Encyclopedia of Philosophy.* Retrieved from http://plato.stanford.edu/entries/ethics-environmental/

Broadbent, J. (1998). The Gendered Nature of "Accounting Logic": Pointers to an Accounting that Encompasses Multiple Values. *Critical Perspectives on Accounting, 9*(3), 267–297. doi:10.1006/cpac.1997.0158

Broadbent, J. (2007). If You Can't Measure It, How Can You Manage It? Management and Governance in Higher Educational Institutions. *Public Money and Management, 27*(3), 193–198. doi:10.1111/j.1467-9302.2007.00579.x

Bruyn, F. D. (2001). The Classical Silva and the Generic Development of Scientific Writing in Seventeenth-Century England. *New Literary History, 32*(2), 347–373. doi:10.2307/20057662

Buhr, N. (2007). Histories of and Rationales for Sustainability Reporting. In J. Unerman, J. Bebbington, & B. O'Dwyer (Eds.), *Sustainability Accounting and Accountability* (pp. 57–69). Oxon: Routledge.

Campbell, D., & Beck, C. A. (2004). Answering Allegations: The Use of the Corporate Website for Restorative Ethical and Social Disclosure. *Business Ethics: A European Review, 13*(2–3), 100–116. doi:10.1111/j.1467-8608.2004.00357.x

Cho, C. H., Roberts, R. W., & Patten, D. M. (2010). The Language of US Corporate Environmental Disclosure. *Accounting, Organizations and Society, 35*(4), 431–443. doi:10.1016/j.aos.2009.10.002

Clare, S., Krogman, N., & Caine, K. J. (2013). The "Balance Discourse": A Case Study of Power and Wetland Management. *Geoforum, 49*(0), 40–49. doi:10.1016/j.geoforum.2013.05.007

Cooper, C., & Puxty, A. (1994). Reading Accounting Writing. *Accounting, Organizations and Society, 19*(2), 127–146.

Cooper, C., & Senkl, D. (2016). An(Other) Truth: A Feminist Perspective on KPMG's True Value. *Sustainability Accounting, Management and Policy Journal, 7*(4), 494–516.

Crane, A., Matten, D., & Moon, J. (2008). Ecological Citizenship and the Corporation: Politicizing the New Corporate Environmentalism. *Organization & Environment, 21*(4), 371–389. doi:10.1177/1086026608326075

Dando, N., & Swift, T. (2003). Transparency and Assurance Minding the Credibility Gap. *Journal of Business Ethics, 44*(2–3), 195–200.

Deegan, C., & Gordon, B. (1996). A Study of the Environmental Disclosure Practices of Australian Corporations. *Accounting & Business Research, 26*(3), 187–199.

Dey, C. (2007). Developing Silent and Shadow Accounts. In J. Unerman, J. Bebbington, & B. O'Dwyer (Eds.), *Sustainability Accounting and Accountability* (pp. 307–326). Oxon: Routledge.

Donaldson, T., & Preston, L. E. (1995). The Stakeholder Theory of the Corporation: Concepts, Evidence, and Implicaitons. *Academy of Management Review, 20*(1), 65–91. doi:10.5465/AMR.1995.9503271992

Georgakopoulos, G., & Thomson, I. (2008). Social Reporting, Engagements, Controversies and Conflict in an Arena Context. *Accounting, Auditing & Accountability Journal, 21*(8), 1116–1143. doi:10.1108/09513570810918788

Gray, R. (2010). Is Accounting for Sustainability Actually Accounting for Sustainability...and How Would We Know? An Exploration of Narratives of Organisations and the Planet. *Accounting, Organizations and Society, 35*(1), 47–62. doi:10.1016/j.aos.2009.04.006

Gray, R., Adams, C., & Owen, D. (2014). *Accountability, Social Responsibility and Sustainability: Accounting for Society and the Environment.* Harlow: Pearson Education.

Gray, R., Owen, D., & Maunders, K. (1987). *Corporate Social Reporting.* London: Prentice Hall.

Greenfield, K. (2008). *The Failure of Corporate Law: Fundamental Flaws and Progressive Possibilities.* Chicago: University of Chicago Press.

Habermas, J. (1987). *The Philosophical Discourse of Modernity: Twelve Lectures* (F. G. Lawrence, Trans.). Cambridge: MIT Press.

Hamilton, C. (2002). Dualism and Sustainability. *Ecological Economics, 42*(1–2), 89–99. doi:10.1016/S0921-8009(02)00051-4

Haque, S., Deegan, C., & Inglis, R. (2016). Demand for, and Impediments to, the Disclosure of Information about Climate Change-Related Corporate Governance Practices. *Accounting and Business Research*, 1–45. doi:10.1080/00014788.2015.1133276

Haraway, D. J. (2004). *The Haraway Reader.* New York: Routledge.

Hawken, P. (1993). *The Ecology of Commerce: A Declaration of Sustainability.* New York: HarperBusiness.

Hines, R. D. (1988). Financial Accounting: In Communicating Reality, We Construct Reality. *Accounting, Organizations and Society, 13*(3), 251–261.

Hopwood, A. G. (1987). The Archeology of Accounting Systems. *Accounting, Organizations and Society, 12*(3), 207–234. doi:10.1016/0361-3682(87)90038-9

Hopwood, A. G. (2009). Accounting and the Environment. *Accounting, Organizations and Society, 34*(3–4), 433–439. doi:10.1016/j.aos.2009.03.002

Horkheimer, M. (1982). *Critical Theory.* New York: Seabury Press.

Horkheimer, M., & Adorno, T. (1987). *Dialectic of Enlightenment* (E. Jephcott, Trans., & G. Schmid Noerr, Ed.). Stanford: Stanford University Press.

IPCC. (2013). *Climate Change 2013: The Physical Science Basis.* Cambridge: IPCC.

Joseph, G. (2012). Ambiguous but Tethered: An Accounting Basis for Sustainability Reporting. *Critical Perspectives on Accounting, 23*(2), 93–106. doi:10.1016/j.cpa.2011.11.011

Kheel, M. (2008). *Nature Ethics.* London: Rowman & Littlefield.

Klein, N. (2015). *This Changes Everything: Capitalism vs The Climate.* New York: Simon & Schuster.

Kolk, A. (2003). Trends in Sustainability Reporting by the Fortune Global 250. *Business Strategy and the Environment, 12*(5), 279–291.

KPMG. (2013). *The KPMG Survey of Corporate Responsibility Reporting 2013.* Netherlands: KPMG.

KPMG. (2015). *Currents of Change; The KPMG Survey on Corporate Responsibility Reporting 2015.* The Netherlands: KPMG.

Kristeva, J. (1986). *The Kristeva Reader* (T. Moi, Ed.). Oxford: Blackwell.

Lakoff, G., & Johnson, M. (1980). *Metaphors We Live By.* Chicago: University of Chicago Press.

Lehman, G. (1999). Disclosing New Worlds: A Role for Social and Environmental Accounting and Auditing. *Accounting, Organizations and Society, 24*(3), 217–241. doi:10.1016/S0361-3682(98)00044-0

Livesey, S. M. (2001). Eco-Identity as Discursive Struggle: Royal Dutch/Shell, Brent Spar, and Nigeria. *Journal of Business Communication, 38*(1), 58–91. doi:10.1177/002194360103800105

Merchant, C. (1989). *The Death of Nature: Women, Ecology, and the Scientific Revolution.* New York: Harper & Row.

Merchant, C. (2006). The Scientific Revolution and the Death of Nature. *Isis, 97*(3), 513–533. doi:10.1086/508090

Miller, P., & Napier, C. (1993). Genealogies of Calculation. *Accounting, Organizations and Society, 18*(7–8), 631–647. doi:10.1016/0361-3682(93)90047-A

Mitchell, J., Lowe, J., Wood, R., & Vellinga, M. (2006). Extreme Events Due to Human-Induced Climate Change. *Philosophical Transactions of the Royal Society, 364*, 2117–2133.

Moerman, L., & Van Der Laan, S. (2005). Social Reporting in the Tobacco Industry: All Smoke and Mirrors? *Accounting, Auditing & Accountability Journal, 18*(3), 374–389.

Morrison, L., Wilmshurst, T., & Shimeld, S. (2018). Environmental Reporting Through an Ethical Looking Glass. *Journal of Business Ethics, 150*(4), 903–918. doi:10.1007/s10551-016-3136-4

Neimark, M. (1992). *The Hidden Dimensions of Annual Reports: Sixty Years of Conflict at General Motors.* New York: Wiener.

Oakes, L. S., & Hammond, T. A. (1995). Biting the Epistemological Hand: Feminist Perspectives on Science and Their Implications for Accounting Research. *Critical Perspectives on Accounting, 6*(1), 49–75.

Oreskes, N. (2004). The Scientific Consensus on Climate Change. *Science, 306*(5702), 1686. doi:10.1126/science.1103618

O'Riordan, L., & Fairbrass, J. (2014). Managing CSR Stakeholder Engagement: A New Conceptual Framework. *Journal of Business Ethics, 125*(1), 121–145. doi:10.1007/s10551-013-1913-x

Plumwood, V. (1991). Nature, Self, and Gender: Feminism, Environmental Philosophy, and the Critique of Rationalism. *Hypatia, 6*(1), 3–27.

Plumwood, V. (1993). *Feminism and the Mastery of Nature.* London: Routledge.

Reser, J., Bradley, G., Glendon, A., Ellul, M., & Callaghan, R. (2012). *Public Risk Perceptions, Understandings and Responses to Climate Change and Natural Disasters in Australia and Great Britain.* Retrieved from Brisbane, Australia.

Roberts, J. (2009). No One Is Perfect: The Limits of Transperancy and an Ethic for 'Intelligent' Accountability. *Accounting, Organizations & Society, 34,* 957–970.

Rodrigue, M. (2014). Contrasting Realities: Corporate Environmental Disclosure and Stakeholder-Released Information. *Accounting, Auditing & Accountability Journal, 27*(1), 119–149. doi:10.1108/aaaj-04-2013-1305

Shafer, W. (2006). Social Paradigms and Attitudes toward Environmental Accountability. *Journal of Business Ethics, 65*(2), 121–147. doi:10.1007/s10551-005-4606-2

Shearer, T. L., & Arrington, C. E. (1993). Accounting in Other Wor(l)ds: A Feminism Without Reserve. *Accounting, Organizations and Society, 18*(2), 253–272.

Spence, C. (2009). Social Accounting's Emancipatory Potential: A Gramscian Critique. *Critical Perspectives on Accounting, 20,* 205–227.

Steffen, W., Grinevald, J., Crutzen, P., & McNeill, J. (2011). The Anthropocene: Conceptual and Historical Perspectives. *Philosophical Transactions of the Royal Society, 369,* 842–867.

Swift, T., & Dando, N. (2002). From Methods to Ideologies. *Journal of Corporate Citizenship, 2002*(8), 81–90.

Tinker, T., & Neimark, M. (1987). The Role of Annual Reports in Gender and Class Contradictions at General Motors: 1917–1976. *Accounting, Organizations and Society, 12*(1), 71–88. doi:10.1016/0361-3682(87)90017-1

Tregidga, H., Milne, M., & Kearins, K. (2014). (Re)Presenting 'Sustainable Organizations'. *Accounting, Organizations and Society, 39*(6), 477–494. doi:10.1016/j.aos.2013.10.006

Tregidga, H., Milne, M., & Lehman, G. (2012). Analyzing the Quality, Meaning and Accountability of Organizational Reporting and Communication: Directions for Future Research. *Accounting Forum, 36*(3), 223–230. doi:10.1016/j.accfor.2012.07.001

Unerman, J., & Bennett, M. (2004). Increased Stakeholder Dialogue and the Internet: Towards Greater Corporate Accountability or Reinforcing Capitalist Hegemony? *Accounting, Organizations and Society, 29*(7), 685–707. doi:10.1016/j.aos.2003.10.009

Walters-York, L. M. (1996). Metaphor in Accounting Discourse. *Accounting, Auditing and Accountability Journal, 9*(5), 45–70.

Waring, M. (1988). *Counting for Nothing: What Men Value and What Women Are Worth.* New Zealand: Allen and Unwin.

WCED. (1987). *Our Common Future* (O. U. Press, Ed.).

Wittgenstein, L. (1953/2010). *Philosophical Investigations.* Hoboken: John Wiley & Sons, Ltd.

Young, J. J. (2013). Devil's Advocate: The Importance of Metaphors. *Accounting Horizons, 27*(4), 877–886.

Young, J. J. (2015). (En) Gendering Sustainability. *Critical Perspectives on Accounting, 26,* 67–75.

Young, J. J., & Williams, P. F. (2010). Sorting and Comparing: Standard-Setting and "Ethical" Categories. *Critical Perspectives on Accounting, 21*(6), 509–521.

4   Operationalising Critique

Introduction

Corporate environmental reporting provides corporations with a means to report on their interactions with the natural environment to their stakeholders and also to the wider community. The underpinning approach of this book rejects the view that corporate reports are simply a reflection of value-neutral and objective information, and instead seeks to identify and analyse their underpinning philosophical approaches. Such an active reading of the text is exemplified by critical discourse analysis. This chapter outlines how a critical approach can help us to understand the corporate relationship with nature.

This chapter explains the means for developing a method of analysis with which to identify and highlight the philosophical approaches which underpin the relationship between corporations and the natural world. First the methodological approach is discussed, including discussions of the critical theories and historical understandings which inform the approach used in this book.

Methodology

McNicholas and Barrett (2005) explain that a research methodology guides how the research engages with the research question and also guides how the research question itself is developed. With this in mind, the first part of this chapter explores the methodological approach of this book, followed by an explanation of the methods applied to gather and analyse the data required to discern how western environmental philosophy is communicated through the corporate environmental report, and also to discover what this means for understanding the corporate relationship with the natural world.

A Qualitative Approach

In this book, a qualitative approach will be taken to explore the notion that western environmental philosophy might inform an analysis of contemporary corporate environmental reporting. The purpose of qualitative research is to "produce knowledge about a particular phenomenon through generating a deepened complex interpretation" (Ellingson, 2011, p. 605). As this book seeks to *produce knowledge* about contemporary corporate environmental disclosures through the *deepened complex interpretation* of western environmental philosophy and its interplay with corporate reporting, a qualitative approach is required.

Qualitative research explores the qualities of phenomena, rather than quantities. In this way, qualitative research is able to more clearly grasp the complexities of real events. Implicitly questioning the perceived value neutrality of much quantitative research, this approach is pertinent in this book for two primary reasons. First, rather than perpetuating the Enlightenment view that the guise of objectivity is somehow more 'true,' in this book I reject the idea that facts can be understood exclusive of values. A research methodology which is underpinned by this approach strengthens the thread which runs through not only this book, but through critical thought more broadly. As critical research, this book builds on the idea that what are considered *facts* have been filtered through the value sets of particular cultures – in this case, western culture.

Second, the already established role of Enlightenment and post-Enlightenment thinking in the domination and devalorisation of nature guides this book to critique artefacts of Enlightenment thought, such as institutions like the modern corporation. In highlighting some of the effects of Enlightenment thought, other world views might be found which can better inform the relationship between the corporate world and nature. A qualitative methodology is equipped for this task, in exploring the qualities of philosophical approaches, and how they manifest in the environmental report to communicate the corporate relationship with nature.

A Historical Perspective

In order to explore how qualities of philosophical approaches could help us to understand the corporate relationship with the natural world, a historical view of western environmental philosophy also contributes to the approach of this book. In Chapter 2, changes to western environmental thought through history were examined to discern patterns which could shed light on contemporary practices. The idea that history could shed light on present practice is based in part on Foucault's conception that the present is not only a culmination of past events, but that the past is ever-present. Similarly, Haraway (2004) proposes the idea of an *amodern* history, which rejects the idea that history presents a teleological path towards the present, and instead views history as ever-present by way of being reflected in the conventions and practices of the present. These conceptions of the relationships between the present and past signal one of the underpinning assumptions of this book – that the past and present continue to inform each other profoundly.

Within the extant accounting literature, the historical analysis of accounting has been used as a method of exploring the diverse issues and events that have led to current practice (Carnegie & Napier, 1996). Buhr (2007) discusses the particular history of environmental reporting, noting that it has generally been undertaken to address the human health issues which often arise from environmental damage. She argues that environmental reporting has contributed to not only the shaping of public discourse about nature, but also the philosophical and practical approaches of environmental management.

Callinocos (1995) demonstrates that as history is retold, the distinction between actual events and the interpretation of these events becomes blurred. He considers history as a narrative which is continually reconstructed from the point of view of each reader's contemporary perspective. Rowlinson (2004) notes that in order to construct a historical narrative, themes need to be identified and connections between events highlighted. Consequently, the historical narrative of western environmental philosophy provided in this book is a further reconstruction of documentary evidence arranged into a single coherent story; not to be understood as a value-neutral activity. This reconstruction sheds light on philosophies which will be used to analyse contemporary corporate environmental reporting.

By way of an exploration of history through the lenses of Foucault and Haraway, the values which have become embedded at different times throughout the history of western culture are brought into focus. By focusing on the impacts of such changes to cultural values, and those values themselves, this book utilises the philosophies which underpin the changing ways that western culture has related to the natural world over time. Through Haraway's *amodern* lens, then, these philosophies are still very much alive in contemporary western culture and continue to profoundly impact the ways in which we interact with nature. Taking analytical themes from a historical perspective in this way allows us to discern not only the ways in which western environmental philosophy underpins corporate environmental reporting, but also what this conveys about the relationship between western corporations and the natural world. Such a historical perspective is in line with the critical traditions to which I seek to contribute with this book, and as such, it is through a historical review of western culture's approach to nature that the philosophical themes have been identified. In this chapter, it will be explained how these themes will be applied to better understand the corporate relationship with nature.

A Critical Approach

Critical approaches to research aim to expose the underpinning values, which are embedded in modern institutions. Growing from a rejection of the positivist thought which has dominated western thought especially since the Enlightenment, critical thought uses this view to critique the dominant western paradigm (Agger, 1991; Horkheimer, 1982; Horkheimer & Adorno, 1987).

Expressions such as 'critical theory,' 'critical accounting,' 'critical accounting literature' and 'critical studies' have variously been used to describe an approach which aims to question conventional accounting and to explore how such conventional accounting practices and theory have emerged (Lodh & Gaffikin, 1997; McNicholas & Barrett, 2005).

Critical approaches in the accounting literature have emerged in response to the failure of positivist accounting research to properly acknowledge the relationships between accounting and society. As discussed in the previous chapter, traditional accounting research has drawn from the positivist approach which claims value neutrality, and views accounting as an objective technique with little or no relation to the context in which it is placed, or from which it has emerged. In contrast, critical approaches in accounting research acknowledge and draw from the contexts surrounding and within accounting theory and practice, recognising the relationships between accounting, society and organisations (Lodh & Gaffikin, 1997).

Mackenzie-Davey and Liefooghe (2004) describe how critical research highlights assumptions which are taken for granted in other approaches to research. Utilising a critical approach in this book entails analysing the values which construct facts. I do so by identifying and questioning some of the underlying assumptions which have guided the western relationship with nature, and consequently contemporary western corporations' relationships with nature.

Case studies provide a rich source of information which is not isolated from its context. Since critical and qualitative research aims to analyse the influence of social structures in the workings of society, context forms an integral part of the lens through which data should be viewed (Travers, 2001). As such, the case study model for research design adopted in this book allows for the evaluation of the relationship between an 'event' (corporate environmental reporting) and its context (western culture, through the lens of western environmental philosophy).

To explore these themes, a diverse range of companies have been selected. Following Yin (2014), small selections of case studies provide the opportunity to explore in depth, as opposed to large surveys which offer broader but shallower insights. These companies were selected on the basis that they illuminate the topic most clearly (Maxwell, 2005). By referring to *western* environmental philosophy, the questions which guide this book ask about *cultural* perspectives, rather than interest in a particular industry. Since the cultural perspective being examined is that of western culture, companies which are rooted in this culture have been chosen. Australia represents a western country, through its colonial past, traditions based on Christian heritage and ongoing cultural links with other western countries such as the UK and the US (Said, 1993). Consequently, companies from a broad range of industries were selected, drawing from the top 200 listed companies on the Australian Stock Exchange (ASX) (ASX, 2015). This selection of companies represents the 200 largest (by market capitalisation) publicly listed companies as included on the ASX at June 2015. The ASX 200 represents 80% of Australia's market by capitalisation (Standard & Poor's, 2015).

In order to achieve a deepened understanding in this project, multiple sources of information were drawn from, including organisational environmental reports and interviews with members of management from the case study companies.

This book focuses on the publicly available environmental reports produced by companies. Many Australian companies are required under legislation to report environmental information to government agencies. The reports examined in this book include information which is provided voluntarily, but also often includes that information which is mandated.

From the ASX 200, it was found that 94 companies had disclosed environmental information voluntarily for the three years subsequent from 2012 (2012, 2013 and 2014). This information was established by searching the internet and the websites of each of the 200 companies. Fifty-one of these companies disclosed environmental information through dedicated sustainability or corporate responsibility reports, while 43 disclosed through the annual report or annual review.

It is relevant to note that of the 94 companies which reported environmental information during the three years from 2012 to 2014, 14 provided only superficial information which amounted to one page or less. This information often consisted of a large image and a small amount of standard text, repeated in consecutive years. These 14 companies were consequently removed from the sample selection, leaving 80 companies in the data set.

Although many of the environmental reports of these 80 companies cited the GRI reporting parameters, specifying that "...the contact point for questions regarding the report or its contents" is provided (Global Reporting Initiative, 2011, p. 21), this often led to a generic email address, or the 'contact us' page on their website, which didn't actually point directly to a particular person, department or contact address. This situation arose for 44 of these 80 companies.

Following a low rate of response (only five companies agreeing to participate), it was decided to expand the data set of companies to the 80 companies which had voluntarily reported more than one page of environmental information for the three consecutive years until 2014. As mentioned, not all of these companies had provided contact details for a dedicated sustainability or environmental officer. Instead either general company-wide email addresses, or shareholder liaison contacts were supplied by the company, through either the company website or in their reports. A second round of invitations were emailed through these channels. After the second round of invitations were sent, another five companies responded positively, with ten companies in total agreeing to participate.

Critical Discourse Analysis

Analysis of the environmental reports and interviews was undertaken through the lens of discourse analysis. Discourse analysis provides a method of garnering the underpinning themes implicit within texts (Wodak & Meyer, 2009). In the context of discourse analysis, texts may include written texts, but also talk, images and other methods of communicating (Grant et al., 2004; Hardy, 2001; Moerman & Van Der Laan, 2007). Given that "a discourse is a particular formation of stories and practices, which constructs both knowledge and power relations" (Kamler & Thomson, 2006, p. 11), the analysis of discourse is one way to explore how philosophy underpins corporate environmental reporting. It is a method of exploring text which allows for the in-depth scrutiny of the implicit underpinnings of communications such as the corporate environmental report. Such analysis acknowledges that discourse is used to communicate not only the explicit object of communication, but also its embedded ideologies (Heracleous, 2004).

Fairclough (1992/2003) outlines how discourse is not only shaped *by* social practices, but also *shapes* social practice by reconstituting current conventions. He argues that discursive practices are often infused with ideologies which perpetuate social power structures. He proposes that while non-critical approaches to discourse analysis tend to describe discursive practices, more critical approaches also show how these practices are shaped by and shape cultural identity and practice. This more critical approach aligns with the approach of this book, and is outlined below.

Critical discourse analysis has been described as critical social research aimed at better understanding how societies work (Fairclough, 2013) and is used to illuminate ideologies which are coded into discourse (Le et al., 2009). A critical analysis of discourse will help to unravel world views which structure approaches towards the natural environment, as expressed through corporate environmental reporting.

Reflecting the same foundations as social construction, and other critical approaches, critical discourse analysis aims to deconstruct these taken-for-granted assumptions. Through analysing the discourse of contemporary corporate disclosure, the constitutive role of language is acknowledged (Tregidga, Milne, & Kearins, 2014). The assumptions that are taken for granted and implicitly built on in such discursive practices are therefore challenged and critiqued, undermining the legitimacy of drawing from such hegemonies as those highlighted through an exploration of western environmental philosophy.

The Discourse

Discourse analysis encompasses not only modes of communication such as written documents, but also websites, interviews, meetings (Lee, 2009), accounting (both financial and non-financial) (Llewellyn & Milne, 2007), non-verbal communication (Wodak & Meyer, 2009), conversations (Nycyk, 2015; Peräkylä & Ruusuvuori, 2011) and images (Hrasky, 2012; Stiles, 2004).

In this book, the written word, images and the visual arrangement of these texts, which constitute corporate environmental reports, are analysed. In addition to the discourse exhibited in the environmental reports, the interviews will provide an alternative viewpoint, thus contributing to what Ellingson (2011) calls the crystallisation of data. This inclusion of multiple perspectives acknowledges Unerman's (2000) call for the examination of a broad range of communications in order to explore a fuller range of corporate reporting.

Environmental Reports

While most companies listed in the ASX 200 have disclosed some environmental information, not all have produced a stand-alone report dedicated to these issues. Since in this book I consider the context of contemporary environmental reporting, attention is given to the ways in which companies communicate information about their environmental interactions. This information is commonly communicated through formal reporting mediums and is usually included in such reports denominated as sustainability, corporate social responsibility, social and environmental, sustainable development, among other nomenclature. Henceforth, reports of this nature will be grouped together as 'sustainability reports' for clarity. The environmental information which makes up part of these reports, as well as environmental information disclosed separately will be called 'environmental reports' in this book.

In order to explore the ways in which western environmental philosophy is communicated through corporate environmental reporting, and how this underpins the corporate relationship to nature, a number of corporate environmental reports will be critically analysed. Three years of recently published environmental reports will be analysed in this book, in order to establish particular contemporary approaches expressed by the case study companies. Within these reports, the written word, images and the visual arrangement of these texts will inform analysis.

Written Word

Central to any discourse analysis is spoken and written language. Fairclough's account of discourse analysis begins with the demarcation of *text* as "any product whether written or spoken" (1992/2003, p. 4). In accordance with Fairclough, the critical discourse analysis undertaken for this book also begins with an analysis of the written word. At a word level, this analysis incorporates word choice, the use of metaphor and representation. For instance, the use of terms such as 'natural capital,' 'natural resources' and 'offsets' imply a sense of interchangeability which reflects a dualistic approach to the natural world.

From a motif level, this analysis incorporates discursive mechanisms such as the direction of readers' attention or the use of case studies or a regulatory focus, for instance. Discursive mechanisms such as these point the analysis towards the underpinning philosophies which inform the corporate report, but cannot be interpreted exclusive of their context (Fairclough, 1992/2003, 2013). Larger contexts such as cultural hegemonies and ideologies are discussed below, but here, context refers to the surrounding text within the environmental reports or from information garnered in the associated interviews which point towards particular understandings. Other contextual information such as the corporate reputation and media reports will also be used on occasion to support findings.

Along with literate communication, numerical information also portrays characteristics that help in the exploration of philosophical underpinnings through a critical analysis. Miller (2001), for instance, argues that the communication of information through numerical methods shapes the way the information is understood and can thus be used strategically. Similarly, numerical expression has been linked to the desire to control (Dambrin & Robson, 2011), to the silencing of alternative accounts (Robson, 1992), to persuasion (Chua, 1995) and to the shaping of world views (Bloomfield & Vurdubakis, 1997). With the potential to express these inherent values, the analysis of numerical communication is an essential aspect of the critical discourse analysis used in this book.

Images

Along with the literate and numeric text written in the environmental reports, discourse also includes other communicative media such as images. Images are powerful transmitters of meaning. Accordingly, the images displayed within the environmental reports will also be considered discourse and consequently analysed.

Charts, graphs and tables are frequently used in corporate reporting. Beattie and Jones (2008) have suggested that while these visual analytical aids are useful for communicating information, they also tend to obfuscate such information. Dambrin and Robson (2011) concur with this observation, adding that in the context of corporate reporting, charts, graphs and tables construct a division between the information portrayed and the reader. Similarly, the shapes, placement and fonts used in these mechanisms convey particular themes (Kress & Van Leeuwen, 2006). These insights will be drawn from to gauge the philosophical underpinnings of such imagery in the environmental reports analysed in this book.

Kress and Van Leeuwen (2002) have explored some of the implicit meanings which colour can indicate in discourse. They demonstrate how colour is used to highlight particular items, de-emphasise others, as well as embed certain characteristics into the discourse. As such, the use of colour in the reports will also contribute to the critical analysis of the discourse.

In addition to text and image-related communication, context such as how these aspects are arranged on the page are also incorporated into the critical analysis of the discourse. Kress and Van Leeuwen (2006) outline the importance of placement in visual communications, claiming that placement choices are inherently meaningful, portraying meaning in subtle and powerful ways.

One example of the power of placement is where the implicit meaning of images conflicts with the message presented in surrounding text. In this case, the meaning of the image has the potential to override the inherent message of the text (Davison, McLean, & Warren, 2012; Zillmann, Gibson, & Sargent, 1999). Images may be used in this way to distract the reader, or to impart a particular idea about the company's environmental impact. These methods of visual arrangement are interpreted in accordance with their context to illuminate the philosophies which underpin their use.

Other examples of how visual arrangement is used in this book include the direction of readers' attention, either away from or within the report. The direction of readers' attention could signify the construction of barriers between the corporate report and impacts, which would point towards certain philosophical approaches regarding the corporate relationship to the natural world. As with the written word, images and other subjects of interpretation in this book, visual arrangements cannot be analysed exclusive of their context.

Other Discursive Mechanisms

Along with written text, images and visual arrangement, the critical analysis of discourse undertaken in this book will uncover discursive mechanisms that are in common use in the environmental reports. These prevalent discursive mechanisms may include such items as certification, mention of prizes, the use of language based on financial understandings and common approaches to topics such as materiality, but will only be discovered in the process of analysis. The close reading that critical discourse analysis needs requires the researcher to pay attention to such repeated discursive techniques in order to unmask the meaning which underpins their use (Alexander & Stibbe, 2014).

Interviews

The aim of the semi-structured interview process utilised in this book is to shed light on the philosophical approaches implicit in the reporting process, from the perspective of a subject closely involved with this process. By interviewing a subject who has an 'insider perspective' about the environmental reporting process of a company, a view which highlights the concealed processes, attitudes and philosophical perspectives of the company becomes more visible. During the interviews, I questioned the participants about the key motivations and values expressed by the company, as well as the participants' own perspectives. Semi-structured interviews allow the researcher to access and record these intangible aspects of reality that are otherwise inaccessible (Peräkylä & Ruusuvuori, 2011).

According to Parker (2014), the personal philosophical and religious beliefs of senior management are a strong indicator of organisational approaches to wider environmental and social responsibilities. Consequently, interviews with members of senior management will provide added depth to the data provided by the case study companies' environmental reporting practices. Senior managers who participated in the process of reporting corporate environmental information were invited to be interviewed. The interviewees were sustainability managers, external corporate affairs managers or other managers directly involved in the environmental reporting process. These managers were considered to have an informed view of both the environmental reporting process, as well as the company's approach to environmental issues. As well as these intimate perspectives, the interviewees had a role in the decision-making process behind the production of the reports themselves. As such, these interviewees were valuable sources of information about the philosophical approaches underpinning the companies' interactions with the natural world and were considered to have perspectives which could shed light on the processes underpinning these reports.

I conducted the interviews with these respondents at their place of work. Semi-structured interviews are considered appropriate for this kind of research, since the structure of the interview is flexible enough to allow for in-depth discussions guided by the interviewees' responses and focus (Erikson & Kovalainen, 2008). In-depth discussion aids in the exploration of the interviewees' philosophical assumptions regarding the natural world, providing rich data which encompasses the experience, values, feelings and knowledge of each participant (King & Horrocks, 2010). For this reason, face-to-face interviewing was necessitated to allow for a wide range of cues to be noted. Such cues include facial expression, body language and other less tangible signals which can guide discussion and provide additional insight (Qu & Dumay, 2011).

Semi-structured interviewing means that although a common set of questions is asked of all interviewees, the discussion may diverge from the initial list of questions. These questions were designed to ascertain the interviewees' attitudes to the company's reporting processes and to the natural environment more generally. Since corporations are made up of individual people, it is the social context of these individuals which drives and guides corporate decision-making. When collecting text from interviews for discourse analysis, the aim is to provide an in-depth perspective.

Qu and Dumay (2011) recognise that qualitative interviews provide rich data which aid in the understanding of complex social and contextual phenomena. They reinforce the idea that the semi-structured interview reflects a social constructivist methodology capable of disclosing hidden aspects of organisational behaviour. Since the context around interviews has been recognised as an important facet of data which can aid qualitative analysis (Qu & Dumay, 2011), my own personal reflections were also recorded as soon as possible after the completion of each interview. This text, along with the transcribed interviews will augment the text of the environmental reports.

Analysing the Discourse

Multiple linguistic devices are used to implicitly inject particular perspectives into discursive communications. The next three sections discuss three key concepts which are useful in understanding critical discourse analysis: metaphor, ideology and hegemony. Following these three sections, the philosophical themes which arose from the review of philosophical literature elucidated in Chapter 2 will be outlined and applied to the methods utilised in this book.

Metaphor

Metaphor is one aspect of language which implicitly but profoundly contributes to the shaping of culture and our understanding of the world. Rather than simply providing poetic flourish and superfluous literary decoration, Lakoff and Johnson argued in their seminal work that metaphors are present in the everyday use of language, due to the fundamental link between human cognition and metaphor (1980). The use of metaphorical language provides a frame through which we perceive our everyday realities. In this way, the use of metaphor influences the way we consider an issue or event. This everyday use of metaphor goes largely unnoticed and therefore unquestioned.

One of the many examples discussed by Lakoff and Johnson is the metaphor of an argument as a battle. In western culture, arguments are frequently described in terms of 'winning' and 'losing,' 'defending one's position' or having a 'weak' or 'strong' argument. This framing is more than a random choice of words, but shapes the way we think about arguments. To illustrate this point, Lakoff and Johnson provide alternative ways that we could think about arguments, such as arguments as dialogue, as learning or as dance. This example illustrates one of the many instances where an apparently insignificant and taken for granted detail of discourse reveals a fundamental message about the culture in which it is situated.

Drawing from Lakoff and Johnson, Walters-York (1996) explores the effect of metaphor in accounting discourse. Contrary to the apparent objectivity of accounting language, Walters-York exposes several metaphors in common use in and about accounting, including the description of accountants as *numbers crunchers*, or referring to accounting as *dry*. Building from these findings, Young (2013) also highlights various metaphors used in accounting discourse such the organisation as a *container*, with business occurring within organisational boundaries, and costs which occur outside these boundaries (such as the costs of secondary environmental damage) referred to as *externalities*. Also evidenced in the language of business are directional metaphors which reinforce hierarchical structures such as *top* managers, *high-flyers* and *the glass ceiling*.

These examples support the idea that rather than inconsequential linguistic decoration, metaphors can inject layers of implied meaning. While Walters-York and Young describe the benefits of accounting embracing the use of metaphor, others demonstrate that particular metaphors have been used to obfuscate the challenge of true sustainability. An example of this argument is Milne, Kearins and Walton (2006), who highlight the use of the metaphor of *sustainability as a journey* in organisational sustainability reports. They claim that true sustainability requires fundamental changes to the ways in which organisations operate. However, the *sustainability as a journey* metaphor perpetually postpones the need for these fundamental changes, allowing business to maintain the status quo of past and current practices. Juxtaposed against the urgency of climate change and other environmental needs, the *sustainability as a journey* metaphor is a potentially dangerous social construction. This is one example of how discourse can shape the way a culture approaches nature and regulates attitudes.

Metaphors are one discursive method which contributes to the construction of social realities, particularly in the case of environmental reporting. The language and metaphors used in organisational reports contribute to shaping the worldviews of users and reflect the organisation's philosophical approaches. With this understanding, environmental reports are shaped by the approaches to the natural environment adopted by the organisation and, and at the same time, are shaping the current and future approaches of users.

Metaphors and other descriptive images and discourses play an important role in establishing and maintaining social norms within a culture. Merchant (1989) explores this role in the relationship between western culture and the natural environment. She argues that as metaphors and the ideas that they convey have changed throughout history, they have subsequently changed the West's attitudes towards, and treatment of nature. In this way, cultural discourse about nature plays as a normative ethical restraint. Metaphors are commonly used in popular discourse and as such guide ethical restrictions and socially accepted behaviour, to the extent that they represent ideologies.

Ideology

Van Dijk (1998) describes ideologies as "political or social systems of ideas, values or prescriptions of groups or other collectives, and have the function of organizing or legitimating the actions of the group" (p. 3). Ideologies have been used in environmental discourse to express and reproduce ways of approaching an issue within particular groups, such as cultures and sub-cultures. Discourse is a powerful tool used by group members to persuasively communicate ideologies within the group and to propagate ideologies amongst others. In order to identify ideologies, Van Dijk deduces that close analysis of their discursive manifestations is the only way to do so.

Ideologies which are explored in this book include attitudes towards nature which have become embedded in western culture. Philosophical approaches to the environment legitimate the actions of the group by normalising certain relationships with the natural world. By building an ideology which has reduced the normative restrictions to harming nature – by prioritising profit, for instance – organisations can continue to exploit the natural world unheeded. Without critical analysis, such ideologies can (and have) become dominant forces within a culture.

Hegemony

Wodak and Meyer (2009) explain that ideologies which have come to take a dominant position in a culture often appear as neutral and objective, thereby avoiding meaningful questioning. In this way, hegemony is created which forms the world view shared by a majority of participants within a society. This world view then contributes to the maintenance of power structures within that society and is maintained through mechanisms such as language, accounting and other institutions.

Tregidga, Milne and Kearins (2014) argue for the analysis of hegemonies used in the construction of organisational interactions with the natural world. They propose that 'true' sustainability is a threat to the hegemonies of business. They call for analyses of corporate environmental narratives to illuminate the ways businesses attempt to appropriate these processes rather than adopt fundamentally different approaches.

While metaphor is a linguistic tool used to inject implicit values into discourse, ideologies are what may be built with such discursive mechanisms. Left unheeded, ideologies which are imparted in this way tend towards becoming hegemonic; dominating and guiding social attitudes in such a way as to normally remain unnoticed. Such hegemonic values include the western approach to nature, which guides the treatment of the natural world. The critical discourse analysis of this book aims to unmask such hegemonic values as they are communicated through corporate environmental reporting, and identify what they convey about the corporate relationship to nature. To do so, the philosophical themes which were elucidated in the review of western environmental philosophies (Chapter 2) have been grouped into three primary discourse groupings, as outlined below.

Discourse Groupings

To employ a critical analysis of the corporate environmental discourse, discourse groupings are utilised. Following Morrison, Wilmshurst and Shimeld (2018), beliefs and assumptions underpinning discourse are more clearly defined through the use of discourse groupings. Through the historical review of the West's philosophical approaches towards the natural environment explored in Chapter 2, a selection of themes were highlighted. These themes are used as the basis for analysing a sample of corporate environmental reports. Other themes have been highlighted in prior literature. For example, Wiman (1990) highlights three distinct themes of thought towards nature: nature as benign, nature as chaotic or cunning and nature as ever-changing; Dryzek (2013) suggests four themes of discourse in green political discourse, and Adams and Belasco (2015) offer two primary motifs of 'Ruthless Nature' and 'Idyllic Nature' in popular contemporary culture. However, in this book I apply themes that more accurately reflect the review of environmental philosophy literature provided in Chapter 2: dualism, transcendence and interconnectivity. These themes also offer a practical advantage, since their comprehensiveness allows them to be used in the analysis of corporate reporting. Also identified from that literature are multiple sub-themes, as in the following diagram (Figure 4.1).

These three themes (primary discourse groupings) are not always distinct, and it is acknowledged that they do in fact overlap. This is not considered a problem, as discourse analysis methods are flexible enough to allow for this (Wodak & Meyer, 2009). These themes are discussed in more depth in the following sections.

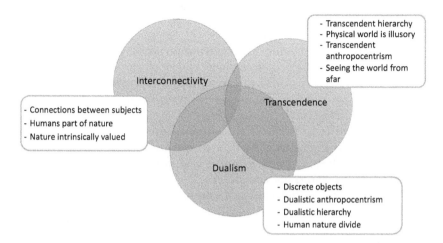

Figure 4.1 Philosophical themes.

Dualism

Dualism is a philosophical approach which considers humans and nature to be inherently different, and as such, separate and distinct from each other. Over time, this separation has developed into a hierarchical relationship, with humans considered superior to other aspects of the natural world. Dualism also encompasses other hierarchical dichotomies, such as those between culture and nature, male and female, mind and body and the universal and the particular. Plumwood established that many of these dualistic relationships are associated with the worldview that humans are superior to nature. It is this aspect of dualism which is considered here.

Plumwood (1993) argues that the hierarchical logic which underpins dualism supports human domination over nature. When humans and the rest of the natural world are separated and dualised, commonalities are erased. With weakened connections to the physical world, people are apt to view themselves as superior to nature, which is viewed as the *background* to the endeavours of human culture. This *backgrounding* is a way to deny our profound dependence on and participation in the natural world, thereby making it appear to be an inessential and incidental aspect of human life.

There is some overlap between dualism and transcendence, in that both of these approaches incorporate a sense of separation and hierarchy. To address this overlap, in this book I focus on the *separation* aspect of dualism, but will also consider hierarchical narratives in context to discern whether they relate more to a dualistic or transcendent approach. It is acknowledged that within the ecofeminist literature the separation aspect of dualism is less important than the hierarchical aspect. For instance, in giving an ecofeminist perspective, Plumwood (1993) explains that the reason dualism devalorises nature is not the distinction itself but the systematic hierarchy and dominance that is a direct consequence of a dualistic worldview. While the hierarchical aspect of dualism plays an important role in ecofeminism, the separation aspect of dualism plays an important part in other environmental philosophies. It is the separation of the human experience from the natural world which is a position which many environmental philosophies consider important to oppose. In particular, deep ecology resists dualism by calling for the erasure of distinctions between members of the biotic community. As such, the dichotomous aspect of dualism plays an essential role in contemporary approaches to the natural environment and, for this reason, will be considered separately to transcendence here.

This theme will be discerned in the corporate environmental discourse through any emphasis on the distinctions between humans and nature, particularly where a higher value seems to be placed on humans, at the expense of the rest of the natural world. The subgroupings which reflect this approach are discussed in the next three sections.

Within the discourse grouping of 'dualism,' four subgroupings are used in order to assist in the analysis of the texts, as illustrated in Figure 4.2, below. The subgroupings are more specific expressions of a dualistic approach, and

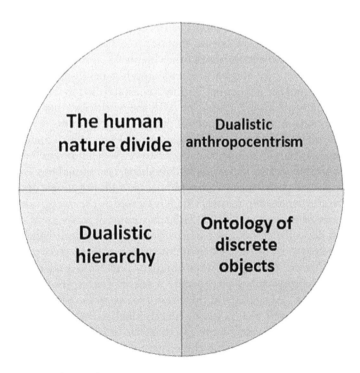

Figure 4.2 Dualism subgroupings.

in this way aid in guiding the analysis. The first of these four subgroupings is the *ontology of discrete objects*.

Ontology of Discrete Objects

Dryzek (2013) articulates the ontology of environmental discourse which implicitly describes natural phenomena as inert and valueless matter. He describes such an ontology as one which has been informed by industrialisation. According to Dryzek, industrialisation produced a view that considers nature as a store of useful matter which can be removed or altered without broad effects throughout the environment. In this way objects are considered *discrete* and unconnected to the wider systems that make up the natural environment.

The ontology of discrete objects is further explained by Latour (2016a) in his description of the differences between an organism and a machine, in that a machine's parts can be removed and reassembled, in contrast to an organism, from which certain parts may not be removed without the destruction of the whole. The ontology of discrete objects exemplifies the view of nature as machine-like, which echoes Descartes' view of nature and the Cartesian split; further supporting the inclusion of the *ontology of discrete objects* within the dualistic discourse grouping.

An *ontology of discrete objects* is demonstrated by the mention of 'environmental impacts' without context which might illustrate the effect of these impacts on living ecosystems within nature. The use of such narratives over-simplifies the contextual environmental effects of those metrics being reported. As such, context-less reporting of greenhouse gas emissions, energy use and emissions reductions illustrate a distance between the factors reported and the reasons behind reporting these factors. This distance renders such reported facts as controllable and somewhat intangible, whereas the local effects of these metrics are entirely tangible and corporeal.

Expressing values in a numerical form also enhances this sense of distance and sterility, removing context thereby giving the impression that these factors are entirely controllable. For example, values such as greenhouse gas emissions, emissions reduction, energy use, energy intensity, recycling rate, packaging compliance, waste and energy use are often presented in exclusively numerical terms. By expressing these issues in this way, context such as raised temperatures from carbon emissions, leading to altered habitat or migration patterns; reduced plastic waste which would otherwise be disposed of in landfill, or contribute to the accidental consumption of plastic waster by marine life or the use of fossil fuels which not only contribute to climate change through emissions, but also directly impact through destructive mining practices, is omitted. While many of these values are commonly understood in numerical terms, it is the absence of any context that expresses a dualistic attitude towards the environmental effects of operations and informs their inclusion in the *ontology of discrete objects* subgrouping.

Dualistic Anthropocentrism

The second of the dualism subgroupings is *dualistic anthropocentrism*. This subgrouping is similar to the anthropocentrism subgrouping in the transcendence discourse grouping, however *dualistic* anthropocentrism represents an approach which focuses on the dualistic relationship between humans and nature. As discussed, a dualistic relationship not only represents a separation, but a hierarchical relationship between two opposing values. In the case of dualistic anthropocentrism, higher value is placed on humans, at the expense of the rest of the natural world. In this book 'human' may equate to 'corporate.'

Dualistic Hierarchy

A dualistic approach incorporates a hierarchical world view in which priority must be given to one set of values at the expense of another. In the analysis of corporate environmental disclosure, this third dualistic subgrouping will be applied to text which imposes this hierarchical worldview on the natural environment, in collaboration with a sense of separation which characterises a dualistic approach. As discussed, the context of this type of discourse will govern whether it is included in either the dualistic or transcendent hierarchy subgroupings, or both.

The Human Nature Divide

The human nature divide is a foundational concept in dualism, and therefore text which demonstrates this approach will be categorised into *the human nature divide* subgrouping. This subgrouping forms the fourth subgrouping for the dualism discourse grouping, and together with *ontology of discrete objects*, *dualistic anthropocentrism* and *dualistic hierarchy*, represents the full range of dualism as it will be analysed in this book.

Transcendence

Both dualism and transcendence offer relatively unhelpful narratives with which to relate to the natural environment, and which have been placed at the heart of the current environmental damage (Hawken, 1993; Merchant, 2010). Despite the failure of these frameworks to adequately provide a narrative which would contribute to a more beneficial relationship between humans and the natural world, these two approaches currently dominate western discourse about the natural world.

The dichotomous hierarchy of Plato's dualism paved the way for a value system which perceives the physical world (nature) to be an illusory and devalorised imitation of a superior 'other' place. This concept is exemplified in Christianity, where the Earth is considered a place of sin, and compared to a transcendent idea of heaven.

An approach which devalorises the natural world diminishes the limitations to its exploitation. Despite this, philosophical approaches which draw from transcendence include those of the American Transcendentalists, who venerated the natural world as a place to find and explore Christian spirituality (Nash, 1973). By drawing on ideas which perpetuate the conceptualisation of a transcendent 'other' (that is, a Christian God who resides 'elsewhere'), the transcendentalists failed to completely transfer inherent value to the natural world, and further reinforced the idea that the source of value remains outside of the natural world.

The *transcendence* discourse theme will be discerned in the text with the aid of three subgroupings which in aggregate comprise of the full range of transcendence to be analysed for this book. These three subgroupings are *physical world less valued than the transcendent, seeing physical world from afar* and *transcendent anthropocentrism,* as illustrated in Figure 4.3, below. Each of these subgroupings is outlined in the following sections.

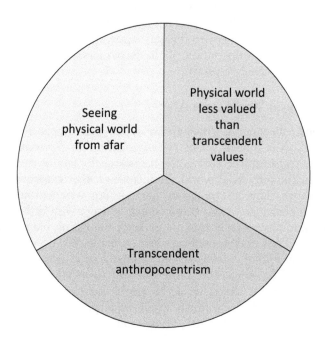

Figure 4.3 Transcendence subgroupings.

Physical World Less Valued than the Transcendent

A subgrouping which encompasses the expression of a sentiment that the *physical world is less valued than the transcendent* aids in identifying a transcendent approach in the environmental reports. Through a transcendent lens, the physical world is devalorised, in reference to any number of transcendent values. The most frequently critiqued of these transcendent frameworks is that of Christian theology. Dodson Gray (1981) describes how inherent structures of Christianity enforce the vision of reality in which God (a transcendent value) is valued at the expense of nature. This is carried out through a chain of authority that valorises men, then women, then children, then animals, plants and nature more generally as least valued. This view of the universe is reflected in multiple Christian narratives, including those which place heaven, and spiritual (invisible, transcendent) values higher, in comparison with the lower (earthlier) planes, which are closer in nature to 'the devil' and 'hell.' In this narrative, that which is *made of flesh* (that is, physical substance) is not spiritual, and thus, by definition, more prone to evil.

In the context of corporate environmental reporting, economic benefit can be seen as a transcendent value. Latour (2014) argues that the salvation once offered by heaven is now conceptually provided by capitalism, drawing parallels between the laws of economics, and the laws of physics, going so far as to claim that the laws of economics are now superior to the laws of physics in the western mind. Accordingly, transcendence will be identified in the environmental reporting discourse through any reference to, or de-valorisation of the Earth in favour of any form of transcendence, including profit.

Seeing Physical World from Afar

The second subgrouping which assists in the discernment of a transcendent approach is that of *seeing the physical world from afar*. Implicit within the transcendent view is the transference of value in some place other than the terrestrial world. In this sense, the transcendent 'gaze' is *from* above. This interpretation corresponds with Latour's (2016b) description of the *globe* as a transcendent concept with little relation to localised and terrestrial events, or in other words, no planetary correspondence. Other correspondences can be made, however, particularly with the concept of 'globalisation.' Globalisation is a universalising concept which Banerjee (2003) links directly to social and environmental harm. Similarly, the view of the world from afar echoes the universal approach which feminists argue underpins the urge to master, or subdue nature (Kheel, 2008; Plumwood, 1993). As such, *seeing the physical world from afar* will assist in the identification of a transcendent approach.

Transcendent Anthropocentrism

The third transcendent subgrouping is *transcendent anthropocentrism*. This subgrouping is similar to *dualistic anthropocentrism*, however *transcendent anthropocentrism* represents a focus on human values within a transcendent context, for instance, if humans are represented as more transcendent, higher, less physical or less earthly than physical or environmental values. Looking at the world through a transcendentalist lens, nature and physical reality lack any inner principle, and therefore any intrinsic value in and of itself (Mathews, 2006). Through this lens, the natural environment is considered passive and in need of human management, since humans are in possession of an intelligence which is superior to that of brute nature (Dryzek, 2013). This chain of authority is also evident in Christian theology, which places the responsibility of the management of nature in the hands of 'man' (Dodson Gray, 1981). The role of humans as the stewards of nature has been critiqued as dangerous and arrogant, in that the capacity of humans to manage nature is greatly overstated (Attfield, 1991). Thus, discourse which expresses *transcendent anthropocentrism* will aid in identifying a transcendent approach in the environmental reports.

Interconnectivity

In contrast to the dualistic and transcendent views which dominate contemporary western narratives about our philosophical approaches to the natural world, interconnectivity represents an approach which recognises the relationships between the multiple subjects within nature, inclusive of humans. First articulated by Heraclitus in Ancient Greece, two contemporary philosophical approaches which build on the idea of interconnectivity are deep ecology and ecofeminism.

A deep ecology perspective incorporates a sense of self within the natural environment. This approach deconstructs the idea of a distinct self in the traditional sense, and questions where the boundaries of self might lie. In this way, distinctions which separate a human from the environment in which they exist are eliminated, and the *self* evolves into what Naess described as a 'Self' (1973). Mathews (1991) explains that if each self is considered as a contained entity which strives for its own continuity, then humans can consider themselves as one part of a larger collective, or 'Self,' in which each part serves to sustain the greater whole.

While deep ecology attempts to deconstruct the perception of barriers between the self and the rest of nature, ecofeminism values the specificity of subjects within nature, and does not strive for the deconstruction of boundaries between humans and other members of the biotic community. Rather, ecofeminism argues that the sense of self should be upheld, and that egalitarian relationships between members of the biotic community should be reinforced and valued (Kheel, 2008; Plumwood, 1993). By focusing on the *connections* between members of the biotic community in this way, the hierarchical view of the human-nature relationship is counteracted and exploitation is diminished.

The *interconnectivity* theme considered in this book encompasses a relational view of nature which is reflected in deep ecology and ecofeminism. In these philosophical approaches, humans are considered to be an integral part of the natural systems and therefore also *made of* nature. As such, interconnectivity will be discerned by three philosophical subgroupings in the corporate environmental discourse which express the inherent value of nature of *connections between subjects*, *humans as part of nature*, and *nature intrinsically valued*, as illustrated in Figure 4.4, and discussed in the following sections.

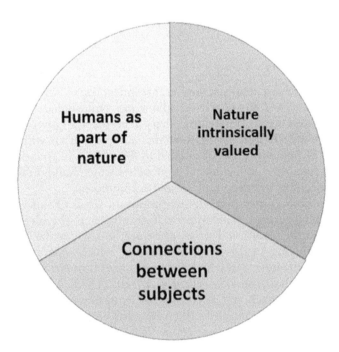

Figure 4.4 Interconnectivity subgroupings.

Connections between Subjects

Implicit in an interconnected approach to the natural world is the acknowledgement that contrary to the mechanical view of nature, where any part of nature can be removed or replaced with little consequence, organisms and systems are a matrix of relationships where each part is integral to the whole. This concept is exemplified by Lovelock (1987), who argues that the world itself is a living being: one huge organism made of multiple parts. As such, parts of the environmental reporting discourse which discuss wider effects such as through life cycle analysis, supply chain issues or other interconnections between systems and objects in the natural environment will be considered to represent the interconnectivity discourse grouping, through the identification of the *connections between subjects* subgrouping.

Humans as Part of Nature

Reflecting the connections between subjects within the eco system, humans must also be considered not only natural organisms, but part of the wider environment. This view is exemplified by the deep ecology perspective of nature in which humans are ordinary members of a larger community which makes up natural eco systems (Mathews, 2001; Naess, 1973). The consideration of humans as a part of nature, rather than separate and distinct, rejects the dualistic approach to nature which valorises humans at the expense of natural values. As with the other subgroupings, the *humans as part of nature* subgrouping can be discerned through any aspect of the discourse – through either text or by images in the environmental reports. By discerning the *humans as part of nature* subgrouping within the environmental reporting discourse, an interconnective approach will be identified.

Nature Intrinsically Valued

The third subgrouping which aids in the identification of an interconnective approach is an approach in which nature is intrinsically valued. This subgrouping represents the view that nature can be valued for its own sake, regardless of any anthropocentric value it might provide. The intrinsic value of nature is a concept which plays an important role in contemporary environmental philosophy (Brennan & Lo, 2011), and as such I have used this concept to assist in the discernment of discourse which represents an interconnective approach to the natural environment.

Application of Discourse Groupings

The three discourse groupings and subsequent subgroupings will aid in the discernment of the various philosophical approaches which were disseminated in the review of environmental philosophy literature presented in the second chapter, and outlined in this chapter. By discerning the different philosophical approaches, an awareness is developed which will highlight the ways in which the corporations are communicating about the natural world. The philosophies which underpin the environmental reports will aid in interpreting the ways in which the companies are relating the natural environment; are these relationships different to what is being purported ostensibly in the reports? Are dualistic barriers being constructed which distance the company from the temporal and physical effects of its environmental impacts? Is the company portrayed as something which is superior, or valorised at the expense of the natural world? Or does the company portray a vision in which it is an integral but humble aspect of the natural world; implicitly respecting the differences of subjects within the environment?

By highlighting the philosophical underpinnings of the environmental reports, the aim of this book is not to simply count the number of phrases or words, numerically assessing the text, but to analyse and interpret what these underpinnings might mean for the corporate relationship to nature holistically. As such, two layers of analysis will take place; the first of which will simply outline which of the philosophical themes is predominant in the environmental reports and interviews of each company, and to what extent. This will provide an overview of the general approach expressed through the discourse of each company.

The second layer of analysis will explore the ways in which these approaches are expressed in more depth. In this part of the analysis, some of the prevalent discursive mechanisms which have been detected during the first layer of analysis will be explored in more detail. Finally, the insights garnered from this two-step process will be analysed to explore how the environmental philosophies have been communicated through the environmental reporting, and what this conveys about the corporate relationship to nature.

Summary

This chapter has explored some of the philosophical assumptions which underpin and guide the methodologies of this book. In doing so, qualitative research, historical perspectives and critical approaches have been discussed, leading to an outline of methods adopted in order to address the important questions which guide this book.

The multiple case study approach, along with sample selection methods, interviewing techniques and critical discourse analysis were explained and justified as appropriate methods to answer this question. The discourse groupings proposed for the critical discourse analysis, and the forms of discourse to be analysed were outlined, as well as some of the linguistic constructions which convey these ideas. The results of these approaches will be discussed in the following two chapters.

References

Adams, D. H., & Belasco, J. (2015). The Mythic Roots of Western Culture's Alienation from Nature. *Tapestry Institute Occasional Papers, 1*(3).

Agger, B. (1991). Critical Theory, Poststructuralism, Postmodernism: Their Sociological Relevance. *Annual Review of Sociology, 17*, 105–131.

Alexander, R., & Stibbe, A. (2014). From the Analysis of Ecological Discourse to the Ecological Analysis of Discourse. *Language Sciences, 41*(Part A), 104–110.

ASX. (2015). 'ASX 200'. *Australian Securities Exchange*. Retrieved June, from www.asx.com.au

Attfield, R. (1991). *The Ethics of Environmental Concern* (2nd ed.), Athens: The University of Georgia Press.

Banerjee, S. B. (2003). Who Sustains Whose Development? Sustainable Development and the Reinvention of Nature. *Organization Studies, 24*(1), 143–180.

Beattie, V., & Jones, M. J. (2008). Corporate Reporting Using Graphs: A Review and Synthesis. *Journal of Accounting Literature, 27*, 71–110.

Bloomfield, B. P., & Vurdubakis, T. (1997). Visions of Organization and Organizations of Vision: The Representational Practices of Information Systems Development. *Accounting, Organizations and Society, 22*(7), 639–668.

Brennan, A., & Lo, Y. (2011). *Environmental Ethics*. Retrieved November, from http://plato.stanford.edu/entries/ethics-environmental/

Buhr, N. (2007). Histories of and Rationales for Sustainability Reporting. In J. Unerman, J. Bebbington, & B. O'Dwyer (Eds.), *Sustainability Accounting and Accountability* (pp. 57–69). Oxon: Routledge.

Callinocos, A. (1995). *Theories and Narratives: Reflections on the Philosophy of History*. Cambridge: Polity Press.

Carnegie, G. D., & Napier, C. J. (1996). Critical and Interpretive Histories: Insights into Accounting's Present and Future Through Its Past. *Accounting, Auditing & Accountability Journal, 9*(3), 7–39.

Chua, W. F. (1995). Experts, Networks and Inscriptions in the Fabrication of Accounting Images: A Story of the Representation of Three Public Hospitals. *Accounting, Organizations and Society, 20*(2–3), 111–145.

Dambrin, C., & Robson, K. (2011). Tracing Performance in the Pharmaceutical Industry: Ambivalence, Opacity and the Performativity of Flawed Measures. *Accounting, Organizations and Society, 36*(7), 428–455.

Davison, J., McLean, C., & Warren, S. (2012). Exploring the Visual in Organizations and Management. *Qualitative Research in Organizations and Management, 7*(1), 5–15.

Dodson Gray, E. (1981). *Green Paradise Lost*. Wellesley, MA: Roundtable Press.

Dryzek, J. (2013). *The Politics of the Earth: Environmental Discourses* (3rd ed.). Oxford: Oxford University Press.

Ellingson, L. (2011). Analysis and Representation across the Continuum. In N. K. Denzin & Y. S. Lincoln (Eds.), *The Sage Handbook of Qualitative Research* (4th ed., pp. 595–610). Thousand Oaks, CA: Sage.

Erikson, P., & Kovalainen, A. (2008). *Qualitative Methods in Business Research*. London: Sage.

Fairclough, N. (1992/2003). *Discourse and Social Change*. Cambridge: Polity Press.

Fairclough, N. (2013). *Analysing Discourse: Textual Analysis for Social Research* (2nd ed.). Abingdon: Routledge.

Global Reporting Initiative. (2011). *Sustainability Reporting Guidelines G3.* Amsterdam.

Grant, D., Hardy, C., Oswick, C., & Putnam, L. (Eds.) (2004). *The Sage Handbook of Organizational Discourse.* London: Sage.

Haraway, D. J. (2004). *The Haraway Reader.* New York: Routledge.

Hardy, C. (2001). Researching Organizational Discourse. *International Studies of Management & Organization, 31*(3), 25–47.

Hawken, P. (1993). *The Ecology of Commerce: A Declaration of Sustainability.* New York: HarperBusiness.

Heracleous, L. (2004). Interpretivist Approaches to Organizational Discourse. In D. Grant, C. Hardy, C. Oswick, & L. Putnam (Eds.), *The Sage Handbook of Organizational Discourse.* London: Sage Publications.

Horkheimer, M. (1982). *Critical Theory.* New York: Seabury Press.

Horkheimer, M., & Adorno, T. (1987). *Dialectic of Enlightenment.* Stanford: Stanford University Press.

Hrasky, S. (2012). Visual Disclosure Strategies Adopted by more and less Sustainability-Driven Companies. *Accounting Forum, 36*(3), 154–165.

Kamler, B., & Thomson, P. (2006). *Helping Doctoral Students Write: Pedagogies for Supervision.* London: Routledge.

Kheel, M. (2008). *Nature Ethics.* London: Rowman & Littlefield.

King, N., & Horrocks, C. (2010). *Interviews in Qualitative Research.* London: Sage.

Kress, G., & Van Leeuwen, T. (2002). Colour as a Semiotic Mode: Notes for a Grammar of Colour. *Visual Communication, 1*(3), 343–368.

Kress, G., & Van Leeuwen, T. (2006). *Reading Images: The Grammar of Visual Design* (2nd ed.). London: Routledge.

Lakoff, G., & Johnson, M. (1980). *Metaphors We Live By.* Chicago: University of Chicago Press.

Latour, B. (2014). *The Affects of Capitalism.* Copenhagen: Royal Academy.

Latour, B. (2016a). Onus Orbis Terrarum: About a Possible Shift in the Definition of Sovereignty. *Millennium – Journal of International Studies, 44*(3), 305–320.

Latour, B. (2016b). *Reset Modernity.* Lecture: University of Tasmania.

Le, T., Lê, Q., & Short, M. (2009). *Critical Discourse Analysis: An Interdisciplinary Perspective.* New York: Nova Science Publishers.

Lee, A. (2009). What Is a Text? Questions of Boundaries and Limits. In T. Le, Q. Lê, & M. Short (Eds.), *Critical Discourse Analysis: An Interdisciplinary Perspective* (pp. 37–48). New York: Nova Science Publishers.

Llewellyn, S., & Milne, M. J. (2007). Accounting as Codified Discourse. *Accounting, Auditing & Accountability Journal, 20*(6), 805–824.

Lodh, S. C., & Gaffikin, M. J. R. (1997). Critical Studies in Accounting Research, Rationality and Habermas: A Methodological Reflection. *Critical Perspectives on Accounting, 8*(5), 433–474.

Lovelock, J. E. (1987). *Gaia: A New Look at Life on Earth.* Oxford: Oxford University Press, cat02831a database.

Mackenzie-Davey, K., & Liefooghe, A. (2004). Critical Research and Analysis in Organizations. In C. Cassell & G. Symon (Eds.), *Essential Guide to Qualitative Methods in Organizational Research* (pp. 180–191). London: Sage.

Mathews, F. (1991). *The Ecological Self.* London: Routledge.

Mathews, F. (2001). Deep Ecology. In D. Jamieson (Ed.), *A Companion to Environmental Philosophy* (pp. 218–232). Cambridge, MA: Blackwell.

Mathews, F. (2006). Beyond Modernity and Tradition: A Third Way for Development. *Ethics and the Environment, 11*(2), 85–113.

Maxwell, J. A. (2005). *Qualitative Research Design: An Interactive Approach.* Applied Social Research Methods Series: no. 41. Thousand Oaks, CA: Sage, cat02831a database.

McNicholas, P., & Barrett, M. (2005). Answering the Emancipatory Call: An Emerging Research Approach 'On the Margins' of Accounting. *Critical Perspectives on Accounting, 16*(4), 391–414.

Merchant, C. (1989). *The Death of Nature: Women, Ecology, and the Scientific Revolution.* New York: Harper & Row.

Merchant, C. (2010). *Environmentalism: From the Control of Nature to Partnership.* University of California Television.

Miller, P. (2001). Governing by Numbers: Why Calculative Practices Matter. *Social Research, 68*(2), 379–396.

Milne, M. J., Kearins, K., & Walton, S. (2006). Creating Adventures in Wonderland: The Journey Metaphor and Environmental Sustainability. *Organization, 13*(6), 801–839.

Moerman, L., & Van Der Laan, S. (2007). Pursuing Shareholder Value: The Rhetoric of James Hardy. *Accounting Forum, 31,* 354–369.

Morrison, L., Wilmshurst, T., & Shimeld, S. (2018). Environmental Reporting Through an Ethical Looking Glass. *Journal of Business Ethics, 150*(4), 903–918.

Naess, A. (1973). The Shallow and the Deep, Long-Range Ecology Movement. A Summary. *Inquiry, 16*(1–4), 95–100.

Nash, R. (1973). *Wilderness and the American Mind.* New Haven: Yale University Press.

Nycyk, M. (2015). The Power Gossip and Rumour Have in Shaping Online Identity and Reputation: A Critical Discourse Analysis. *The Qualitative Report, 20*(2), 18–32.

Parker, L. D. (2014). Corporate Social Accountability through Action: Contemporary Insights from British Industrial Pioneers. *Accounting, Organizations and Society, 39*(8), 632–659.

Peräkylä, A., & Ruusuvuori, J. (2011). Analyzing Talk and Text. In N. K. Denzin & Y. S. Lincoln (Eds.), *The Sage Handbook of Qualitative Research* (4th ed., pp. 529–543). Thousand Oaks, CA: Sage.

Plumwood, V. (1993). *Feminism and the Mastery of Nature.* London: Routledge.

Qu, S. Q., & Dumay, J. (2011). The Qualitative Research Interview. *Qualitative Research in Accounting and Management, 8*(3), 238–264.

Robson, K. (1992). Accounting Numbers as "Inscription": Action at a Distance and the Development of Accounting. *Accounting, Organizations and Society, 17*(7), 685–708.

Rowlinson, M. (2004). Historical Analysis of Company Documents. In C. Cassell & G. Symon (Eds.), *Essential Guide to Qualitative Methods in Organizational Research* (3rd ed., pp. 300–311). London: Sage.

Said, E. W. (1993). *Culture and Imperialism.* London: Chatto & Windus.

Standard & Poor's. (2015). *S&P/ASX Australian Indices: Methodology.* McGraw Hill Financial.

Stiles, D. (2004). Pictorial Representation. In C. Cassell & G. Symon (Eds.), *Essential Guide to Qualitative Methods in Organizational Research* (pp. 127–139). London: Sage.

Travers, M. (2001). *Qualitative Research through Case Studies*. Introducing Qualitative Methods. London: Sage, cat02831a database.

Tregidga, H., Milne, M., & Kearins, K. (2014). '(Re)presenting 'Sustainable Organizations'. *Accounting, Organizations and Society, 39*(6), 477–494.

Unerman, J. (2000). Methodological Issues – Reflections on Quantification in Corporate Social Reporting Content Analysis. *Accounting, Auditing & Accountability Journal, 13*(5), 667–681.

van Dijk, T. (1998). *Ideology: A Multidisiplinary Approach*. London: Sage.

Walters-York, L. M. (1996). Metaphor in Accounting Discourse. *Accounting, Auditing and Accountability Journal, 9*(5), 45–70.

Wiman, I. M. B. (1990). Expecting the Unexpected: Some Ancient Roots to Current Perceptions of Nature. *AMBIO, 19*(2), 62–69.

Wodak, R., & Meyer, M. (2009). *Methods for Critical Discourse Analysis* (2nd ed.). London: Sage.

Yin, R. (2014). *Case Study Research: Design and Methods* (5th ed.). Thousand Oaks: Sage.

Young, J. J. (2013). Devil's Advocate: The Importance of Metaphors. *Accounting Horizons, 27*(4), 877–886.

Zillmann, D., Gibson, R., & Sargent, S. L. (1999). Effects of Photographs in News-Magazine Reports on issue Perception. *Media Psychology, 1*(3), 207–228.

5 Predominant Corporate Philosophical Approaches

Introduction

By articulating the relationship between the corporation and the natural world, corporate environmental reporting implicitly draws from western attitudes towards nature. Since this relationship is associated with current environmental damage, it is useful to closely examine the values with which it is informed. In order to explore these underpinning values, in this chapter I examine the corporate relationship with nature through the lens of western environmental philosophy. This chapter explores how western environmental philosophy is conveyed in contemporary corporate reports.

In order to explore the relationship between western environmental philosophy and organisational environmental reporting, the reports of a sample of companies listed in the ASX 200 were analysed. This analysis was undertaken through the lens of three themes which have guided the evolution of western environmental philosophy from Ancient Greece to the present day: dualism, transcendence and interconnectivity. The previous chapter explored how these themes would be sought; this chapter explores how they were found. The case studies are examined one by one, and specific examples are provided in order to demonstrate the ways in which the themes were expressed by each company: through their reports and interviews, and surrounding contextual issues. These findings are laid out in this chapter and explored in more depth in the next. Chapter 6 further develops the analysis by exploring some of the discursive mechanisms which are commonly used by many, and in some instances, *all* of the case study companies.

The process of analysis undertaken can be described as a spiral, or hermeneutic circle, where understanding increases and interpretation deepens with each additional piece of information (Prasad, 2002). Thus, analysis in this project undergoes several stages, each reiterating and extending from the previous stage. While the initial methods provide a *lineal* 'plan' for the analysis, in actuality, this plan developed *cyclically*, with new information and therefore new interpretations gradually altering the initial analysis until this final set of results and subsequent analysis was arrived at. One example of this process is the initial rejection of companies which had repeated the same relatively superficial text in their environmental reports from year to year. Initially these companies were excluded from the selection process, as such repetition appeared to represent a relatively meaningless discourse. However, since expanding the selection process to include a number of these reports, the verbatim repetition of text was able to be analysed in context, so that even the relative superficiality could provide meaning to the findings. This hermeneutical process of analysis is reflected in the structure of this chapter and the next, which begins with a preliminary presentation of results, and then leads to a more in-depth and complex analysis of findings in the following chapter.

Multiple Case Studies

Multiple case studies were drawn from within the ASX 200. A proportion of these companies agreed to participate in this research anonymously. To apply this consideration evenly, this book has de-identified all of the companies by using pseudonyms in the place of company names. These pseudonyms have been randomly chosen and do not purposefully represent the companies in any way. The companies will henceforth be labelled with the following pseudonyms:

- Phi
- Alpha
- Delta
- Sigma
- Kappa
- Beta
- Zeta
- Theta
- Psi
- Gamma

The ten companies were of varying positions within the ASX 200 (ASX, 2015), ranging from a company within the largest ten, to one within the smallest ten. Market capitalisation of the companies ranged from over $80 billion to over $450 million (exact figures may risk company anonymity). The average market value of the case study companies was $12,851,218,200, with a median value of $2,929,075,000. Companies were from diverse industries, as illustrated in the following table. Also included in Table 5.1 is an indication of the comparative ranking of each of the companies, their pseudonym for the purposes of this book and whether these particular companies are also listed in the ASX 100.

   The proportion of industry sectors within the ASX 200 is aligned to the proportions evident in the multiple case study used in this book. The relationship between the proportion of companies in each sector in the ASX 200 as compared to those included in this book is illustrated in the chart below, where the y axis represents percentages, and the x axis outlines the industry sectors (Figure 5.1).

Table 5.1 Industry diversity of case study companies

Industry sector	Number of case study companies	Pseudonym	Ranking in terms of size	ASX 100
Real estate	1	Kappa	4	Yes
Consumer discretionary	3	Sigma	5	Yes
		Beta	8	No
		Theta	7	No
Consumer staples	1	Psi	10	No
Energy	0			
Financials	1	Zeta	1	Yes
Health care	0			
Industrials	1	Delta	6	No
Information technology	0			
Materials	2	Alpha	2	Yes
		Gamma	9	No
Telecommunication Services	0			
Utilities	1	Phi	3	Yes

ASX (2016).

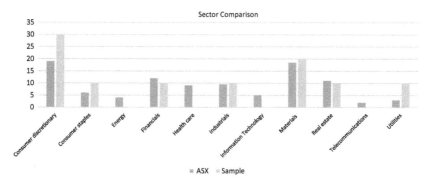

Figure 5.1 Comparison of ASX 200 and multiple case study industry sectors.

The Environmental Reports

The first layer of information collected was the publicly available environmental reports of the multiple case studies. In aggregate, this composed of 393 pages from within 30 environmental reports published between 2012 and 2014, inclusive. These reports varied in form and included dedicated environmental reports, sections of sustainability reports and pages of annual reviews.

Interviews

The second layer of information collected involved in-depth semi-structured interviews with senior management involved in the environmental reporting processes of the case study companies. All of the participants interviewed for this book had a central role in the preparation of the environmental reports. Interviews were all undertaken face-to-face at the interviewees' place of work. Genders were almost equally represented, with six female participants compared to four male participants. Although the expected interview length was 60 minutes, and all participants were asked the same set of core questions, interview times ranged from 35 minutes to 91 minutes, at the behest of participants, and depending on the depth with which the participants wished to discuss their responses. Most interviews involved additional discussions which grew from the core set of questions, in order to capture the specific perspectives of the participants and the contextual issues of the particular companies involved.

After each interview was conducted, I recorded my reflections of the process. This allowed for additional, contextual topics such as impressions and general atmosphere of the interview to be noted.

During the interviewing process, it was established that the participants came from a wide variety of professional and educational backgrounds. For instance, some participants' career paths were directed towards becoming involved in the 'sustainability reporting' industry. This career path was often signalled by the participants' completion of an accounting degree or 'sustainability' major or similar educational pathway. This career pathway was also signalled by previous roles within the sustainability reporting industry, often at other organisations, for dedicated sustainability firms, or as independent sustainability reporting consultants. Six of the participants had this kind of career path.

Three participants came from a background of environmental or marine science. Two of these participants had moved into the sustainability reporting industry early in their careers and can therefore also be considered part of the previous group.

Conversely, two participants had made their way through a single organisation's employment ladder, and therefore had working experience exclusively within the case study company. One of these participants had begun in a different field and crossed over to sustainability reporting three years prior to the interview. The other had begun as a science officer and worked their way to the sustainability department.

These diverse backgrounds appeared to have direct impact on how the participant approached the environmental reporting process. These differing approaches became evident through the type of language used when discussing the environmental report, and through the perspective the participant took towards the case study company's environmental impact, ranging from a broad perspective of environmental issues using sophisticated 'corporate' language, to a narrow focus bordering on defensive, using more 'layperson's' language. The following passages from two of the interviews provide examples of these differences:

We are a very carbon intensive company, carbon constrained, however you want to define it, through... carbon tax ... is a critical issue that is facing this company but equally because of my background in the social responsibility side of things, I'm able to see that – what I call... the confluence, where the essential service, social obligation nature, and the environmental impact of energy ... come together, and you throw in an economic thing and it's like a perfect storm. So my role in the sustainability report is about framing that – about setting up saying these are the core issues, how are we going to respond to them?

(Phi interview)

Um, well, I think it is good, I think that people are passionate about it. Again, apart from the waste, electricity, packaging, type of thing, I think that people are quite mindful, you know, things that we buy – even office supplies for example you know, I had this question the other day – why did we change from x percent recycling to x percent – well I don't know, ask procurement, you know, but just by having this question, it's something, its wow, for someone to be going to the printer, and checking up what is the percentage of recycled paper that we have there.

(Theta interview)

The first of these two quotes comes from an interview with a participant who had an accounting and sustainability education and had worked in the sustainability field at another large Australian company before moving into their current role. Their use of accepted corporate style language and persuasive style reflects this background. In contrast, the second quote is from a participant who had worked within the case study company in varying roles not directly related to environmental reporting for seven years and had taken their current role three years ago with no other environmental or sustainability reporting experience. Notice this participant speaks in narrower terms, on a more personal and particular level. This relationship between background and patterns of speech and language use was evident across the other participants as well.

Other variances of interviews ranged from relaxed and chatty to short and defensive responses, with the approach also impacting on the analysis of the interview data. Prior literature has defined good quality interview participants as relaxed and open (Barriball & While, 1994; Whiting, 2008), however in this research, all participants' conduct was useful in contributing to the overall analysis.

Of particular note in most of the interviews was that the interviewees seemed able to express their views in a less guarded way in comparison to the reports. One result of this relaxation is that the interviews incorporate a much more interconnected view overall, particularly in comparison with results from the environmental reports analysed in this book, which were largely expressed in terms of dualism. The relationships between the themes evident in the environmental reports, and those evidenced through the interviews is illustrated in Figure 5.7, presented towards the end of this chapter.

The first seven of the case study companies presented here reported their environmental issues largely through a dualistic lens, the next through a more balanced approach and the final two case study companies presented in this chapter reported their environmental interactions predominantly through an interconnected approach.

Zeta

Zeta is one of Australia's 'Big 4' banks, operating in Australia, New Zealand, Asia, the UK and the US. It was listed on the ASX as a member of the 'financials' sector in 1974 (ASX, 2016). Zeta produced a standalone environmental report in 2012 and 2013, of 30 and 36 pages, respectively. In 2014, this report developed into a more broadly based Corporate Social Responsibility report, with environmental information taking up 10% of a total 69 pages. Of these environmental reports, as in most of the other reports from within the sample, the predominant approach is that of dualism.

Zeta Environmental Reports

A pattern detected in these reports, and found repeatedly in the other reports examined for this book, is the direction of the reader's attention towards other sources of information, particularly to Zeta's website. This is considered as a way to separate and obscure information, and as such, is considered to be a dualistic mechanism.

Similarly, the regular reference to the environmental management standard ISO 14001 is considered representative of a dualistic approach, since it implies that humans are well placed (presumably because of our superior intelligence or powers of reason) to 'manage' nature. It implies this in not only the title of the standard ("environmental management"), but also through the concept of a standard which implies universality, a concept which is associated with the masculinist rationality of Enlightenment thought. In the text of the standard, terms such as the development of greenhouse gas accounting, verification, emissions trading and carbon footprint measurement are used (ISO, 2015) – all terms which are associated with a dualistic approach to the environment by way of construction of a barrier between the company and the actual, temporal effects on the environment. These concepts will be discussed in more depth in the following chapter. It is important to note that the importance of such standards is not being challenged here, only that they represent a dualistic approach to the environment.

The extract below from the Zeta 2012 environmental report demonstrates both the view of carbon neutrality being objective and value neutral and of the motif of directing the readers' attention away from the report itself. Narratives around carbon neutrality and carbon counting have been explored by Nerlich and Koteyko (2009) and Koteyko, Thelwall and Nerlich (2010), who discuss the discursive implications of carbon in the public discourse. They argue that such terms are commonly associated with a moral value and used to perpetuate a moralistic attitude. The term 'carbon neutral,' as used in the environmental reports analysed in this book, is based on an accounting treatment of carbon and carbon equivalent emissions. Like accounting itself, carbon accounting is a far from a value-neutral concept (Ascui & Lovell, 2011), which obfuscates the physical impact of carbon emissions. As such, discourse such as this exhibits a dualistic approach. The following is an example of dualistic text in the 2012 Zeta environmental report:

Carbon Neutral – What Does It Mean to Us?
We define carbon neutrality as a process
  Involving five steps:

  i defining and measuring our carbon (greenhouse gas) inventory;
  ii reducing our greenhouse gas (GHG) emissions through energy efficiency, demand management (employee behaviour change) and transitioning to lower emissions energy sources, where it is practicable;
  iii avoiding emissions through the purchase of renewable energy (where it is necessary to support our strategy to invest in local emissions abatement);
  iv offsetting remaining emissions through the purchase of quality carbon offsets (including co-benefits from selected projects); and
  v verifying and reporting on our progress by:

  • regularly assessing our carbon neutrality and reduction targets;
  • obtaining annual external verification and assurance of our carbon accounts (inventory and offsets) and carbon neutral commitment; and
  • reporting regularly to key internal stakeholders and annually to external stakeholders.

  (Zeta, 2012)

In these reports there is a recurring mention of 'clean' renewable energy and 'dirty' coal. Analysing these words in terms of environmental philosophy, *dirty* implies a closeness to the Earth; literally like dirt, soil or earth. Through the lens of environmental philosophy, the implications of the double terms of *clean* and *dirty* are reversed, so that *dirty* begins to take on the positive connotations of being analogous to the Earth, and *clean* becomes an attempt to be rid of dirt (or earth). The use of terms which indicate 'cleanliness,' identifies a dualistic approach to the environment. The following extracts from Zeta's various environmental reports demonstrate the repeated use of this term (underline added):

> [subsidiary of Zeta] Bank wins Clean Glasgow – Business Award.
>
> (Zeta, 2012)

> ...a concentrated focus on energy efficiency and the use of cleaner energy sources....
>
> (Zeta, 2012)

> ...continued our support of Australia's transition to cleaner energy sources.
>
> (Zeta, 2013)

> It is also an opportunity to innovate and grow new business as clean technology is developed....
>
> (Zeta, 2013)

> Renewable energy has a positive environmental impact because it generates clean power.
>
> (Zeta, 2013)

> ...and lower emissions to assist the transition to cleaner technologies....
>
> (Zeta, 2014)

> ...as we continue to look for further ways to integrate clean and alternative technology into our operations and decrease our dependency on fossil fuel consumption.
>
> (Zeta, 2014)

> We believe ongoing investigation into clean technology is important to identify innovative and cost-effective ways to reduce energy use and GHG emissions....
>
> (Zeta, 2014)

> ...will require the scaling-up of private-sector investment in clean technology applications and systems for natural capital management around the world....
>
> (Zeta, 2014)

Over the three years of environmental reports analysed for this book, Zeta expressed a predominantly dualistic approach to the natural environment. This theme was expressed through terms such as *clean* energy, but also through the frequent use of financial style language to express environmental values, claims and discussions about the neutrality of carbon being attainable through a mechanistic view of the physical world, and through the direction of readers' attention away from the report. The dualistic theme was also repeated throughout the interview.

Zeta Interview

The dominant theme evident during the interview with an environmental sustainability manager at Zeta is dualism. This is in part due to the way they described their approach to the environment in terms of 'natural capital,' from a very analytic and quantitative perspective, which as discussed, indicates a dualistic method of communication.

In the passage below, this quantitative approach is highlighted. By focusing on quantitative data, the participant constructs a barrier between the company and the natural environment which demonstrates a dualistic approach.

> ... we used to report on number of suppliers who, who've signed up to our principles, then we break it down by different categories of suppliers, then we break it down by different spend groups, it's like, no one cares about that information. All they want to know is how many have signed up, and then what's the total spend with those guys, what's that as a proportion of our whole, you know like those sorts of juicy numbers as opposed to, yeah, going into minute details...

Balancing this perspective, an interconnective approach was also taken by the participant, in remarks such as the following. This quote represents interconnectivity by acknowledging the direct connection between an aspect of human life (farming) and the effect of climate change and other environmental damage.

> ...they're important to stakeholders in the sense that you know, the farmers are going to be hammered by this stuff if it's not taken care of.

Despite this peppering of interconnectivity, Zeta's environmental reports demonstrate a predominantly dualistic theme. This finding is reinforced by the largely dualistic nature of the interview results. Zeta is one of the companies which expresses environmental issues at the most dualistic end of the spectrum of possible approaches. This spectrum is illustrated at the end of this chapter, in Figure 5.7.

Gamma

Gamma was listed on the ASX in 2000 when it was split from another large minerals company. It is a diversified metals and mining company specialising in the mining of iron ore, metal recycling and steel manufacture. At the time of writing, Gamma had gone into voluntary administration. Prior to suspension, it was listed on the ASX as part of the 'metals and mining' sector (ASX, 2016).

Gamma has released information about its environmental impact in its annual reports since its first annual report in 2001. Its first standalone sustainability report was produced in 2010. The 2012, 2013 and 2014 reports analysed in this research include the environment section of the standalone sustainability reports for those years. The environmental section makes up 17.5% of a total of 40 pages in 2012 and continues with similar coverage in 2013 and 2014.

Gamma Environmental Reports

Gamma communicates its environmental impact most commonly in terms of a dualistic approach, with some exceptions. In Gamma's 2012 environmental report, the tables provided on page 25 without context would be considered as illustrating an ontology of discrete objects, and therefore a dualistic approach. However, since the page provided context and background information in a way that focused on Gamma's role within a larger system, the table and accompanying figures can also be considered to communicate the connections between subjects, and therefore part of an interconnective approach.

One pattern of this report, and also noted in other reports across the multiple case studies, is that of titles and images portraying an interconnected approach, with the text underneath revealing an ontology of discrete objects, and therefore a dualistic approach. See, for instance, the image below – a picture which communicates the intrinsic value of a tiny native bird – which represents interconnectivity in part due to its reflection of the intrinsic value of this creature. This image is followed by a list of ISO 14001 certified sites, which considered on its own reflects a dualistic approach. The list of sites which have achieved certification itself represents dualism since the list reflects a 'site specific' perception of environmental impacts. By conceptually confining the effect of environmental management, Gamma fails to recognise the flow on and interconnected nature of environmental impact. This is an example of the ontology of discrete objects, and therefore dualism (Figure 5.2).

Similarly, in this report there is a distinct focus on the company's adherence to regulations and mandatory governmental reporting, exclusive of any contextual discussion, as demonstrated in the following quote from Gamma's 2013 environmental report:

> The [Gamma] Group's operations are subject to various environmental regulations at a National, State and local level. Where this regulation is particular and significant, compliance is assured through Environmental Management Systems to the ISO14001 standard.

ENVIRONMENTAL MANAGEMENT SYSTEMS

Environmental Management Systems (EMS) are a key tool in maintaining environmental compliance and managing environmental risk. The following is a list of Arrium's major facilities that are externally certified to Environmental Management System standard ISO 14001.

Environmental Management System ISO 14001 Certification

Australia	North & South America
Dolomite Quarry	- Edmonton, Canada
- Acacia Ridge	- Kamloops, Canada
- Newcastle	- El Salto, Mexico
- Somerton	- Lima, Peru
Traklok	- Arequipa, Peru
Wire Mill	- Mejillones, Chile
Steel Mill	- Santiago, Chile
Mining – Middleback Ranges	- Talcahuano, Chile
Rod Mill	
Wire Mill	
Steel Mill	
Steel Mill	

Environment
ISO 14001
SAI GLOBAL

Figure 5.2 Image conflicting with text in Gamma 2013 environmental report.

> Compliance with this regulation was generally achieved in FY13 with the exception of unrelated releases of contaminated water at separate locations that resulted in the receipt of an Infringement Notice (with associated fine of $2,200) and a Penalty Notice (with associated fine of $1,500.)

Since this discourse fails to demonstrate a particular connection or reason for completing the report, other than because it was required, this approach is considered to represent an ontology of discrete objects, and therefore a dualistic approach.

In common with many of the other reports within the sample, targets and goals are mentioned with no discussion of context – no reason which could relate the target back to the natural environment. These types of lists neglect any linkage to the environment, and therefore are also considered to be representative of a dualistic approach which favours a view of the company as one with only tenuous links to the natural world.

Gamma's 2014 report utilises case studies to explain some of the interactions Gamma has with the natural environment. Case studies allow

████████participated in an urban forestry project together with the non-profit association Patrulla Ecológica in Arequipa. The project consisted of the production of a guide book on tree planting in the Arequipa City area, with an emphasis on species that assist in mitigating pollution. The project also included a tree planting campaign.

"Trees and Shrubs of Arequipa" is the book produced with the assistance of ████████ to promote tree-planting in the Arequipa area.

Figure 5.3 Case study in 2014 Gamma environmental report.

for contextual information to be included and as such are generally classed as displaying the interconnectivity theme, as in the example above (Figure 5.3).

Despite some reflection of an interconnective approach, Gamma demonstrated a predominantly dualistic approach to the natural world in its 2012, 2013 and 2014 environmental reports. This was the philosophical theme most frequently communicated in all of the environmental reports analysed in this book.

Gamma Interview

The interview with a senior environmental manager in Gamma is one example of a participant who expressed a good deal of dualism, in similar proportion to the environmental reports. This might be explained by the participant's direct and relatively singular role in producing these reports.

The following statement from the Gamma interview illustrates a dualistic approach which is linked to the managerial branch of stakeholder theory, which holds that a company will only be accountable to powerful stakeholders who can financially impact on the company (Donaldson & Preston, 1995). This implicit ranking of stakeholders depending on what they can offer the company (in this case investment) reflects a dualistic approach.

...professional investor community, they certainly want to know and they're – they are adept at looking at reports and drawing conclusions about the company, and we get from time to time we get assessments from analysts to that effect, about how – about what they think of our reporting. And then there might be individual investors that are interested in specific issues, that might have a look, and they're one example. And they're the ones – one of the more important ones...

Similarly, the quote provided below represents the dualism theme by diminishing the relevance of the natural environment in comparison to business operations, and also by making reference to the regulatory environment in order to justify Gamma's position in terms of environmental impact.

...so we are an iron ore miner, and a steel producer – a steel products producer, and a metal recycler. All of those activities have an unavoidable degree of impact on the environment. And you can't run those businesses without accepting that degree of impact. Having said that, I am very confident that we are a solid corporate citizen, so we have a commitment to compliance in all of the countries we operate in.

Again, in the next quote, the participant justifies environmental damage in terms of business operations and justifies this damage with reference to global demand.

... if you accept that there has to be mining, and in our case its open cut mining, then you accept that there is – that there will be unavoidable and irreversible impact. You know steel – steel making and its role in greenhouse gas production for example is a – is a hot topic, and we – the bottom line is, the world demands steel.

Dualism is again reflected in the following quote which demonstrates the view that one aspect of the environment can be substituted for another. The dualistic approach is also demonstrated here by the participant's reference to government-imposed regulations as motivation for undertaking this offset.

So there are standards set by the state government on rehabilitation. And they're mostly around, well, around, let's talk about – there are standards set to do with biodiversity and mining, so the first one is if you're going to destroy any area because you're going to dig it up, you must have acquired an offset area of equivalent or greater biodiversity value. So this has been going on for years, ever since we've been mining and I don't think I put the – the details in here, but we have bought over the years an area adjoining our mining lease which is about ten times as big as the mining area, and it was it was um rangelands, so it was basically fairly much unmodified landscape but it had been subject to some grazing over the years, and what we're doing now is managing that and improving that so that it improves in biodiversity value and then compensates the area that we have to mine...

The next quote reinforces a dualistic perspective of the participant towards the natural environment by justifying environmental impact in terms of economic and social benefit. This quote is an interesting contrast to the quote provided in the *Phi* interview (discussion provided below), where the economic, social and environmental aspects are also compared, however in the Phi interview the relationship between the three aspects was highlighted, rather than a combative ranking system where each aspect is in competition with the others.

...we accept that there is some irreversible impact due to our operations. We do everything we're obliged to do to manage that, and we go beyond that in a lot of ways. And at the end of the day we consider that the value that is generated by the business, that is – economic and social – outweighs the impact of those operations.

This reduction of environmental values in comparison to social and economic values is reinforced in the following quote. The dualistic nature of this quote is highlighted by the participant's use of the phrase "*you have to put a line around it,*" which portrays a very dualistic image of separation.

You have to put a line around it, and um and you know what I'd say is – whilst that's important and it's a big deal for us, you know is a – it's not the major component of sustainability. So our major components of sustainability are business sustainability especially while our business is under threat and if the next component would be social ... we go to extraordinary lengths to protect our employees and we're leaders in safety. It's hard to – for some people it's hard to understand that sustainability is not just environmental sustainability...

However elsewhere in the interview, the participant highlights some more positive links between environmental performance and economic outcome, as in the following quote:

...you won't find a company that has solid economic sustainability without a reasonable environmental track record. Um you

know the likes of – if you look at some of the big disasters in recent years, the Deepwater Horizon oil spill, BHP 's performance,
even um Volkswagen's emissions control disaster, you know, they
are all going to have massive impacts on their bottom line, and
that's just the way it goes. Any company that doesn't deal with
environmental risks the same as it deals with any other risk is
completely mad.

In contrast to this dualistic view, the participant expressed an interconnected approach when discussing his personal views about important
environmental issues, as demonstrated below.

...so the top list is global warming and its associated impacts. Yeah
so personally for me, um next would be loss of biodiversity due to
various causes, and there's a whole bunch of causes, big ones – land
use changes, and over exploitation of various resources.

Gamma's environmental reports, as well as the interview text, draw
principally from a dualistic philosophical perspective. This is balanced
somewhat with a moderate proportion of interconnectivity expressed in
both the reports and the interview, and minimal expression of a transcendent view. This pattern is continued by the following case study
company, Beta.

Beta

Beta operates Australia's largest department store group. It is a well-
known retail brand with outlets in all major Australian cities. Beta was
officially listed on the ASX in 2009, however has been operating since
1900. The ASX includes Beta in the 'consumer discretionary' sector
(ASX, 2016).

Beta's Annual Review has included some environmental information
since 2008, however standalone sustainability reports were not provided
to the public until 2013. The environmental reports which I analyse in
this book include a section of the 2012 Annual Review (1 page of a
total 115 pages), and the environment sections of the 2013 and 2014
sustainability reports, which accounted for 13% of 15 pages and 12.5%
of 24 pages, respectively.

Beta Environmental Reports

Beta's environmental reports demonstrate a bias towards looking at
the natural environment as separate and distinct from human life. It
has done so principally by expressing environmental factors in the absence of any contextual explanation. This approach is reflected in the

predominant use of quantitative information, which as discussed, is seen as an attempt to further strip contextual issues from the discourse.

Beta's 2012 environmental report consists of a single page within its annual report. On this page, numerous positive steps are discussed, such as a reduction in packaging waste and an increase in recycling rates. The text presented on this page is considered largely dualistic, since there is virtually no reference to the natural world.

The 2013 report continues in this vein and is underpinned by the two images chosen for inclusion in the environment section, which, like the text, omit any reference to the natural world.

The 2014 report maintains a dualistic perspective by focusing on this somewhat narrow view of the environment. By confining images to those taken inside the retail outlets, the images reinforce this narrow perspective. This approach is representative of the predominantly dualistic approach demonstrated within the three Beta environmental reports analysed here.

Beta Interview

Despite being relatively guarded and uncommunicative at the beginning of this interview, the national sustainability manager of Beta demonstrated a moderate degree of interconnectivity in terms of their approach towards the natural environment. Overall, the interview data is almost evenly divided between interconnectivity theme and dualism in its thematic interpretation.

As the following two passages demonstrate, the participant highlighted the supply chain and life cycle issues of the products Beta sell:

> ...whereas energy and emissions, climate change yes we do have a part to play in that, particularly around product stewardship issues – yes we are selling stuff, therefore the responsible end of life for those things is something that we see as important.
> ...things like deforestation or you know, how that filters through to the fibre that we would use to print catalogues, so we are working, you know all of those things are being done as a responsible business but may not be highlighted in the report.

While there seems, in the transcriptions, to be a generous amount of interconnective discussion, the context around this interview supports a sense that overall, this participant was very guarded and distant, approaches which are more closely related to a dualistic perspective. The following remarks made by the participant during the interview confirm this approach by focussing on the economic benefits of the environmental decisions being made in the company, rather than any benefits to the environment itself.

...and to be honest, the environment issues have dollars attached to them.

...I'd say there's three. Compliance tick box would be the lowest one on our priorities, but it's always there. I think around cost, so we're wanting to reduce our waste cost and increase our recycling rebates. We're wanting to reduce our energy costs, so I think that's extremely important for our business...

Further to this, the extract from the interview below illustrates how the participant distanced the company from the concept of a relationship with the natural environment.

RESEARCHER: How would you describe your company's relationship with the natural environment?

PARTICIPANT: The company's relationship with the natural environment? [pause] I don't even know how you would put that into words. Um we have our approach to the environment, which I could probably talk to, but as far as...

RESEARCHER: OK, so tell me about the approach.

PARTICIPANT: So the company has relationships with people, and I guess, and our approach to environment is around maximising positive impacts, minimising negative impacts um and influencing the people that we have relationships with...

In this instance, while the textual data alone suggests that an interconnective approach was taken by the participant, context such as the body language, vocal tone and overall tone of the interview and the preceding communications of the participant aggregate to point towards a more dualistic approach overall. In Beta's case, the analysis of the environmental reports was similarly reflected throughout the interview.

Phi

Founded in 1837, Phi is one of Australia's oldest companies. Originally founded in order to provide Sydney with gas lights, Phi now provides gas, electricity, solar and related products and services across Queensland, New South Wales, Victoria and South Australia. While this company is now the largest listed provider of renewable energy, it is also Australia's largest emitter of carbon and carbon equivalents (Australian Conservation Foundation, 2016). The ASX lists Phi as a member of the 'utilities' sector (ASX, 2016).

Phi reports extensively on environmental issues and has released a standalone sustainability report since 2007. The 2012 report analysed in this research project focuses on the 'climate change,' 'environmental risk' and 'water' sections of the sustainability report. In aggregate, these sections make up 25% of total pages within the sustainability report. In 2013, these sections were renamed 'sustainable energy' and 'environment,' and continued to constitute one quarter of the sustainability report. The structure and presentation of the 2014 environmental report differs from the previous two years, however much of the wording remains the same.

Phi Environmental Reports

The primary approach in the Phi environmental reports was that of dualism. Some of the ways in which the philosophical approaches are communicated through the reports are presented below, in order to demonstrate how western environmental philosophy is communicated through Phi's 2012, 2013 and 2014 environmental reports.

Within these reports, there is some discussion of the risks of climate change, however rather than representing an approach which recognises the interconnected nature of this phenomenon, it is expressed from a company specific perspective. For instance, 'carbon exposure' is discussed in relation to the introduction of a carbon price, in terms of how this could affect the company financially; similarly, the development of sustainable energy generation is discussed in the context of the possible introduction of a carbon price and any subsequent financial effects. While climate change would otherwise be considered in terms of interconnectivity, in this context, Phi discuss it from a very removed perspective – what costs will they face if a carbon price is introduced? This is particularly so in the 2012 report, on the first page of the climate change section, presented below:

> Carbon exposure: Risks to [Phi] presented by climate change mitigation policies (for example, carbon pricing) could become significant over time. To pre-emptively manage these risks and work towards minimising exposure, the emissions intensity of new electricity generation plant built by [Phi] is included as a key performance indicator.

As such, the approach to climate change demonstrated in this report is considered a reflection of dualism. This interpretation is supported by the considerable amount of space in this climate change section dedicated to measurement in numerical terms, which also reflects a dualistic perspective.

Environmental risk is similarly discussed not in terms of risks to the environment, but risks posed to the company as a consequence of climate changes. This motif of parring the company against the environment is repeated throughout the 2012 report through the mention of offsetting devices:

Includes scope 1 and 2 greenhouse gas emissions for assets where [Phi] had operational control. This does not include Oakey or Yabulu power stations, or [Phi]'s nonoperated Upstream Gas joint ventures. While emissions from [Phi]'s corporate and retail activities have been included (calculated in accordance with the National Greenhouse and Energy Reporting Act) it should be noted that these emissions have been partially offset by purchasing 100% Green-Power at [Phi]'s main offices in Sydney, Melbourne, Adelaide and Mount Beauty.

As discussed earlier, offsetting one object for another implies that aspects of the natural environment are replaceable and interchangeable, an approach which disregards the particularity of specific places or parts of the environment. This approach reflects an ontology of discrete objects which neglects the interconnected characteristics of nature. This dualistic motif was repeated throughout all three of Phi's environmental reports.

Much of the material used in the 2012 report was repeated in the 2013 report. This is a practice used by several of the case study companies analysed in this book. Minor changes to the 2013 report include the 'climate change' section being renamed as 'sustainable energy.' Other relevant changes include discussions of water management which was coded as interconnectivity in the 2012 report, as it included environmental contexts of the natural cycles and conditions of drought and high rainfall. However, in the 2013 report, only numerical information is included, with environmental context removed. As such, this section was considered dualistic in the 2013 report.

There is a change in the presentation of Phi's environmental report in 2014, however much of the wording remains the same. The discrete objects aspect of the dualistic theme is based on Mathews' (1991) explication of Newtonian and mechanistic science, where one 'part' of nature can easily be replaced by another with little or no consequence. This approach is evident in Phi's discussion of 'produced water,' which is extracted as a by-product of coal seam gas mining, and either disposed of elsewhere, or mixed with fresh water and used as irrigation for salt resistant crops. The report mentions 'minimal increase in salt levels to soils,' and by doing so disregards the effect of even minimal increased salt levels in soils on the natural environment.

In the 2014 report, there is mention of breaches of laws and the payment of penalties by Phi. This topic is considered to articulate an ontology of discrete objects, as these fines have been exchanged for environmental damage. Again, this reflects Mathews (1991) understanding of the dualistic approach of mechanistic science.

Reinforcing the sense of separation evident in this report are multiple instances where the reader is directed towards other sources of information. This represents a limiting of the scope of responsibility. Many of these alternative sources of information are within the Phi website, but such direction is a device which succeeds in distracting the reader's attention, effectively placing a barrier between the reader and the data.

This dualistic approach is the predominant philosophical theme evidenced in Phi's 2012, 2013 and 2014 environmental reports. The approaches evident in the reports provide a contrast to the approaches evident in the interview with Phi's environmental manager, as outlined below.

Phi Interview

This interview took place in the Phi offices in central Melbourne. To meet with this participant, there were some technological barriers to entry, which included a tablet at the ground floor reception, with which to type out the researcher's name, and the interviewee's name. To access the meeting room, the participant used a passkey to allow access through some large metal stalls. Looking at this process through the lens of the three philosophical themes, these barriers to entry clearly symbolise a dualistic approach which separates the company and its corporate employees from other members of society.

The Phi participant expressed a largely interconnective approach towards the natural environment during this interview. The following remarks, which are part of a larger discussion in which the participant was expressing his motivations for working in the energy industry, exemplifies this approach:

> ...if you have a Venn diagram of sort of economic, social and environment, and do that across a range of industries, electricity is one of those ones that is purely right at that centre point because it doesn't, you know if you're talking to anybody about social policy the cost of electricity comes up. If you're talking to anybody about environmental policy, the emissions are environmental, if you're talking to anybody about economic policy the cost of energy comes up so you have that triumbra [sic] of core political issues.

This quote illustrates interconnectivity through the acknowledgment that environmental, social and economics are inherently connected. The interconnected approach continued to dominate the interview, and the following statement articulates another aspect of the interconnected theme as expressed by the participant:

> ...if you assume that Mother Nature, or Gaia or however you pronounce it is sitting there going 'You've really got to stop pumping these tonnes of carbon into the atmosphere', then particularly from

an Australian perspective she's sitting there going 'Yes, I'm talking about you!' You know, and I'm being flippant, but that whole thing of if you're talking specifically about the relationship between the environment and [Phi]? At the moment we are contributing significantly to an issue that is a significant contributor to fundamental climate change. So, you couldn't say that we're on an A1 relationship – it is strained, but we recognise that it is strained, if that makes sense, so 'Hey we know we're causing you some pain, and we're trying to do our best to reduce it'. So it's a – I would suggest that I would describe our relationship as an acknowledged strained relationship, with a promise and an open commitment to try and ease the pressure.

This quote expresses interconnectivity in response to a question about Phi's relationship with the environment. The participant imagines the natural environment as a feminine 'Mother Nature' archetype, with whom Phi enters dialogue. He imagines that she is unhappy with Phi, but patient enough to understand that it promises to do better in the future. This image of the maternal relationship between the natural environment and the company exemplifies how the connections between subjects within the natural world can be conceptualised.

While interconnectivity overshadowed the other themes during this interview, there was also a subtle appearance of a dualistic theme, as illustrated by the following quote, which is part of the participant's description of environmental reporting.

It's purely risk management, and shouldn't be viewed as anything more or less.

This second dualistic quote is part of the participant's response to being questioned about the decision-making process involved in deciding which information is included in the environmental report. The participant's response draws from a dualistic view that the report is heavily influenced by regulations and guidelines. As discussed, these topics are representative of a dualistic approach since they involve the participant 'stepping back' from the actual effects of environmental impact, and focusing instead on the company's regulatory obligations.

So obviously the law would be the first disclosure thing. The GRI would be the second. So we report to the relevant GRI standards and pretty much what's in there, and then once all that's done, what else is material and relevant.

This third dualistic themed quote follows from the statement above in which the participant is imagining a conversation between 'Mother Nature' and the company. Viewing the natural environment as an inanimate receptacle for waste product clearly fails to acknowledge the physical effects of such waste, and therefore represents dualism.

> Because at the moment the environment is very much a – from one side, so from our coal generating side, the environment is fundamentally just a receptacle for our refuse. We try and minimise that refuse...

Despite expressing this dualistic view at various times throughout the interview, this interview overwhelmingly expresses an interconnected approach to the natural environment. This is in contrast to Phi's environmental report, which is overwhelmingly dualistic in its approach. This juxtaposition was found in other companies and will be discussed in more depth in the following chapter.

Delta

Delta is an Australian company which supplies transport services, utilities services, engineering, construction, maintenance, mining and rail in Australia, as well as several other countries. Delta has been listed on the ASX as a member of the 'industrials' sector since 1990 (ASX, 2016). Delta has released an annual sustainability report since 2009. The environmental section constitutes 20% of the 2012, 2013 and 2014 sustainability reports. Most of the wording in these three reports is almost identical.

Delta Environmental Reports

Delta's environmental reports were distinctly dualistic, with the majority of the discourse within the reports expressing this theme. Following a pattern that is repeated in other environmental reports analysed in this book, these reports make use of images which have a contrasting theme to the surrounding text. Often the images portray more interconnectivity than the text. This is so on page 12 of the 2014 report which shows a sepia picture of a desert-type landscape. Highlighting the interconnected theme of the image, the perspective of the viewer is from a low position close to the ground, symbolically connecting the viewer of the picture with the terrestrial landscape.

This image is followed by the words:

> Environment
>   There are three foundations to the Delta environmental sustainability strategy: compliance and risk management, minimisation of environmental and sustainability impacts and improvements to resource efficiency

As discussed earlier in this chapter, compliance, risk management, minimisation of environmental impacts, resources and efficiency are all considered to represent a dualistic approach. As such, the text which accompanies the image contrasts with the interconnective approach of the picture by using a largely dualistic view.

Overall, the environmental reports for 2012, 2013 and 2014 express Delta's predominantly dualistic approach to the natural environment. This section has presented some examples of the approaches communicated in the reports. Next, the findings associated with the interview with Delta's environmental manager are presented.

Delta Interview

Echoing findings from other case study companies within this book, the interview with the senior environmental manager of Delta demonstrated a more interconnected approach in comparison with its environmental reports. The interview with senior environmental management of Delta extended for more than 90 minutes, at the behest of the interviewee, who enthusiastically discussed environmental and philosophical issues with me at length, which itself reflects an interconnected tendency.

An interconnective approach was demonstrated throughout the interview in particular by a focus on recycling and intelligent design which can impact on environmental interactions, as in the following passage:

> ...because one of the things that we do is actually do the development within the mine, so structure the haul roads, so that the roads are designed to maximise the efficiency of the vehicle, so that they're not having to accelerate, you know if you have a flat bit, a steep bit, a flat bit a steep bit then you're doing lots of acceleration, so you'll, we tend to try and develop the mines so that there is a slow general incline to come out of the pit or wherever, so you can maintain the speed of the vehicle without accelerating so you actually reduce emissions. And whilst it doesn't sound much on each vehicle, because they use so much fuel and there's so many trips that you can actually maximise that.

Again, supply chain issues were discussed by the Delta participant, which indicates an interconnective perspective, as in the next two quotes.

> ...one of the things that we've tried to do is increase the amount of recycled material that we use in our asphalt and we've just, not that long ago, its actually on world environment day they did a trial down in Melbourne and we've managed to produce an asphalt that's made from 99% recycled material, on average.

...we're trying now to actually push that further into other aspects of it too to understand, and have a bit more information about what our activities had generally, our indirect activity, it's sort of the indirect impact of our activities on the environment, so we're trying to influence our suppliers and our contractors as well to try and take that into consideration.

When discussing climate change denial, the participant responded by highlighting the relationship between human activity and climate changes, as in the following remarks:

Yeah, I think I would have thought it's kind of a no brainer, it is happening, it's happening partly because of a cycle that we're in and it's accelerated by the fact that there's human impacts, and it's quite clear and you know everyone's saying oh well we've just had the coldest week in Victoria how can that be global warming? Well on an average, we have had – is it 19 of the hottest years in the last 20? That would tell us that something is happening. Now, does it really matter whether all of that is just natural variation? Well there's some things that you might be able to do about that, but maybe not. But there's enough evidence to say that it's not all natural variation, that a very large proportion of that is caused by humans who tend to do things, so wouldn't the sensible thing be to acknowledge it and then think about what you can do to reduce it?

While there is ample evidence of the interconnected approach in the Delta interview, this is contrasted by a moderate proportion of dualistic perspective. The dualistic theme is demonstrated in the following quote, which considers climate changes in terms of business opportunities for Delta and its clients. This distinctly dualistic approach separates human activity (or company activity) with the causes of climate change, and instead views it as an opportunity to generate revenue.

In terms of climate change, I think our opportunity is around you know we produce a lot of material that gets used in areas that are subject to potential inundation, so for us it would be around better bridge building, you know, better road fabrication – when we're working for a client, a coastal council or something, and they want you know here, fix the road, well how about we fix the road so that if we do it in a particular way then it's going to resist the potential from adverse storms or so on. So I think that's where our opportunity to respond to potential – I mean ultimately, depending on who you believe, we could end up with an ETS [emissions trading scheme] again, I think there will be a price on carbon in Australia again, if not in the short term, then in maybe the medium term – we'd be smart and looking at how we can reduce our emissions to make us a lower carbon organisation…

Overall, the Delta interview demonstrated a balance between dualism and interconnectivity. This balance differs starkly with its environmental reports, which are predominantly dualistic in their approach, reflecting themes also found in Alpha's environmental reports.

Alpha

Alpha is a multinational company which is based in Australia. Another old Australian company, it was founded in 1860 when it was established as Victoria's first paper mill. Currently focusing on manufacturing packaging, it is the world's largest supplier of flexible packaging. Alpha is listed on the ASX as operating in the 'materials' sector (ASX, 2016).

Alpha has been producing a standalone sustainability report, including a dedicated environmental section since 2010. The reports analysed in this research were the environmental sections of the sustainability reports of 2012, 2013 and 2014. In these sustainability reports, the environmental section constitutes around 10% of the total pages dedicated to sustainability issues.

Alpha Environmental Reports

Alpha's primary philosophical approach towards the natural environment is that of dualism. This approach is expressed in the 2012, 2013 and 2014 environmental reports through a focus on company policies and government regulations. Of interesting note are the images used on the covers of these reports, which represent a strong interconnective approach (see Figure 5.4 on the following page). Figure 5.4 reflects an interconnective theme by presenting an image of three children, all barefoot and physically connected to the Earth. These children are similarly connected to each other by holding hands. They seem to be embarking on a childhood adventure through a natural setting – all indicating a deep connection with nature. This contrasts with the contents of the reports, which are largely dualistic.

Alpha Interview

A contrast between the approaches demonstrated in the interview and report data is also reflected in Alpha. Alpha's environmental report was largely dualistic in its approach, however the interview with a senior manager directly involved in the production of the report demonstrated a principally interconnected approach towards the natural environment.

Figure 5.4 Interconnective image from Alpha's 2012 environmental report.

During the interview, the participant frequently referred to supply chain and life cycle issues, demonstrating Alpha's focus on environmental issues which are both directly and indirectly connected to their operations. This approach is illustrated in the following quote from the interview:

> Yeah so it's very focused on the value chain, so not just looking at what your business is doing within its four walls but what's happening in your supply chain up and down.

The following quote illustrates Alpha's awareness of environmental impacts which can occur at any point in the life cycle process. This is considered an interconnective approach.

> ...we do process a lot of plastics, so we buy in little resin plastic beads, so if they spill into your storm water they're out in the ocean. So it's not just liquid spills but we don't want to be spilling small particles of plastic either.

Amongst these largely interconnected responses to the interview questions are interspersed dualistic approaches, such as in the following quote, which refers to the ranking of environmental impacts and events.

> We have a reporting matrix so if something rates as a high enough significance then it would be reported. Anything that's minor, if it's contained, I don't have all the details exactly, but there is a sliding scale that would rate the different – an incident – an environmental incident, so that ones that are a certain level would be publicly reported – we'd need to report it to the EPA or and we would certainly report anything that was significant in our reports.

In this way, the pattern of dualistic reporting in conjunction with more interconnected interviews continues. Overall, Alpha's environmental reports for 2012, 2013 and 2014 were predominantly dualistic in nature, compared with a more interconnected interview discussion. This pattern continues in the discourse from the following company.

Kappa

The Kappa Group was listed in 1971. It was Australia's first property trust, and went on to split from its parent company and become The Kappa Group in 2005. As a property trust, Kappa manages the construction, rent and management of business properties within Australia. Properties managed by Kappa include shopping centres, office buildings and warehouses. Some environmental information has been communicated through the Annual Report since 2008. Similarly, the 2012, 2013 and 2014 environmental reports analysed in this research form part of the Annual Reviews of those years, making up less than 5% of the total pages of the annual reviews of those years. The wording is much the same from 2012 to 2014. ASX lists Kappa as part of the 'real estate' sector.

Kappa Environmental Reports

Kappa's 2012 environmental report repeatedly uses the terms 'positive contribution' and 'positive contributor.' Realistically, to be a positive contributor to the natural environment, a company would have to not only be carbon negative (that is, absorbing more carbon than they emit), and not only *not* impacting at all on the environment, but somehow increasing the quality of the natural environment. This claim demonstrates a dualistic anthropocentrism as it displays a sense of arrogance or denial about the company's impact on the environment. This is considered a 'self-congratulatory' approach, which is a reflection of dualism. The following quote, from Kappa's 2012 environmental report provides an example of this type of discourse:

> [Kappa] is committed to reducing its environmental impact, aspiring to be an overall positive contributor to environmental sustainability.

The self-congratulatory motif is reinforced by an image of six different awards which Kappa has received. The displaying of environmental and sustainability awards is common amongst all of the environmental reports analysed.

The motif of being a positive contributor to the natural environment is continued in the 2013 report. The following quote is the same as the quote given above from the 2012 report, and repeated in the 2013 report exactly. The 2014 report maintains this repetition, with much the same text as the 2012 and 2013 reports.

> [Kappa] is committed to reducing its environmental impact, aspiring to be an overall positive contributor to environmental sustainability.

Overall, the Kappa environmental reports communicate a strong sense of dualism which is in contrast to the company's interview data. As previously discussed, this is a common approach within much of the companies' discourse analysed for this book.

Kappa Interview

The trend of an increased interconnective approach in the interviews compared to the environmental reports continues with the Kappa interview. The following statement is an example of how the interconnective approach was expressed during the interview. In this statement, the participant is responding to a question about Kappa's motivation to report on environmental issues. In their response, the interviewee draws attention to a range of stakeholders who have indicated an interest in environmental issues. Further to referring to the relationship between Kappa and its stakeholders, the participant also comments about the relationship between Kappa's buildings and the wider environment.

So of all of our stakeholder groups there is an interest, whether that's through employees, through community, through customers, through buyers, investors, they've all in different ways expressed an interest in our environmental impact. So in having that level of interest, coupling that with the inherent recognition of our long term success will be linked to a sustainable future and [Kappa] is in a position where it can take that where it must take that sort of long term view, we're investing in assets that are material parts of cities, cities are growing in their impact on the nation as a whole, the world as a whole.

In the next passage, the interviewee acknowledges the environmental impact which is already embedded in the materials Kappa utilises in its operations. Again, he mentions a long-term timeframe, and the life cycle of the buildings and materials they are constructed with. This part of the discussion exemplifies an interconnected approach to environmental issues.

...there's a lot of embedded energy and a lot of embedded emissions in the construction of this building, but this building will probably provide very productive space from the community perspective, highly productive space for a hundred years. So the lifetime embedded emissions are really amortised over the hundred-year period. And if it got to the point where we actually pulled this building down, the materials will be largely recycled reused.

Despite demonstrating a predominantly interconnective approach during the interview, the interviewee also drew from dualism in parts of the discussion, for instance in the passage below, where the financial reward for making positive environmental choices is highlighted.

... if we went "we're carbon neutral" today, which stakeholder would give us a reward? There might be a community stakeholder – NGOs – "oh great, good on you!" Good on you's don't go far. [laughter]. Tenants might look at it and say you've spent too much money somewhere, somehow, what's going on? Investors might think the same thing; we're not sure, so we get some feedback so there's some deep green investors who [would say] we'd encourage you. Well, money on the table please.

As such, the Kappa discourse reinforces the approaches expressed in many of the other companies analysed for this book, by adopting a predominantly dualistic approach in their 2012, 2013 and 2014 environmental reports in contrast to a predominantly interconnective approach expressed during the semi-structured interview. The predominantly interconnective approach displayed during this interview is reiterated again in the interview with Psi's sustainability manager, however Psi is one of the few companies which express a somewhat higher degree of interconnectivity through their environmental reports.

Psi

Psi is an Australian aquaculture company listed on the ASX in 2003 in the 'consumer staples' industry sector. The company was first established in 1986 and has produced a standalone sustainability report since 2011. The environmental reports analysed in this research account for 22% of 59 pages in 2012, 23.7% of 59 pages in 2013 and 28.6% of 63 pages in 2014.

Psi Environmental Reports

By including detailed life cycle assessments in its environmental reports, Psi incorporates a significantly interconnected approach to its reporting. Similarly, by including discussion about operational, 'on the ground' (or on the water, as the case may be) and temporal issues such as the impact operations have on local birdlife and steps Psi is undertaking to address these impacts, these reports succeed in integrating an interconnected approach.

In addition to displaying a distinctly interconnected approach in much of their reports, Psi also demonstrates a transcendent approach, in particular through some of the imagery used. Such imagery presents a wide angle from a perspective high above, and in doing so constructs an image where the salmon ponds appear to be small and inconsequential aspects within a much larger and robust environment. This imagery minimises the appearance of visual, and also environmental impact. Two such images are presented below and on the following page in Figures 5.5 and 5.6.

Figure 5.5 First example of transcendent imagery in Psi's 2014 report.

Figure 5.6 Second example of transcendent imagery in Psi's 2014 report.

Echoing the dualistic sentiments that appear in other reports, there is a sense of distancing some information rather than integrating it into the discussion. In the 2014 Psi report, this is done by using appendices, which present details of the proximity of each of Psi's operational leases to marine reserves and conservation areas, rather than within the section within the body of the report, which is dedicated to marine reserves and conservation areas. This tendency to construct a distance between the reader and salient information reflects a dualistic approach.

In Psi's 2014 report reference was made to the 'ecological footprint,' which implies the idea that environmental impact can be limited to a particular area, specifically that which is situated underneath the salmon ponds. This quote is presented below:

> Visible impacts of solid waste deposition tend to be confined to directly under stocked pens, evident as distinct 'footprint' zones.

Dualism is also represented in these reports, through mention of certification and awards. See in particular the following two extracts from the 2014 report, where the self-congratulatory theme is evident:

> Key achievements for [Psi] in FY14 were: [Psi] benchmarked as the world's best Salmon or trout farming business in corporate, social and environmental reporting...
>
> With a milestone of the [Psi] and WWF partnership being the certification of all [Psi] aquaculture operations by 2015, the certification of these two areas represents impressive progress towards this important target.

The ontology of distinct objects is evident elsewhere in this 2014 sustainability report, where the salmon are valued instrumentally in terms of financial rewards:

> The health and welfare of [Psi]'s fish is a top priority for the company, as our fish are in fact our business.

Overall, while the reports of Psi clearly demonstrated a dualistic approach to the natural environment, they were one of the few companies to also demonstrate a significantly interconnective approach to the natural world in their 2012, 2013 and 2014 environmental reports. These balanced results are juxtaposed against the interconnective themes demonstrated by Psi's senior sustainability manager, as expressed in the semi-structured interviews.

Psi Interview

A largely interconnective approach was evident in interviewing the sustainability manager of Psi. In the following passage, which, through its focus on Psi's dependency on the natural environment, and the connections between the company, its customers and the environment, demonstrates an interconnected approach which is evident in much of the interview.

> ...I think it's important, again, because we're so dependent on the environment, so it works both ways, right? We have to have a healthy environment to grow good products. We're not just using the marine environment we're growing food in it, which people are going to feed to their families. So I think that sense of if you are using waterways or land, or whatever, there's multiple users of that area, you know, you need to communicate what you're doing, right? And the environmental interactions obviously are important, and now it goes beyond a local scale, then we have the broader climate change discussion, and what will business and food production, food security, what's that going to look like into the future?

When asked about the company's relationship with the natural world, the interviewee responded with an emphatically interconnected reply, given below. This reply fundamentally connects the company's operations with the natural world.

> Well, I think respectful, um, one that's not of ownership, this is a real cultural thing in our company so we feel like we're being allowed, to use it, like privileged to use it, so and that we're here temporarily to use it and we'd like to leave it in the same shape that we found it, or better...

Again in the following discourse, the interviewee expresses the company's relationship with the natural world in an explicitly interconnected way.

> ...it's probably just that, a little but more connectedness. It's also the reliance on it, the respect for it, the respect of what it can do to you, and the respect that you have to... you can't control everything, nor should you try to. Yeah. You can't modify everything – you've got to work with it sometimes.

This interview was the most fundamentally interconnected interview examined for this book. This approach supports those found in Psi's 2012, 2013 and 2014 environmental reports which, while still predominantly dualistic, displayed a relatively balanced dualistic/interconnective approach to the natural world.

Theta

Theta was listed on the ASX in 2004 as a member of the 'consumer discretionary' sector. Theta operates a number of well-known retail stores in Australia. First established in 1972 as a family-run business, it was listed in 2004 and has grown into one of Australia's ten largest retail companies. Theta communicates its environmental issues within its Corporate Review, and has done so since 2012. Within the Corporate Reviews of 2012, 2013 and 2014, the environment is discussed on 5.6% of 38 pages in each year's review.

Theta Environmental Reports

Along with Sigma, Theta represents the only other case study company for which dualism is not the predominant philosophical approach expressed in the environmental reports. A bias towards interconnectivity is expressed in Theta's environmental reports by discussions of the connections which are an inherent aspect of our natural environment. The subsequent passage which is repeated verbatim in all three of Theta's reports analysed for this book exhibits an interconnective approach through its acknowledgement of environmental impacts beyond Theta's immediate operations, and their attempts to address some of these life cycle issues. However, the repetition with which it is presented identically for three years is reflective of a more distant relationship with the environment, indicating a dualistic approach.

> In accordance with our Environmental Policy, the Group continues to explore options to offer our customers the ability to return directly to our retail stores selected products which will be collected

and distributed to recycling facilities. [Theta] now accepts used car batteries in all retail stores. These are collected and returned to a recycling facility where the lead and plastic is reused in manufacturing new products. In addition to this, the Group continues to explore other recycling opportunities as an added service and convenience to our customers in support of the environment.

In contrast, this next quote represents a dualistic anthropocentrism, because of the implication that being profitable comes before being sustainable, and that group can't be sustainable without being profitable; environmental initiatives are conflated with social initiatives, rather than standing on their own, and all for the benefit of humans.

> We are committed to achieving and demonstrating profitable and sustainable growth in a manner consistent with our group values and with our commitment to social and environmental initiatives for the benefit of our team, customers and trade partners and the communities in which we operate.

As mentioned, Theta was one of only two case study companies which exhibited a predominantly interconnected approach in their 2012, 2013 and 2014 environmental reports. This was contrasted somewhat by the approach of the sustainability manager during the interview.

Theta Interview

In interviewing the Theta national sustainability manager, it became apparent that they communicated about environmental issues through a balanced mix of all three of the philosophical themes being considered in this book. Of all the interviews, it was this one which expressed the most transcendent approach, as demonstrated in the following excerpt from the interview. This excerpt represents a transcendent approach through its focus on the trade-off between financial and environmental issues, with the dominant value being financial.

> …the board was very keen to invest in solar, but then when we got the numbers together, it was like, well really? Is that really what you want to do? We don't own any of our sites, so to be investing in this technology – yeah it's great, but if you own the buildings, if you're leasing, try to liaise with your landlords and to see what their views are on that, because otherwise it just doesn't make financial sense. So I think that the company is always very mindful of doing something good, but also having the cost benefit assessed, especially for us because we are a public company. So whatever we do we still have to think about our shareholders and the nature of our work is

basically, we are retailers, so they expect us to make a profit from selling.

Where financial and environmental issues are in competition, and where the financial value is considered more important, this represents a transcendent approach. This relates to Latour's conception of profit as a transcendent value and filters down through the organisational processes which contribute to the creation of profit. This is particularly so where tangible values such as the natural environment, are sacrificed for profit.

The next passage illustrates an interconnective approach through its focus on the connections between subjects within the organisation, and how this can have a positive effect on engagement with environmental issues.

> ...I think it brings a benefit for us as well because we are doing something about it. And I've got to say because the CEO he is quite passionate about sustainability in general and I think that is something that helps because if he didn't really care, I don't think other people around the business would. So I think when it comes from the top you have better chances to have some more engagement...

Although this interview expressed a transcendent approach towards the natural world more than other interviews in this book, overall, it primarily communicated in terms of dualistic and interconnected approaches in a more balanced way than other interviews, including that with the sustainability manager of the following company.

Sigma

Sigma operates hotels, casinos and a convention and exhibition centre, all based in Australia. First listed in 2011 (ASX, 2016), Sigma has released some environmental information annually since 2012. 2012 and 2013 environmental information was released as part of the Annual Review, totalling two pages out of a total of 120 pages, and three pages in a 130-page 2013 Annual Review. Similarly, in 2014 the company dedicated three pages of a 114-page Annual Review to environmental issues. Much of the space in these pages is taken up with images. The ASX lists Sigma as a member of the 'consumer discretionary' sector (ASX, 2016).

Sigma Environmental Reports

For Sigma, the most frequently communicated approach was that of interconnectivity. Sigma represents only one of two case study companies for which dualism is not the predominant approach expressed in the environmental reports.

The 2012 environmental report consists of two pages of environmental information. Of these, one page is taken up entirely with an image which is considered to represent transcendence, since the direction of the image is upwards, away from the terrestrial environment, and is focused on a human made construction. The only two aspects of the image that reflect the 'environment' to which the title refers are the out of focus flowers and the distant sky. Superimposed across the top pat of this image are the words "HELPING OUR ENVIRONMENT" (all capitals in the original). As discussed, the motif of humans helping the natural world supports the interpretation of the transcendent theme. In this case, it is unclear how Sigma plans to 'help' the natural world.

The second page of the 2012 environmental report is overshadowed by another image which takes up one-third of page space. This second image further reinforces the theme of transcendence by being entirely taken up by modernistic human made structures. In this second image, representations of the natural world have reduced considerably – now only visible as a small slither of sky and some greenery in the foreground.

The 2013 report continues with the theme of disregarding the natural world in favour of human made structures with a large image of an employee replacing the light bulbs of an extravagant interior lighting system.

The 2014 report continues the theme of employees changing light bulbs, with another large image of another male worker happily changing light bulbs. This unbalanced focus on taking small steps is a theme further taken up in the 2014 report, with images as well as text focusing on 'household' type steps to reducing energy use and increasing recycling. This 2014 report makes repeated reference to 'tangible' effects, which as discussed, relates to an interconnected approach, however these are effectively empty words, since there is no mention of what these 'tangible' effects might actually be. Overall, Sigma's environmental reports are principally transcendent and interconnective in approach – Sigma is one of only two of the case study companies which demonstrate this pattern.

Sigma Interview

In comparison to its environmental reports, the Sigma interview is more dualistic. Sigma is the only company in this book which follows the pattern of more interconnectivity in the environmental reports than in the interview.

In addition to the discussion of the interview demonstrating a dualistic approach, the general approach of the interviewee during the interview was one of defence, with short and sharp mannerisms, indicating an attempt to separate and distance – an indication of dualism. In contrast to most of the other participants interviewed for this book, this interviewee did not at any point seem relaxed during the interview, and maintained an 'on guard' mood. This is highlighted by the length of the interview, which was one of the shortest in duration, lasting only 35 minutes. Despite all of the core questions being answered, there was no banter or relaxed discussion like that which occurred in most of the other interviews. This mode of conversation underpins a dualistic approach as it is a device to construct a barrier between the participant and the researcher. This interpretation is supported in the following quotes, which demonstrate an attempt to separate Sigma and the participant herself, with the environmental effects of the company's activities.

> Yes, so I look after all of the environment and sustainability issues and all of the disclosures that go along with that: our Dow Jones sustainability index reporting, and other surveys and compliance. That's right, I look after all of that.

This quote demonstrates duality through reference to indexes, surveys and compliance issues, rather than the natural environment itself. When asked about the importance of environmental reporting to Sigma, the participant responded in a detached manner, by listing the regulatory requirements Sigma adheres to, mentioning targets and directing the researcher towards information available on Sigma's website.

> Of course. I think it's fundamental and there's an expectation that we need to be reporting on our carbon emissions we also qualify under the national greenhouse and energy reporting, so we're already calculating our carbon emissions and we put those figures on our website already. So we're trying to make sure that – we're a listed company – that we're letting all of our stakeholders know that we have a strategy, we have targets, and we're holding ourselves responsible under those targets.

Again, in the next two quotes the participant directs the researcher towards information on the website. This attempt to draw attention elsewhere is a device noticed in several of the environmental reports, and recognised as dualistic, since it serves to separate and distract, rather than draw close and connect. However, this is the only instance where this manoeuvre was used during an interview.

> So on our website, we went through a materiality process where we looked at what were the key environmental inputs and implications, and what our impacts and aspects were, and we looked at that from an employee point of view so what did our employees think? What was the cost around these things? What do we have a level of influence on? And what are the biggest environmental impacts coming out of our property? So as part of that materiality assessment

that we published, we identified energy consumption, water consumption, waste generation and carbon emissions as our four key material impacts so our strategy was built around managing those buildings. So then we have a target for each of those things, and then we report annually against those in our report.

...carbon and waste, it's all on our website as well, so if you have a look on there it actually has our materiality assessment, and it's got the process that we went through so we spoke to stakeholders, we considered the feedback so we've got all that there in a diagram, and then how we came up with those issues.

When asked about her own relationship with the natural environment, the participant resisted discussion, and immediately drew the conversation back to Sigma. The defensive nature of this response draws from the same logic as dualism, in the form of a metaphorical barrier, separation or defence which protects one subject from another. The dualistic approach of this part of the interview is illustrated in the following quote:

Personally my relationship with the natural environment is fantastic. We're always out bushwalking, those sorts of things. And that's the sort of thing we try to bring – our sustainability programme focuses on sustainability at work and at home, and I think because we don't have an opportunity, we don't have landscaping, I mean traditionally we're quite concrete – there's a few gardens but there's not a lot that we can interface the natural environment with our properties.

In response to being asked if the motivation for Sigma to report on environmental issues is based on the profit motive, the following quote highlights the dualistic viewpoint which underpins this interview:

Oh sure, I mean businesses are around to make money and we need to be very clear that you need to make good commercial decisions. But I believe the sustainability is a commercial decision and I believe we've come a long way from just doing the right thing – it's a risk, and you need to manage it that way...

This interview was distinctly dualistic in its approach to the natural environment, and represented one end of a spectrum of possible approaches. The context of the participant's approach to the interview, and the dialogue of the interview itself all point towards a separation between the participant (and by extension, Sigma) and the natural environment. These findings contrast the data found in Sigma's environmental reports, and represent the company with the widest divergence between the discourse of the reports and interview. This interesting juxtaposition is discussed in more depth in the following chapter.

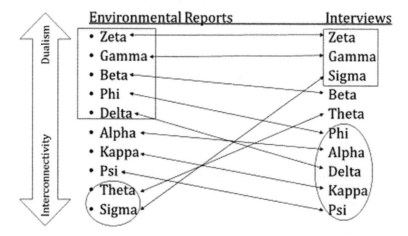

Figure 5.7 Comparison of themes found in reports and interviews.

Comparison

Overall, the reports and interviews expressed the three primary discourse themes to varying extents. The reports were predominantly dualistic, with a minority of reports demonstrating more interconnected or transcendent approaches. In contrast, generally the interviews were expressed in predominantly interconnected terms, with only a minority using a more dualistic approach. Transcendence, conversely, is only marginally reflected in either reports or interviews, with the exception of the Theta interview and Sigma reports.

The diagram above (Figure 5.7) illustrates the spectrum of approaches demonstrated in the reports, in comparison to the interviews. Since transcendence was evident in relatively small proportions in both environmental reports and interviews, it has been omitted from this diagram. The companies which are boxed are those which have a principally dualistic approach towards the natural environment, in either reports or interviews. Those which are circled have are largely interconnective, and those which are not outlined have a more balanced approach.

The relationship between the approaches evident in the environmental reports compared with those evident in the interviews is explored in more depth in the following chapters.

References

Ascui, F., & Lovell, H. (2011). As Frames Collide: Making Sense of Carbon Accounting. *Accounting, Auditing & Accountability Journal, 24*(8), 978–999. doi: 10.1108/09513571111184724

ASX. (2015). *ASX 200.* Retrieved from www.asx.com.au

ASX. (2016). *ASX Company Information*. Retrieved from http://www.asx.com.au/prices/company-information.htm

Australian Conservation Foundation. (2016). *Australia's 10 Biggest Climate Polluters*. Victoria: ACF.

Barriball, K. L., & While, A. (1994). Collecting Data Using a Semi-Structured Interview: A Discussion Paper. *Journal of Advanced Nursing, 19*(2), 328–335. doi:10.1111/j.1365-2648.1994.tb01088.x

Donaldson, T., & Preston, L. E. (1995). The Stakeholder Theory of the Corporation: Concepts, Evidence, and Implicaitons. *Academy of Management Review, 20*(1), 65–91. doi:10.5465/AMR.1995.9503271992

ISO. (2015). *ISO 14001:2015*. Retrieved from https://www.iso.org/obp/ui/#iso:std:iso:14001:ed-3:v1:en

Koteyko, N., Thelwall, M., & Nerlich, B. (2010). From Carbon Markets to Carbon Morality: Creative Compounds as Framing Devices in Online Discourses on Climate Change Mitigation. *Science Communication, 32*(1), 25–54. doi:10.1177/1075547009340421

Mathews, F. (1991). *The Ecological Self*. London: Routledge.

Nerlich, B., & Koteyko, N. (2009). Compounds, Creativity and Complexity in Climate Change Communication: The Case of 'Carbon Indulgences'. *Global Environmental Change, 19*(3), 345–353.

Prasad, A. (2002). The Contest over Meaning: Hermeneutics as an Interpretive Methodology for Understanding Texts. *Organizational Research Methods, 5*(1), 12–33.

Whiting, L. S. (2008). Semi-Structured Interviews: Guidance for Novice Researchers. *Nursing Standard (through 2013), 22*(23), 35–40.

6 Prevalent Discursive Mechanisms

Introduction

By repeating certain discursive mechanisms, discourse actively perpetuates particular hegemonic ideals (Alexander, 2009; Davison, 2014; Spence, 2009). In this chapter, the environmental reports and interviews will undergo a second layer of analysis, in which the discourse of corporate environmental reporting is examined through the lens of western environmental philosophy. To highlight the ways in which the reporting process communicates these philosophies, some of the more prevalent discursive motifs – and the mechanisms with which they are communicated – will be considered and discussed. How these motifs relate to the philosophical themes used in this book will also be examined. After the discursive motifs and mechanisms have been outlined and considered, the following chapter will explore the repercussions of these findings.

Discursive Motifs

Alexander (2009) notes that by repeating certain words or themes, texts accustomise readers to particular notions, thus normalising certain approaches to the natural environment. Similarly, others have noted that despite being perceived as objective and neutral statements, corporate reports are social constructs which are embedded with the corporation's values (Benschop & Meihuizen, 2002). By repeating themes within an environmental report, the corporation implicitly adopts a rhetorical technique which attempts to persuade the reader (Davison, 2014). It is argued that these themes not only communicate the company's approach to the natural environment, but contribute to the construction of particular ways of interacting with the natural environment (Dryzek, 2013; Nerlich, 2010). The discursive motifs explored in this book are expressions of the three primary philosophical themes which reflect particular underpinnings in the relationship between corporations and the natural world. The motifs are expressed through discursive mechanisms which are common to many (sometimes *all*) of the environmental reports analysed for this book.

Prevalent Discursive Mechanisms

Archel, Husillos and Spence (2011) outline how organisations come to resemble each other through the process of institutionalisation through the shared sense of meanings, values and practice. In this book, I uncover some of the discursive mechanisms that reflect the institutionalisation of various approaches to the natural world. The mechanisms outlined below were found in many (sometimes all) of the environmental reports analysed for this book, and therefore reflect not only a shared understanding amongst the sample of corporations examined in this book but also the discursive mechanisms these corporations use to shape cultural views about nature.

Discourse actively shapes cultural views. This is particularly so in discourses about the natural environment. Discourse is not only text, but also design, layout and images. All of these aspects of discourse can be analysed to uncover implicitly communicated meanings enshrined in organisational documents such as those analysed here. The discourse analysed for this book demonstrates some repeated discursive techniques elucidating the philosophies at play in corporate communications about nature.

Some of the discursive mechanisms discussed are visual in character. Davison, McLean and Warren (2012) illustrate the communicative power of images and visual techniques in framing the content of a corporate report. They argue that visual devices have great influence in how the user of the report views the content and are often more compelling than the content itself.

Other discursive mechanisms discussed utilise both visual and textual techniques. The ways in which these techniques communicate particular philosophies will be explicated and analysed, in the context of the organisation. Also discussed is what these techniques are communicating about the corporate approach to nature.

Dualism

Many of the most prevalent discursive mechanisms used in the reports were in keeping with a dualistic approach. As discussed in the previous chapters, a dualistic approach reinforces the idea that humans are separate and distinct from the natural world, and also that objects within the natural world are distinct from each other. Since interdependencies between subjects are ignored in this way of thinking, this brings about the notion of hierarchical relationships, inevitably leading to the view that human interests should be at the top of this hierarchy. This view is embedded into much of western culture, and has become somewhat ubiquitous, however this first section of this chapter aims to bring to light some of the ways dualism is discursively expressed, particularly in contemporary corporate environmental reporting.

To assist with the textual analysis, a list was created as a reference tool in order to group some of the more often repeated motifs which were expressed in the environmental reports. The fact that these approaches were frequently found in the environmental reports reflects what Archel et al. (2011) describe as the institutionalisation of particular beliefs and values which leads to organisational homogeneity. Some of the more frequently referred to discourses reflecting a dualistic approach are listed below.

Common Dualistic Motifs

Ontology of Discrete Objects

- Charts, tables and graphs
- Obfuscation of reality through use of graphs; language which distracts
- Focus on numbers
- Financial language
- Cost effective
- Natural capital
- Risk
- Materiality
- Offsets
- Images minimising apparent impacts
- Carbon accounting
- Carbon neutrality
- Images which conflict with text
- Direction of readers' attention elsewhere
- Legislation/Regulatory focus
- Compliance
- Targets/Goals
- Indexes
- Future-proofing
- Efficiency
- Certification
- Monitoring with no context explained
- Standards
- Site specific effects (that is, immediate effects, with no ongoing or wider effects mentioned)
- Fences, delineation

Dualistic Anthropocentrism

- Nature as a resource
- Environmental risk
- Environmental market

- Environmental prizes
- Awards
- Self-congratulatory
- Business opportunities (from environmental changes)
- Accreditation – business being lauded
- Positive effect on environment
- Control
- Signing agreements

Dualistic Hierarchy

- Grading stakeholders' importance
- Grading environmental issues
- Eliminating certain environmental issues as irrelevant
- 'Little or no impact' especially when compared to others (for example, to mining)

These motifs share a common thread of linguistic and conceptual mechanisms, which contribute to the separation of human (or corporate) values, and those of the rest of the natural world (Alexander, 2009). Different ways in which these mechanisms function include a focus on metrics, as opposed to the physical effects of an action. By focusing on the metrics, a barrier is formed between the responsibility of the corporation and the natural environment. The corporation becomes responsible for producing appropriate measures, and attention is distracted from what effect these measures have on the physical world (Pollock & D'Adderio, 2012). Some of the dominant discursive themes listed above are discussed in more depth in the sections below.

Use of Charts, Graphs and Tables

The corporate environmental reports analysed here frequently utilised visual analytical aids such as charts and graphs. Beattie and Jones (2008) outline the types of graphs typically used in corporate reporting, and propose that while graphs are useful for communicating concepts in a simple, visual way that is easy to understand, they often obfuscate meaning.

Dambrin and Robson (2011) draw from Latour's notion of *action at a distance* in outlining the effects of reducing information to mechanisms such as charts and graphs. They describe how these linguistic techniques stifle some modes of being, while giving voice to other elements. Through reducing the particularities of events, charts and graphs construct a division between the physical event and the reader. This act of separating the terrestrial effect with the reader's understanding of it manifests a dualistic approach, since dualism itself describes a separation between the natural world and the human experience.

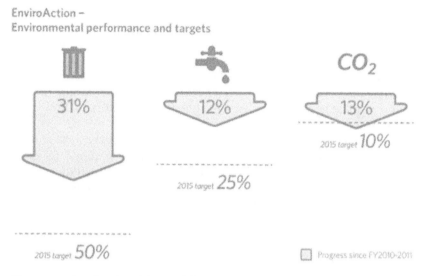

EnviroAction –
Environmental performance and targets

Figure 6.1 Graphic detail from Alpha's 2013 environmental report.

The chart above (Figure 6.1), from Alpha's 2013 environmental report, illustrates a simplified version of events, removing awareness of the terrestrial effects of these measures, how they came about or even identifying their base measurements. This image displays some key symbols – a garbage bin, a dripping tap and the chemical symbol for carbon dioxide. It is left to the reader to interpret the meaning of these symbols, for instance, the garbage bin could represent waste to landfill, but equally could symbolise overall waste, including recycling. The dripping tap might represent overall water usage, or more literally, dripping taps and therefore water wastage. "CO_2" might represent the anthropogenic emissions of carbon dioxide, methane, nitrous oxide, chlorofluorocarbon and hydrofluorocarbon, or perhaps only carbon dioxide. The reader is left to decipher these images for herself. Beneath these three symbols are three downward facing arrows of varying sizes representing the percentage reduction of those three materials. The reader is not provided with baseline data, and is therefore left to her own devices as to how much of a reduction 31%, 12% and 13% actually is. The colour green here implies that these measures are good for the environment (Kress & Van Leeuwen, 2002).

By obfuscating the meaning of this graphic, Alpha communicates a very generalised message about environmental measures taken by the company, thereby reducing the capacity for a more critical reading of the report.

Zeta used a pie chart in its 2014 environmental report to illustrate the company's greenhouse gas emissions for the year. The chart has been presented against a narrative of how Zeta is addressing climate change, and sits above a table of energy efficiencies which have been investigated (but not necessarily implemented). This chart does not indicate whether these are direct (scope 1 or 2) or indirect (scope 3) emissions[1] and makes no reference to which calculation methods have been used in preparing this chart. In common with the previous chart discussed, there is no baseline data provided, so the reader cannot discern the amount of overall greenhouse gas emissions, or what quantity 55%, 26% or 10% might actually indicate.

The use of bright red draws the reader's attention to the 55% of emissions which has been emitted through the energy required in Zeta's buildings. The reader isn't told whether this includes all buildings, since data centre emissions have been given separately – or whether 'building energy use' includes the buildings which house the data centres. The purpose of breaking the data up into these categories is unclear; what is silenced in this process? A more useful graphic might present data from various branches, or departments, however Zeta have chosen to categorise emissions by building energy use, data centres, air travel, other, hotel stays and car fleet in a seemingly random selection of sources.

Through the mechanisms of colour and positioning, attention is drawn to the energy use of buildings. This may be linked to Zeta's significant investment in a new Melbourne building with a "Six Star Green Star Design" rating; perhaps Zeta would like to highlight this investment and its environmental utility. Similarly, in the narrative provided around this graph there is mention of an expected decrease in emissions attributed to the data centres, with a move to a new "LEED Platinum certified" data centre. By presenting the pie chart in such a way that these two areas represent the highest proportion of greenhouse gas emissions, it may appear that the two significant investments undertaken by Zeta are justified.

While a justification of Zeta's investments may underpin this graphic, by presenting the information as a pie chart a sense of objectivity is achieved (Kress & Van Leeuwen, 2006). This sense of abstraction achieves a distancing which is associated with a dualistic approach to the environment.

Delta's 2013 environmental report presents a set of charts and graphs. In comparison to the Zeta graph, Delta's information graphic provides information about the scope of greenhouse gas emissions, what it means by emissions ($ktCO_2e$, or kilotonnes of carbon dioxide and equivalent gasses) and the quantity emitted. It also provides some comparative data, and adds a sense of legitimacy through providing some unfavourable information about increased emissions in the current year, however the presentation of the 2009/10 and 2010/11 data in this graphic does appear to minimise the current year's increase in emissions. While the image provided in the top part of the graphic provides this more legitimate information, the image in the lower part of the graphic suffers the same ambiguity as Zeta's pie chart, in that greenhouse gas emissions by the type of fuels is not essentially of use to the reader. By balancing the more negative information in the top graphic with a less meaningful chart, attention is diverted. Similarly, the use of a circular shaped chart carries with it a sense of organic, natural order (Kress & Van Leeuwen, 2006).

This information graphic is on the right-hand side of a page otherwise filled with written narrative, alongside a table which reports a total of 97 separate spills of large volumes of toxic materials. Kress and Van Leeuwen (2006) have demonstrated how information provided to the left often represents information that is 'given,' whereas information provided to the right is 'new' information. This tendency is based on the left to right pattern of western reading and writing, and differs in cultures with other patterns of reading and writing. By utilising this placement, Delta implies that although there have been some significant spills of toxic materials (on the left of the page), the reader's attention should be drawn to the new information provided by the pleasant looking graphs in which current year emissions are visually minimised, and the eye is drawn to a circular graph which provides information of questionable use. Using the colour green here reinforces the sense that the actions being reported are good for the environment.

The use of pie charts and graphs to present information in this way was almost ubiquitous amongst the environmental reports analysed in this book. Similarly, tables formed a major part of the language which corporations use to communicate environmental information about their operations and impacts.

Kress and Van Leeuwen (2006) propose that tables present information in a way which draws from a hierarchical view of information. Information which is presented on the left represents that which is 'given,' while information on the right represents new information. By presenting the years in the order of 2012, 2013 and 2014 (top to bottom), Psi draws on a hierarchy which highlights older data (FY 2012) above more recently acquired data (FY 2014). Since the 2014 data informs the reader that more rubbish attributable to salmon farms was found in 2014 than in the previous two years, it stands to reason that Psi would accentuate the earlier years' data.

In addition to the emphasis on favourable information, tables which are constructed of squares and rectangles draw legitimacy from the association western readers have of these shapes, which reflect not only objectivity, but stability and rationality (Kress & Van Leeuwen, 2006; Ledin & Machin, 2016).

Another table from Phi's 2012 environmental report demonstrates many of the attributes which are commonly highlighted in critical discourse analysis literature. For instance, Kress and Van Leeuwen (2002, 2006) examine how colour is used to highlight particular items of information, and de-emphasise others. Different shades of pink are used in the hierarchical chart at the top of this image, drawing attention to the term "Climate Change" through a brighter shade of pink. Similarly, the colour pink can be used to relax hostility (Kress & Van Leeuwen, 2002), perhaps in an appeal to the 'feminine.' In this context, the pink can be interpreted as a way to calm the readers' anxiety in the face of climate change. Four boxes outline some of the ways Phi is likely to be affected by climate change (literally) *pales* in comparison through the use of a paler shade of pink. The steps Phi is taking to generate energy from sustainable sources sits in between these two ends of the spectrum. This chart succeeds in expressing the idea that Phi has climate change issues under control, and categorised neatly into rectangular shapes, which as discussed above, help to portray a sense of reason, modernity and control.

The term 'climate change' is often used in favour of 'global warming.' Poole (2006) demonstrates how this choice of words has been deliberately chosen to diminish the apparent threat and to reduce controversy. Phi's chart also favours this term, and coupled with the use of shape, colour and word choice in this hierarchical chart, the effect of presenting environmental information in this way underscores Phi's portrayal of these issues as 'under control.' Other aspects of this chart which underpin this analysis is the use of the term 'footprint,' which implies an environmental impact which is restricted, and therefore that there are no repercussive effects to the wider natural world, whereas the scientific consensus is that climate change is a difficult to control occurrence with far reaching consequences (Steffen, Grinevald, Crutzen, & McNeill, 2011).

The hierarchical chart is followed by a table which outlines a summary of Phi's environmental 'performance.' By drawing attention to these issues (carbon exposure and sustainable generation sources), Phi successfully silences the myriad of other environmental impacts the company has, and focuses attention on two very specific attributes.

By again utilising Kress and Van Leeuwen's (2006) analysis of tables, the columns to the left indicate the 'given.' As the reader views the columns to the right, the information becomes more 'new.' This table demonstrates this tendency with the established 'vision' to the left, the original 2012 target next, the actual performance of 2012, followed by the following year's targets on the extreme right.

The text in this table appears to show how Phi has decreased emissions intensity during the 2012 financial year, and how they intend to continue this trend in 2013; however, as with other graphic images provided in the corporate reports analysed here, not all is as it appears. For instance, the first large print *>50% below* indicates that Phi's emissions are significantly less than the Australian average, however by reading the notes provided in very small print below the table, the reader learns that not all of the electricity sold by Phi has been included in this calculation.

A factor which has been excluded from this formula are the emissions from a particular coal fired power generation plant and coal mine purchased by Phi in 2012. Phi's purchase of this power station was controversial due to its status as the highest emitting power plant in Australia (Ummel, 2012). As such, the omission of "[g]eneration from [name of power plant] is not included in these figures for either the period prior to, or following the [Phi] acquisition" (Phi, 2012) is significant, and potentially misleading.

Similarly, the switch from percentages to absolute measures in the right-hand column conceals the news that from 2013, the base line data will change to only include "new generation capacity." This choice of words indicates that the target will only relate to new investments, and not include emissions from existing plants. The information provided in this table is in deep contrast to other versions of reality, such as an Australian Conservation Foundation report (2016) which lists Phi as Australia's largest emitter of CO_2e in absolute terms.

Charts, graphs and tables used in this way express an environmental dualism in corporate reporting. Shapes, positioning and colours have the capacity to not only obfuscate important environmental information, but to underpin an approach to nature which deepens the divide between humans and the natural environment, in the process reducing the apparent responsibility of corporations towards the beneficial treatment of nature.

Focus on Numbers

The previous examples demonstrate how quantitative information can be presented and manipulated to express a favourable impression. Such manipulation is possible due to the sense of objectivity and authority which is communicated through quantitative information. These qualities are directly associated with a dualism and therefore when environmental issues are expressed in this way, it is considered a dualistic approach to the natural environment.

Miller (2001) has argued that expressing issues through calculative processes shapes social and economic relationships, and implicitly communicates a particular strategy. Others have linked numerical expression with the desire to control (Dambrin & Robson, 2011); to shape a particular view of the world (Bloomfield & Vurdubakis, 1997); to silence alternative accounts (Robson, 1992) and to persuade readers to consent with the actions they express (Chua, 1995). This silencing, control and shaping of a world view which omits the contextual information which is integral to environmental values are approaches which conform to dualism. Ruth Hines articulates this effect:

> Through the accounting gaze reality is seen to be divisible and quantifiable. Particular aspects of reality are identified, named and

so separated and delineated – assets, liabilities, expenses, revenues, capital – and these realities are combined, recombined, added and subtracted. In combination they create and delimit the boundaries of organizations....

(Hines, 1992, pp. 313–314)

Expressing environmental issues quantitatively is a common approach in all of the environmental reports analysed in this book. Alpha's 2012 environmental report provides one example of the ways in which companies commonly communicate environmental issues. In this example, Alpha lists several quantitative environmental targets for future years. Except for one ("implementation of water management plans in other regions"), all of these targets are discussed in a numerical manner.

Robson (1992) asserts that by expressing a value as a number, qualitative variations are suppressed, allowing the number to 'stand in' for the object it counts. He argues that this function allows for the control of what is being counted. Similarly, Qu and Cooper (2011) explain how the reduction of objects and events into numbers plays a crucial role in of the way institutions exercise power. Analysing environmental reports in this light opens up a new way of understanding the corporate relationship with the natural environment.

Read on its own, the previous example (Figure 6.1) lists targets for future years. The green table below (Figure 6.2) is provided on the same page in the 2012 Alpha environmental report, and seems to respond to the target data, however read in conjunction, the two sets of numbers do not easily correlate. For instance, in the image above, one of the targets is a "10% reduction in GHG emissions intensity from 2010/11 by 2015/16." In the table below, the first row of percentages actually relates to an older set of targets from 2005/06 to 2010/11. To compound confusion, it is not clear whether the percentages provided in the green table are targets or outcomes. Regardless of the actual meaning of these numbers, their use achieves a sense of objectivity and trust that such things are being measured. The arrows provided alongside the percentages indicate that most of these items have decreased (although as stated, it is not clear if these are outcomes or targets). Using bright green draws to reader's

Figure 6.2 Table in Alpha's 2012 environmental report.

attention to the table, and implies that what is being reported is good for the environment due to a common association between the colour green and the environment (Kress & Van Leeuwen, 2002).

By using numbers to express environmental issues, corporate environmental reports draw attention to specific aspects, for example, the reduction of emissions, while silencing other aspects not measured numerically (for example, the effect of emissions) (Badiou, 2008; Robson, 1992), and in this way, shape a particular view of the world (Bloomfield & Vurdubakis, 1997; Miller, 2001). This shaping of reader's perceptions plays a crucial role in of the way institutions exercise power and control (Dambrin & Robson, 2011), two qualities which are reflective of a dualistic approach to the natural world.

Rose (1991) furthers this argument by demonstrating the political power inherent in the quantification of objects and subjects. He argues that the use of numbers is critical in the attempt to appear legitimate in the public domain, and is inherent in constructing a perceived reality. This understanding of numerical communication can be applied to the expression of environmental values. In the context of environmental reporting, a focus on numerical values constructs a view of the natural world that can be reduced to something non-descript and exchangeable. Rose discusses the ways in which the quantification of things reduces the perceived importance of more qualitative aspects, and in the process, establishes a sense that the calculations are above question.

Expressing values in numerical form enhances a sense of distance and sterility, removing context thereby giving the impression that these factors are entirely controllable (Latour, 2004; Robson, 1992). Values such as greenhouse gas emissions, emissions reduction, energy use, energy intensity, recycling rate, packaging compliance, waste and energy use are generally presented in exclusively numerical terms in the absence of context. As such, this discursive mechanism expresses a dualistic attitude towards the environmental effects of operations, and towards the natural world more broadly.

In the same way, the expression of environmental values through financial assessment is considered to communicate a dualistic approach. In line with using quantitative values to express environmental values, the use of financial language offers the same protective barrier between the actual effects of corporate actions through the reporting process. As such, financial language including 'natural capital,' 'cost effectiveness,' 'offsetting' and 'resources' is considered an extension of the dualistic approach expressed through numerical communication.

Financial Language

The link between quantification and the language of finance is clear. Spence (2007) argues that when problems are reduced to economics, decisions which may have pernicious environmental consequences begin to appear rational and even desirable. When reducing complex issues into financial terms, a bias towards economic benefit is created. Examples of using a financial style of language include comparing the costs and benefits of environmental ventures; attributing monetary terms to environmental values (for example, carbon pricing); using terms which are associated with finance to describe natural values (for example, capital, resource). Using these discursive mechanisms to describe and interact with the natural environment is frequent in the reports and interviews analysed for this book. The following two passages from an interview with the sustainability manager from Sigma exemplify the close connection between the environment and financial values that many of the case study companies shared.

> Oh sure, I mean businesses are around to make money and we need to be very clear that you need to make good commercial decisions. But I believe the sustainability is a commercial decision and I believe we've come a long way from just doing the right thing – it's a risk, and you need to manage it that way...
>
> There's been a number of studies that talked about value and shareholder value, and investor returns being linked to sustainable development. So it's my view that for investors to – savvy investors – who want to buy shares in our company, they want to know that we're managing all of our risks and sustainability and environmental management is a risk and we need to manage that.

Similar views were demonstrated in other interviews, such as in the following quote where a decidedly cost benefit approach is taken by Gamma to justify irreversible environmental damage.

> ...we accept that there is some irreversible impact due to our operations. We do everything we're obliged to do to manage that, and we go beyond that in a lot of ways. And at the end of the day we consider that the value that is generated by the business, that is – economic and social – outweighs the impact of those operations.

The environmental reports analysed for this book shared this way of discussing the natural environment in financial terms. For instance, this next excerpt from Phi's 2012 environmental report outlines the regulatory environment of carbon pricing.

> In November 2011, the Federal Parliament passed the Clean Energy Act 2011 (Cth), which introduced a price on carbon from 1 July 2012 as part of the Clean Energy Future legislative package. The scheme is designed to operate at a fixed price for the first three years

and then transition to a cap and trade emissions trading scheme from July 2015. FY2013 was the first year of operation for the scheme, and the fixed carbon price was $23/tCO_2e$.

Zeta also draws on this approach by focusing on the company's financial investments in environmental initiatives.

Also in Zeta's 2014 report, environmental values are discussed in financial terms, such as in the following Figure 6.3, in which Zeta converts environmental issues into economic effects. In reference to climate change, Zeta explains the potential need for increased *climate finance*; the natural world is described as a *scarce resource*, a term commonly associated in economics with the factors of production; here, Zeta views the erosion of the natural world in purely economic terms, and in the third section, Zeta commandeers the natural world by reducing it to *capital*, with the potential to impact on *assets* and *business value*. This approach to communicating environmental values in economic terms reflects the tensions between the economic base of corporations and their environmental responsibilities highlighted by Spence (2009).

By reducing environmental values into currency and its equivalents, this type of narrative reflects a dualistic approach towards nature.

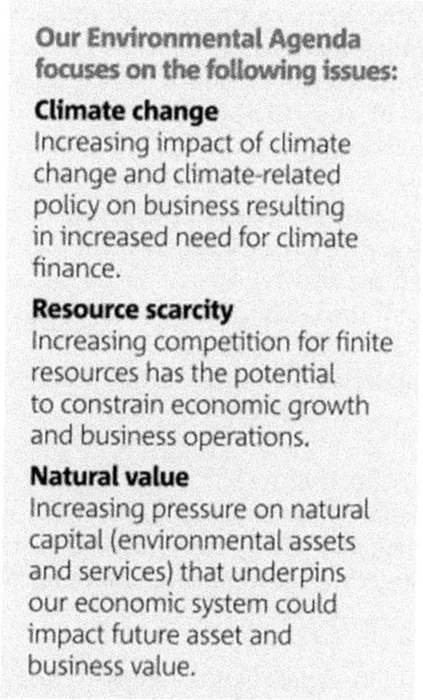

Our Environmental Agenda focuses on the following issues:

Climate change
Increasing impact of climate change and climate-related policy on business resulting in increased need for climate finance.

Resource scarcity
Increasing competition for finite resources has the potential to constrain economic growth and business operations.

Natural value
Increasing pressure on natural capital (environmental assets and services) that underpins our economic system could impact future asset and business value.

Figure 6.3 Extract from Zeta's 2014 environmental report.

It does so first by the reduction of the context and particularities of such aspects of the natural environment, and second by implicitly referring to the environment in terms of something that is uniform and exchangeable. As discussed in the previous chapter, the perception that aspects of the natural environment can be removed and replaced like parts of a machine reflects what Mathews (1991, 2001) describes as a dualistic approach which devalues the interconnected nature of the environment. Similarly, Cooper and Senkl (2016) explain how the desire to express environmental issues in monetary terms represents the urge to reduce and control the issues at hand. They argue that by reducing complex systems such as the natural world into capital, currency and other financial terms, the company seeks to minimise and obscure the underlying issues. These tendencies point towards a dualistic approach to the natural world.

Materiality

Similarly, grading the importance of environmental issues in the environmental report reflects a dualistic approach since it explicitly refers to a hierarchy of values within nature. Hierarchy is identified as a fundamental aspect of dualism, and as such, in the detection of dualism any hierarchical frameworks are considered. Most of the environmental reports and associated interviews referred to the concept of materiality. In terms of accounting, materiality "depends on the size and nature" of an item, which is considered material if it has the capacity to influence the economic decisions of users (AASB 108, para 5). Similarly, materiality in environmental reporting refers to the GRI, which notes that materiality is "the threshold at which aspects become sufficiently important that they should be reported" (Global Reporting Initiative, 2015, p. 17). In most of the cases where materiality is mentioned in the reports and interviews analysed for this book, it is in reference to the materiality assessment process of the GRI:

> The rigorous materiality assessment of the new GRI G4 framework supports this.
>
> (Psi, 2014)

> Our new materiality focus using the GRI G4 guidelines has been transformational. We really are starting to understand how to identify and target the most material issues for our business.
>
> (Psi, 2014)

Psi's 2014 sustainability report lists the steps to their materiality process, in which the process of hierarchically grading issues becomes clear. The steps are as follows, with italics added to highlight the hierarchical logic.

1   Topics from key external stakeholder engagement activities throughout the reporting year informed *a list of 60 topics.*

2   These topics were circulated to the heads of each of the following departments: Environment and Sustainability, Human Resources, Sales and Marketing, Workplace Health and Safety and Quality departments *who then prioritised the topics.*

3   Specific engagement was undertaken with the Sustainability Report Advisory Committee (SRAC) to represent external stakeholder interests. The SRAC is comprised of a diverse range of community representatives.

4   Each [Psi] representative and SRAC member was asked to *rank the topics in order of their view of the importance of the topic* to external stakeholders and to [Psi]'s ability to deliver on their business strategy.

5   The responses were collated and separated into three categories: (1) agreement in *topic ranking* by both internal and external stakeholders, (2) material to internal stakeholders only and (3) material to external stakeholders only.

6   The topics were then mapped against the GRI reporting framework's 'Aspects,' including those in the Food Processing Sector Supplement (Psi, 2014).

The materiality assessment process which Psi outlines is part of the Global Reporting Initiative's G4 reporting guidelines, which has been taken up by almost all of the case study companies in this book. This process has influenced the topics which are being reported on. In this way, the GRI has shaped the content of many companies' environmental reports, specifically to a more dualistic shift. This shift was mentioned during many of the interviews, as demonstrated below by the project manager responsible for Gamma's environmental reporting:

> …therefore the whole point about GRI 4 is if there's a topic that's material then you've got to report on it, so as part of moving towards GRI 4, for the first time we had to move to a materiality – we had to do a materiality assessment, that we hadn't done before. And so that changed a bit of the content. It moved us away from certain things and into other things.

Again in the following two interview excerpts from the Delta and Sigma interviews, respectively, the issue of what guides the inclusion of specific content is demonstrated to be the materiality assessment process, which is itself a part of the GRI guidelines.

> RESEARCHER: …the voluntary environment section of the sustainability report, how is it decided which information gets included in that report?

PARTICIPANT: ...effectively it's based on materiality really. It's what we see as being important to show our shareholders and our board effectively, and also to report to the community on – yeah, it's around the material issues.

(Delta interview)

Materiality decides the focus of our strategy. So our strategy is a five-year strategy and it's based on those material impacts. So it's got six strategic areas which is our community, our suppliers, our team members, environment, governance and one more – it's on our website.... carbon and waste, it's all on our website as well, so if you have a look on there it actually has our materiality assessment, and it's got the process that we went through so we spoke to stakeholders, we considered the feedback so we've got all that there in a diagram, and then how we came up with those issues.

(Sigma interview)

As Plumwood (1993a, 1993b, 2002) has argued, a hierarchical view of nature is implicit in the dualistic approach, thereby supporting the domination and exploitation of the natural world. The materiality assessment process required by the G4 guidelines explicitly impose the need to hierarchically grade environmental issues, and thereby perpetuates a dualistic view of nature in the corporate reporting process.

Nature as a Resource

Also perpetuated through discourse about the natural world is the concept that nature is a 'resource' for human use. This anthropocentric view is endemic throughout the environmental reports analysed in this book, as illustrated in the following excerpts and images from the environmental reports of case study companies (italics added) (Figure 6.4).

Governments and communities expect the energy industry to act responsibly so that *water resources* are not harmed by exploration and development activities, or energy production operations.

(Phi, 2013)

Our global database allows us to compare the environmental performance of different sites to identify improvements in *resource* use.

(Alpha, 2013)

The following section details our performance in environmental areas as we seek to use energy, fresh water and other *resources* more efficiently where economically viable.

(Gamma, 2012)

> ## Did you know?
>
> Since 1971, Earthwatch has conducted 1 400 research projects in 120 countries and 100 000 individuals have joined field trips to connect with research expeditions. Often in stunning and protected areas, these expeditions allow us to understand how best to preserve and improve wildlife habitats, cultural knowledge, and the natural resources that we all rely on.

Figure 6.4 2013 Alpha environmental report image.

...to create a platform for future growth, we continue to seek opportunities to improve our own *resource* efficiency, and to be innovative in the technologies and services that we provide to our clients.

(Delta, 2012)

Developing a stakeholder engagement program to work with our retailers to reduce *resource* consumption....

(Sigma, 2013)

Plumwood (2009) discusses the logic which underpins the description of nature as a 'resource,' illustrating how the ideology of dualism reduces the natural world to "mere matter" (p. 119). She argues that once nature is reduced in this way, the treatment of non-humans as slaves or tools for human use is naturalised. She places this kind of thinking at the heart of ecological exploitation.

Offsets

Linked to the reduction of the natural world that underpins the description of nature as a resource for human use is the approach which sees the natural world as made up of an aggregate of interchangeable parts. Mathews (1991) connects this view with a reductionist understanding in which systems (including ecosystems) can be explained completely in terms of the aggregate of their parts. Conversely, a deep ecologist's view would consider the autonomy of the whole as something above the total of its parts. To exemplify this thinking, consider yourself: you are likely to think of yourself as more than a collection of body parts. You may consider your personality, your whole body, your mind, but probably not as two legs, two arms, a torso and head!

The concept of interchangeable parts is exemplified in the environmental reports by discussion of 'offsets,' particularly, but not exclusively in terms of carbon accounting, where carbon offsets are part of the carbon accounting formula. Other reflections of this logic are found where different places can be used to offset mined land, as in the following passage:

> ...if you're going to destroy any area because you're going to dig it up, you must have acquired an offset area of equivalent or greater biodiversity value.
>
> (Gamma interview)

This view is also reflected when in the following passage, the Phi report discusses 'produced water':

> Deep groundwater is brought to the surface (or 'produced') as an unavoidable by-product of upstream gas exploration and production activities.
>
> (Phi, 2012)

Phi is not the only company which uses this dualistic logic in the context of water, as seen in the following phrase used in Gamma's 2014 environmental report:

> ...assessment of extended use of Caster Dam recycled water to offset Murray River water.
>
> (Gamma, 2014)

More commonly, though, this perception of the interchangeability of natural objects is represented with reference to carbon, where it is considered normal practice to exchange an action which results in x emissions of carbon and carbon equivalents (CO_2e), with the purchase of an offsetting mechanism which will theoretically absorb x CO_2e. Reference to carbon offsetting is commonplace in the environmental reports, as exemplified in the following statement from Zeta's 2014 environmental report:

> Our requirements for the purchase of quality carbon offsets and the management of our offset portfolio are documented in our Environmental Reporting and Offsets Management Standard.
>
> (Zeta, 2014)

...there'll be a few emissions that we'd need to sweep up around refrigerants and some materials, and then we would use offsets as our last resort....

(Kappa interview)

Aside from research which finds many of these carbon offsetting mechanisms invalid and even fraudulent (Cacho, Hean, & Wise, 2003), the underpinning logic that considers one aspect of the natural environment exchangeable for another is dualistic in its approach.

Images Minimising Apparent Impact

Preston, Wright and Young (1996) illustrate how the images within corporate reports transmit messages to the reader. They explain how these messages are portrayed through symbolism and metaphor, in an attempt to mislead the reader. This is particularly so through the use of photographs, since photos are seen as value neutral and objective, despite their capacity to portray deceptive or manipulated images and concepts.

The image below (Figure 6.5) of a thick-billed grasswren, appears in Gamma's 2013 environmental report. Through displaying such a close and detailed image of a small and delicately proportioned bird, Gamma presents the idea that it is sensitive to even the smallest aspects of the ecosystem. The implication is that Gamma has minimal environmental impacts, despite being a mining company.

In the next photograph (Figure 6.6), Gamma presents an image of their Senior Sustainability Scientist against a backdrop of what appears

Figure 6.5 Photo of grasswren in Gamma's 2013 environmental report.

Figure 6.6 Image from Gamma's 2013 environmental report.

to be a mangrove lined waterway. Beneath the image are the words "Senior Sustainability Scientist [name]'s passion for the environment helps drive his dedication to continually improve our environmental performance." This is followed by a narrative about his work at Gamma. In particular reference to the mangroves, the narrative lists dust control and minimising impact on the marine environment as part of their achievements. While these achievements shouldn't be understated, it is important to consider the range of backdrops a mining company could provide in their environmental report. Rather than setting this scientist against a backdrop of an open cut mine or other similarly damaged environments, Gamma has chosen to use a backdrop of a natural area that it has avoided damaging. This provides a positive reflection of Gamma's environmental impact, which is at odds with the majority of its actual impacts. The use of images to portray an overly positive view of environmental impact is repeated in many of the reports analysed for this book, for instance in Psi's environmental reports.

The following two images are taken from Psi's 2014 and 2013 environmental reports (Figures 6.7 and 6.8). Photographs that have been taken from a distance appear to minimise the visual impact of the salmon farm ponds which are in shallow estuaries. The visual concept communicated in these images is that the salmon farm ponds are inconsequential in comparison to the environment in which they are situated.

Delta uses a similar narrative in an image which appears in its 2012 environmental report. Although this image focuses on the large ship and other infrastructure in the marine environment, has also used a waterway which appears clear and healthy. The message portrayed here is that although Delta may be responsible for operating large industrial

Figure 6.7 Landscape image from Psi's 2014 environmental report.

Figure 6.8 Landscape image from Psi's 2013 environmental report.

machines, the natural environment remains intact and undamaged by such operations.

Another image with appears in Delta's 2014 environmental report highlights the natural environment within which Delta operates. Like the images of the grasswren in Gamma's reports, this one uses a detailed view of some grasslands, which highlights the delicate nature of such an ecosystem. Like Gamma, Delta is involved in the mining industry, and this image seems to portray the message that although Delta is involved with mining and infrastructure development, these delicate ecosystems are left unharmed by operations. While this image on its own represents an interconnected approach, set within the context of this report, it also minimises the apparent environmental impact of operations.

These images exemplify the common discursive mechanism of minimising apparent environmental impact, which is a dualistic device. As Davison et al. (2012) argue, images play a powerful role in constructing organisations. In the context of environmental reporting, images portray messages more powerfully than words alone, and it is important to examine what those messages are.

Carbon Accounting

By placing an accounting framework on aspects of the natural environment, another set of values slips through largely unnoticed. The values which are associated with financial accounting, such as the universal value of money which allows for its interchangeability, are thereby also imposed onto nature. In the instance of carbon accounting, the focus is removed from the temporal and physical effects of CO_2e emissions, and instead CO_2e is considered interchangeable and tradable. This thinking opens up the possibility of then exchanging financial values for carbon. The interchangeability that carbon accounting introduces to natural values is reflective of Mathews' (1991) account of a mechanistic view of nature, itself a dualistic view.

Due to legislation such as the Clean Energy Act and the National Greenhouse Energy Reporting scheme (which is now known as the Clean Energy Regulator), many large companies in Australia are obliged to use carbon accounting methodology to account for and report their CO_2e emissions to the Clean Energy Regulator (Australian Government, 2016). Since corporate CO_2e emissions are of interest to many stakeholders, it is a logical step to then publicly report on this data. The relevance of these legislated requirements is illustrated in the following quote from Phi's 2014 environmental report.

> In July 2014, the Commonwealth Government repealed the Clean Energy Act and subsequently removed the applicability of carbon pricing in Australia.

Other companies also use carbon accounting data to report on their CO_2e emissions, such as Delta, who report aspects of this data annually in their publicly available environmental report.

In the following passage, three examples are provided from Alpha's 2013 environmental report which illustrate the use of information derived from the carbon accounting process. These types of emissions reporting are common in all of the environmental reports analysed for this book.

> Two years into our second five-year EnviroAction period, I am pleased to report excellent results. We have delivered a 13% reduction in GHG emissions intensity...
> One of the initiatives, the redesign of our popular PowerBlock beverage container, saved 1,880 tonnes of CO_2-e emissions.
> Greenhouse gas (GHG) emissions
>
> - 10% reduction in GHG emissions intensity from FY2010–2011 by FY2015–2016; and
> - 60% reduction in GHG emissions intensity from FY2005–2006 by 2030
>
> (Alpha, 2013)

By reducing aspects of the environment to numerical values, this discursive mechanism also draws form the views outlined above, that expressing environmental issues numerically shapes the way such issues are perceived. Dambrin and Robson (2011) have argued that this is a method of control. These are characteristics which conform with a dualistic view.

Carbon Neutrality

The motif of separation (and therefore dualism) is expressed through the use of carbon accounting, in particular the claim of carbon neutrality, which is a product of carbon accounting. Nerlich and Koteyko (2009) and Koteyko, Thelwall and Nerlich (2010) discuss the discursive use of the word *carbon*, as well as some of the many compound words which include *carbon* (for example, carbon counting, carbon footprint). The discussion of carbon in these reports reflects Nerlich and Koteyko and Koteyko et al.'s arguments that the discourses around carbon reflect a moralistic attitude. In these reports, the use of the term 'carbon neutral' is considered to reflect a dualistic view, since the use of the term *neutral* is based on the accounting treatment of carbon and carbon equivalent emissions. Like accounting itself, which has historically made ill-founded claims to neutrality, the term *neutral* in this context is equally deceptive. The calculations and assumptions which guide carbon accounting measurements are based in part on politically motivated decisions (Ascui & Lovell, 2011). For instance, in countries where powerful industries like agriculture have a strong influence on environmental policy, land clearing and vegetation burning are not included in the carbon equation (Cacho et al., 2003; Hurteau, 2008). It has been argued that carbon accounting has different meanings for different user groups, and as such, is far from a neutral concept (Ascui & Lovell, 2011). Following these arguments, a claim of carbon neutrality is here considered to be an attempt to 'neutralise' the reader – to use terminology which masks the underlying contestations. In this case, such misleading terms are considered as an attempt to mask and separate the company from the physical reality of carbon emissions, and as such, are dualistic. Some examples of the expression of this motif are provided below in the following three excerpts.

[Kappa] is committed to carbon neutrality in areas within its control.
(Kappa, 2014)

Additionally, uncoated paper (office paper) should be carbon neutral.
(Zeta, 2014)

...can we design a carbon neutral packaging solution in the long-term? What are the steps involved in achieving this?
(Alpha, 2014)

As it is expressed in the corporate environmental reports analysed in this book, carbon neutrality reflects a dualistic approach to the natural environment. The dualistic motif is further expressed in the reports by discussion of 'environmental risk.'

Environmental Risk

In terms of corporate reporting, environmental risk refers to the risks environmental factors pose to the business, rather than any risks the business may pose to the natural environment. This approach is exemplified in the following passages which were drawn from the environmental reports analysed in this book.

> To future-proof our business, we aim to play a leading role in the transition to a sustainable economy, where…environmental risks are understood and opportunities captured to achieve positive outcomes for customers, business and environment.
>
> (Zeta, 2014)

> The understanding and management of risk is crucial to the ongoing success of any business. The management of environmental risk is particularly important to [Phi] given the company holds long-term leases on land used by third parties for other purposes and also operates in sensitive environments such as National Parks.
>
> (Phi, 2013)

> Environmental Management Systems (EMS) are a key tool in maintaining environmental compliance and managing environmental risk.
>
> (Gamma, 2014)

By focusing on the risk apparent to the business, mention of environmental risk reflects a hierarchical view where corporate interests are valorised at the expense of natural values. The repetition of this discursive mechanism contributes to the construction and maintenance of a dualistic approach to the natural world. The dualistic theme is further reflected in the self-congratulatory and repeated mention of prizes and awards won by the reporting companies.

Awards, Self-Congratulatory

Hawken (1993) argues that while companies congratulate themselves with awards and certification, the world continues on its trajectory of degradation and environmental damage. He articulates that the structure of business itself is antithetical to the wellbeing of the environment, and that congratulating organisations with awards while they continue to cause environmental damage, regardless of their intentions, highlights the disparity between business practice and environmental benefit. As such, the display of prizes, awards and similar certification is considered in this book to be an expression of a dualistic attitude towards nature.

Dualism is also characterised by an anthropocentric outlook, which values the human over environmental values (Plumwood, 1993a). There are some common expressions of a dualistic anthropocentric motif which are frequently repeated in corporate environmental reports, including the 'self-congratulatory' motif, as expressed through the discussion of awards, accreditation to specifically environmental groups of 'elite' performers, the signing of agreements and the winning of prizes for environmental performance, as exemplified in the images below. It has been argued that these types of ranking devices serve as a way to interpret a situation and construct artificial hierarchies (Pollock & D'Adderio, 2012).

Many of the case study companies analysed for this book have listed prizes and awards in their environmental reports. This reflects the findings of earlier research, which noted the self-laudatory tendencies of environmental reporting in the 1990s (Deegan & Gordon, 1996). The following is a selection of how these awards and certifications are displayed in environmental reports (Figures 6.9–6.11 and an extract from Gamma's 2014 environmental report).

Figure 6.9 Certification in Psi's 2014 environmental report.

Awards, memberships and certifications

Recognition we received in 2013:

- Listed as one of the 2013 Global 100 Most Sustainable Corporations in the World by Corporate Knights. ▉ was listed as 55, from an initial field of over 4,000 companies.

- Included on the Ethisphere Institute's 2013 list of the 'World's Most Ethical Companies' for the third consecutive year.

- Ranked No. 5 in Newsweek's Worlds Greenest Company rankings – the only Australian company in the top 25 (October 2012).

- Rated 29 out of the top 40 World's Greenest Banks in the 2012 Bloomberg rankings (April 2013).

- Included in the 2013 CDP Climate Disclosure Leadership Index (4th consecutive year in a row).

- Our Company Secretary, ▉ ▉ received the Climate Alliance's Award for Company Secretary of the Year.

Figure 6.10 Awards, memberships and certifications in Zeta's 2013 environmental report.

Figure 6.11 Award in Gamma's 2014 environmental report.

Extract from Gamma's 2014 environmental report:

Case Study – [Gamma] wins regional award for Sustainability
[Gamma] Steelworks and [Gamma] Mining have been recognised for their exceptional commitment to the environment and local community, being named the winner of the Sustainability category in the South Australian Regional Awards in late 2013.

While there are critics of such award winning in the accounting literature, who see the winning of prizes as often distant from operations (Herzig & Moon, 2013), others have reiterated these concerns with attention on the role such prizes play in the legitimisation process (Hopwood, 2009). For instance, Deegan and Gordon (1996) note that companies tend to report positive and self-congratulatory information regardless of whether their operations have been damaging to the environment. The disparity between awards and (in some cases) actual operations reflects the dualistic tendency to separate and distinguish. Similarly, the self-congratulatory nature of such awards, and the hierarchical approach this draws from, points towards a dualistic view, which valorises the company over the natural environment in an anthropocentric dualism.

Images Which Conflict with the Surrounding Text

Prior research has illustrated the use of images in corporate reports which conflict in message with the surrounding text. For instance, David (2001) found that the use of images in annual reports could change readers' perceptions of the company. She found this even when the content of the report conflicts with the message given in the picture. She pointed out that the use of graphics and pictures foregrounds certain aspects that the designer would like to highlight, even to the extent of distorting the truth. This capacity of images to create or manipulate meaning is supported by Davison (2010). Further to this, Hrasky (2012) notes that sustainability reports often rely on images that reflect sustainability themes but which are unrelated to actual operations.

Zillmann, Gibson and Sargent (1999) point out the mechanisms which make the use of images which conflict with surrounding content useful in corporate environmental reporting. They point out that readers' perceptions are powerfully influenced by images, particularly photographs, and that when text is accompanied by biased photographs, readers will tend to believe the image over and above the text.

In the first image below, Alpha visually introduces its sustainability report with an image which powerfully conveys an interconnected approach (Figure 6.12). The image below is on the cover page of Alpha's 2013 sustainability review (with company name and details removed), which includes the environmental report. This image incorporates text,

Figure 6.12 Cover page of Alpha's 2013 environmental report.

and is considered interconnective in its approach, since it illustrates connections between the person, her thoughts and the other symbols. The hand drawn effect underpins this approach by giving the appearance of a personal account. Since images which evoke emotions have been found to more powerfully influence the effect on readers (Zillmann et al., 1999), the 'happy' message in this image functions as an indicator for the reader as to their perception of the content of the report. In contrast to this interconnective image, the environmental report was found to be predominantly dualistic in approach through its focus on disclosing company policy and environmental regulations. Prior research has found that companies reporting primarily on these aspects are reactive, as opposed to proactive about environmental issues (Cañón-de-Francia & Garcés-Ayerbe, 2009), in a distinctly defensive approach (Morrison, Wilmshurst, & Shimeld, 2018).

Stiles (2004) argues that pictures enable messages to be quickly understood and in doing so, are powerful communication tools. By using images which present a message which is different to, even conflicting with, the theme of the surrounding text, these environmental reports attempt to convince readers that their approach is interconnected. Where the text reinforces this approach, the report can be interpreted as reflecting an interconnective approach to the natural world, however, if the text is found to be dualistic, or transcendent in its approach, the images are used to deflect from, rather than reinforce the text. The attempt to divert attention is itself reflective of a dualistic approach, since it constructs a barrier and aims to control the readers' perception of the environmental interactions of the company.

The image below (Figure 6.13), which appears in Psi's 2014 environmental report reflects the concept of biomimicry, where human made objects

Figure 6.13 Landscape image from Psi's 2014 environmental report.

draw from the workings of nature. In this image, the shape of the salmon pond net in the foreground mirrors the shape of Mt Wellington in the background. The message of this image is that the salmon pond reflects the natural order of things, and fits in with the existing ecosystem. The use of repeating patterns is discussed by Kress and Van Leeuwen (2006), who illustrate how such visual techniques portray associations between subjects. As such, the image represents the interconnectivity between the natural environment (Mt Wellington), and Psi's operations. Contrary to this messaging, the image is followed by table of bird 'interactions' including how many birds have died in their interactions with Psi. In this instance, the image draws the readers' attention away from the table.

Similarly, an image is found in Beta's 2014 environmental report which reflects a transcendent theme. It does so by its focus up and away from the terrestrial plane, and also through the symbolism of stairs, which are a common object depicted in religious images leading to heaven. Ledin and Machin (2016) also draw parallels between the depiction of stairs and the core values of neoliberalism, such as improved profits. While the image depicts transcendence, it is followed by text of a dualistic theme.

Through the use of images which portray a conflicting philosophical message compared with the context within which they sit, these environmental reports attempt to distract the readers' attention from the content (David, 2001; Hansen & Machin, 2008; Zillmann et al., 1999). Where a conflicting message is presented between text and image, the image proves more influential (Zillmann et al., 1999) and capable of constructing perceptions (Davison et al., 2012). The fundamental ontology informing dualism is that of separation and hierarchical distinction. A discursive mechanism such as this, where an image is used which conflicts and distracts from the text is a reflection of an ontology of separation. The literature which points out the hierarchies within discourse highlight the bias that is given to images in the readers' perception of the text. This bias reflects the ontology of hierarchical distinction which signals a dualistic approach. In this way, the use of conflicting images constructs a barrier between the reader's perception and the actual environmental impacts; again, a dualistic approach.

Direction of Readers' Attention Away from the Report

In many of the environmental reports which are analysed as part of this book, readers are directed away from the reports themselves, towards other sources of information. This discursive mechanism is considered to be a dualistic method of diverting attention away from the environmental report. This is an act of delineating the boundaries of responsibility, particularly when the reader is directed towards external sources of information. In some cases, the reader is directed towards other webpages within the corporate website, or towards other areas of the report itself.

Within Psi's 2014 environmental report there is a section entitled "Marine Reserves and Marine Conservation Areas." Information which would be considered critical to this topic is not directly presented in this section, but either on an external site, as in the first paragraph, or in an appendix, as in the second paragraph.

> These areas are either solely managed by Tasmanian Parks and Wildlife Service or in conjunction with the Marine Resources Branch of DPIPWE. Specific Information regarding the natural values of these marine reserves and marine conservation areas is available on the Parks and Wildlife website at www.parks.tas.gov.au/indeX. aspX?base=397.
>
> Appendix 1 details the proximity of each of [Psi]'s operational leases to the above marine reserves and marine conservation areas.
>
> (Psi, 2014)

The following examples illustrate how Phi directs readers away from their 2014 environmental report. The underlined words in these quotes are hyperlinked to sections of their website.

> The Camden Gas Project groundwater management plan provides a framework for early assessment of changes in the groundwater systems...
>
> We also prepare annual water resource status reports. All are detailed on our website.
>
> Visit the data centre to view or download the amount of water produced at each of [Phi]'s coal seam gas facilities.
>
> (Phi, 2014)

This discursive device is also used in Zeta's 2012 environmental report. The following example demonstrates how Zeta uses hyperlinks to direct readers' attention.

> Further detail is provided in our Group Environmental Reporting and Carbon Offset Standard, available at [Zeta website address].
>
> (Zeta, 2012)

By creating a division between the environmental report and the reader, this common discursive mechanism is considered to be a dualistic device.

Regulatory Focus

Mention of the adherence to laws and regulations provides a barrier between organisational decisions and responsibilities, effectively stating that the company isn't responsible for the regulations, and is simply abiding by the law. This allows the company to step away from their direct impact on the environment, instead focussing on the regulation. As such, a focus on the regulatory environment reflects a dualistic approach to nature. This interpretation is supported in the following passages from the interview with Gamma's sustainability manager.

> Having said that, I am very confident that we are a solid corporate citizen, so we have a commitment to compliance in all of the countries we operate in.
>
> So there are standards set by the state government on rehabilitation. And they're mostly around, well, around, let's talk about – there are standards set to do with biodiversity and mining, so the first one is if you're going to destroy any area because you're going to dig it up, you must have acquired an offset area of equivalent or greater biodiversity value.
>
> (Gamma interview)

Again, in the interview with one of Zeta's sustainability managers, the role of regulation in their relationship with the natural environment, particularly through their environmental reporting processes is highlighted, below.

> ...predominantly decided by regulation and reporting bodies, and then if there's no guidance then we'll look at our own internal determination of what we should be using.
>
> (Zeta interview)

This role is highlighted in many of the environmental reports, for instance, in the following excerpts from Phi's 2013; Alpha's 2013 and Gamma's 2014 environmental reports.

> [Phi] met all of its regulated targets under the Victorian Energy Savings Initiative, the South Australian Residential Energy Efficiency Scheme and the New South Wales Energy Savings Scheme for the 2012 calendar year.
>
> (Phi, 2013)

> We have achieved high levels of compliance with our Environmental Policy and environmental regulations.
>
> (Alpha, 2013)

> [Gamma] seeks to comply with applicable environmental laws, regulations and mandatory standards.
>
> (Gamma, 2014)

Morrison et al. (2018) argue that a focus on environmental regulatory requirements indicates a deontological approach to nature, which centres on the obligatory duties of the company. This regulatory focus creates a barrier between the company and its actions, since the impetus for making the decision is based on the regulation rather than because of any direct response to the environment itself.

Positive Contribution to the Environment

Hines (1992) calls for accounting to embrace 'negative,' feminine or 'yin' values. She perceives accounting tradition as overly biased towards 'positive,' masculine or 'yang' values. Her call to incorporate negative values into the accounts of business is a call to step back from the continuous growth (particularly economic) which characterises western culture. Gray (2010) similarly calls for a stepping back from claims of sustainability, in order to acknowledge that there is very little that could authentically be labelled as 'sustainable' in modern, western society. As Gray argues, it is difficult to know what might be sustainable except a dramatic shift in values and lifestyles. Western society is increasingly becoming aware of how difficult sustainability would be to actually achieve (Giddens, 2008; IPCC, 2013). Parallel to this realisation is the plethora of businesses claiming to be sustainable (Gray, 2010; KPMG, 2013). Making such claims is a 'positive' statement in terms of Hines' discussion of *positive* and *negative* accounting, since it is a forceful statement of what the company is *doing*, rather than *not-doing*.

Prior research has argued that the claim of positive environmental interactions underpins sustainability reports in general (Gray, 2010). Similarly, some of the reports and interviewees make the claim that they are having a *positive* influence on the environment. Rather than minimising their negative impact (not-doing, or negative), these examples claim to have improved the natural environment (doing, or positive). The following excerpt from the interview with the sustainability manager from Theta demonstrates how these claims were made.

> RESEARCHER: So how well do you think your company interacts with the environment? Would you say it's got a positive, negative, or neutral impact?
> PARTICIPANT: I think very positive. Actually very positive, and I think you know we always talk about – we need to educate, we need to do different things and recognition is one of the things that sometimes gets a little bit lost. But I think that since we started to get some awards the business has started to get, you know to put a little bit more focus.
>
> (Theta interview)

Again, in the interview with the sustainability manager form Sigma, a similar claim was made in terms of their personal relationship with the natural world.

> Personally my relationship with the natural environment is fantastic. We're always out bushwalking, those sorts of things.
>
> (Sigma interview)

The theme of positive contribution to the environment was implicit in all of the environmental reports, as evidenced by some of the other common discursive mechanisms, such as awards. The following example (Figure 6.14) demonstrates how this mechanism was explicitly communicated in Alpha's 2014 report.

The image below, a full-page picture from Alpha's 2014 report, demonstrates how a 'positive' environmental impact can be expressed through both image and words. The image is reflective of the joyful and energetic themes of many soft drink advertisements, the most well-known of which is Coca Cola. The sunshine, the youthful and healthy model, and the enjoyment she displays are all implicitly 'positive.' As discussed above, images are powerful methods for communicating

Figure 6.14 'Positive' image in Alpha's 2014 environmental report.

messages. Along with this image are the words "Lighter packaging means better environmental outcomes." Although the truth of this claim is not disputed, the implication is that lighter packaging equates to a positive environmental impact. The context of this message is supported by the interview with the sustainability manager of Alpha, who stated numerous times that:

> I would say that packaging on the whole as a positive impact, but it's often not well perceived. We see the main role of packaging is in protecting the product, making sure it gets safely to consumers and then it gets used for whatever it was created for. If packaging doesn't work well then you get a lot more food waste, you've got to grow more food, so up the supply chain you get a lot more impact, so we certainly see that packaging is a very valuable part of the supply chain.
>
> (Alpha interview)

The discursive mechanism of expressing a positive impact on the environment, while not commonly expressed *explicitly* in the environmental reports analysed, is a theme which runs through all of the reports *implicitly*, and as Gray (2010) argues, is a fundamental theme of environmental and sustainability reports more generally.

A claim that a positive environmental contribution has occurred as part of normal business operations without justification, demonstrates a distance between the claimant and the reality of the physical world. As such, this discursive device reflects a dualistic attitude towards the natural world. While many of the most commonly evident discursive devices reflect a dualistic approach, there are some repeated throughout the environmental reports analysed for this book which also reflect the other two primary discourse themes: transcendence and interconnectivity.

Transcendence

Transcendence is evident in the environmental reports analysed for this book. Some of the commonly used discursive motifs and mechanisms which portray a transcendent approach are outlined in the following list.

Common Transcendence Motifs

Physical world less valued than the transcendent ($)

- Focus on profit

Transcendent Anthropocentrism

- Financial trade off where financial overrides environmental concerns
- Management of environment – EMS and ISO 14000

Focus on Profit

In the context of corporate reporting, profit can be considered as a surrogate for transcendence (Latour, 2014). Consequently, a focus on profit, or a financial trade-off where profit is given precedence are both considered representations of a transcendent approach.

Transcendence is defined as a state of being that exceeds the limitations of the physical world (Oxford Dictionary, 2016). From this perspective, the continual growth of western economies and profits are states of being which exceed the limitations of the physical world. More specifically, transcendence refers to the valorisation of such a transcendent state at the expense of the physical world. Examples of transcendent discourse include those of a Christian heaven, a Buddhist nirvana and of human reason from an Enlightenment perspective. The equivalent of these states of being in the contemporary era is that of profit. Like the Christian view of heaven, the modern view of profit is that of a higher state of being, which is fiercely sought after. Latour (2014, p. 1) argues that capitalism and profit have become the modern transcendent values:

> No wonder: the transcendent world of beyond has always been more durable than the poor world of below. But what is new is that this world of beyond is not that of salvation and eternity, but that of economic matters.

A focus on profit in the environmental report is considered evidence of a transcendent approach to nature, since while it is usual practice for companies to aim towards profit, and is therefore expected in the financial reports, it is not as relevant for an environmental report to consider profit to any great extent.

The following example is from the 2014 Phi environmental report, and refers to 'the interests of shareholders.' In this example, Phi is framing the risks of climate change in terms of profit (that is, the interests of shareholders).

> **Carbon exposure:** [Phi] is committed in the interests of Shareholders to reducing the financial risks associated with existing and emerging climate change policies.

Again, by framing environmental impacts in terms of economic decision-making, Psi reinforces the idea that the profit margin is an important aspect of environmental decision-making. This is evident in the following excerpt from their 2014 environmental report.

> [Psi] is also looking at economically viable and environmentally sustainable alternative options.

During the interview with Theta's sustainability manager, this point was also raised. This interviewee explained the tensions that exist between making a profit and decisions that would reduce environmental impacts.

> ...otherwise it just doesn't make financial sense. So I think that the company is always very mindful of doing something good, but also having the cost benefit assessed, especially for us because we are a public company. So whatever we do we still have to think about our shareholders and the nature of our work is basically, we are retailers, so they expect us to make a profit from selling. So I guess if we don't have a good business case to back up all the environmental initiatives that we have, we might get in a little bit of trouble...

The sustainability manager at Kappa reiterated the view that the purpose of the environmental report is to increase profits in the next passage.

> RESEARCHER: ...reporting on environmental issues, do you see that as adding to the company's profit margin... improving the bottom line? Do you think that's one of the motivations for reporting on environmental issues?
> PARTICIPANT: Of course it is [laughter]. Ah so yes, it must. And it does, through a range of different mechanisms, as a for instance, the NABRS rating of an office property is material in occupancy and rent, for an office building, so that has material impact and as I said if it we're privileged that we have a mechanism for internalising the cost. Other industries don't, and we do so that gives us a much more direct connection to profitability in relation to emissions which is a good thing.

The 2014 environmental report of Beta also draws from this approach to the environment in the following selection. Here, Beta justifies the continued use of plastic bags in terms of their economic benefit:

> Q: Why does [Beta] still provide plastic carry bags?
> A: [Beta] carry bags are made from low density polyethylene. They are strong, cost effective, and fit for the purpose of protecting and carrying customer purchases. We continue to investigate and trial alternatives.

It is written into the corporate structure that the primary purpose of a company is to increase profits (Greenfield, 2008), and as such, companies are restricted from making environmental decisions which would decrease profits materially. This is a legislated transcendent approach, which directs companies to make decisions which valorise profit over the environment, and leaves companies relatively powerless to make decisions which would valorise the environment at the expense of profits (Greenfield, 2008). However, this decision-making process has been internalised by many companies, when they utilise the argument that decisions are made on this basis. When the environmental reports explicitly state that a decision was made which damaged the environment in favour of profit, it is evident that the company has embedded this transcendent viewpoint into their decision-making processes.

Management of the Environment – EMS & ISO 14000

Mention of environmental management systems (EMS) and the International Organisation for Standards (ISO) is an example of a discursive mechanism which can be interpreted as reflecting either a dualist or transcendent approach. As mentioned, these two themes overlap somewhat. In common with dualism, transcendence can also be portrayed through anthropocentrism. While similar in some respects to a dualistic anthropocentrism, transcendent anthropocentrism represents a focus on human values within a transcendent context, for instance, if humans are represented as more transcendent, higher, less physical or less earthly than the natural environment. In the context of corporate reporting, a patriarchal or protective approach towards nature based on perceived human superiority is considered part of the transcendent theme. This approach is reflected in the expression of a caretaking, or stewardship role of humans towards the natural environment. In the context of corporate environmental reporting, this approach is commonly expressed by discussion of 'environmental management,' including the ISO 14001 environmental management standard. The inclusion of ISO 14001 as representative of either a transcendent or dualistic anthropocentrism is supported when considering the wording used in the standard which reduces the natural world to 'natural resources,' 'ecosystem services' and focuses on the benefit of managing the environment for human purposes (ISO, 2015). In such an example, the context is taken into account to decide on its inclusion as either dualism or transcendence. In some cases, mention of EMS or ISO 14000 was considered as *both* dualistic and transcendent.

Corresponding with the transcendent approach to the natural environment is the reasoning that humans are superior to nature. This superiority is most often justified in terms of human intelligence, which is commonly perceived to be exceeding that of other species (Singer, 1990/1975) and of nature itself (Plumwood, 2002). Such a sense of superiority leads humans to see a need for 'managing' the natural world. In the context of the research in this book, the idea that humans should, or even *could* manage nature is considered to be a transcendent approach, since it involves a perceived hierarchy of (western) human reason over and above the autonomy of nature (Plumwood, 2009).

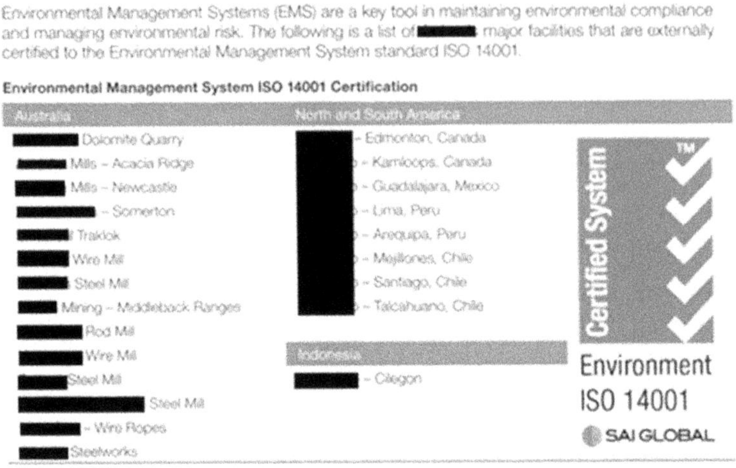

Environmental Management Systems (EMS) are a key tool in maintaining environmental compliance and managing environmental risk. The following is a list of ██████ major facilities that are externally certified to the Environmental Management System standard ISO 14001.

Environmental Management System ISO 14001 Certification

Figure 6.15 Extract from Gamma's 2014 environmental report.

In terms of corporate environmental reporting, there are copious examples of this approach, particularly since the ISO 14000 series of standards are in common use. These standards relate to best "environmental management" practices (ISO, 2015). The image above (Figure 6.15), and the following two extracts (a quote from Alpha's 2012 environmental report and a quote from Psi's 2012 environmental report) present some of these examples.

Extract from Alpha's 2013 environmental report:

> With over 300 sites across the globe, we have a responsibility to manage our environmental impacts. To achieve this, we focus on:
> > implementing environmental management systems and continuously improving environmental performance at our sites
> [Alpha] maintains environmental management systems appropriate for each site's operations and for the country in which the site is located.
> (Alpha, 2012)

> In the reporting year, the Environment and Sustainability team began the review of [Psi]'s Environmental Management System (EMS) in order to prepare for third party certification to ISO14001 standard. The process of review highlighted the need to streamline the alignment of our EMS and additional eco-certifications with [Psi]'s Integrated Management System (TIMS) resulting in the EMS being delayed.
> (Psi, 2012)

The philosophical approach that places humans in a position to 'manage' the environment is underpinned by the assumption that humans *can* manage the environment. The benefits of environmental management systems are not being debated however, these underpinning assumptions are.

Interconnectivity

Like dualism and transcendence, the philosophical theme of interconnectivity is represented repeatedly in the environmental reports. This would seem to indicate that the companies are not attempting to obscure their relationship with the natural world. Some common motifs are outlined in the list below, and explained in more depth in this section.

Common Interconnectivity Motifs

Connections between Subjects

- Recycling
- Geography specifics
- Biodiversity
- Case studies in general
- Stakeholder engagement
- Leadership
- Supply Chain
- Procurement
- Employee engagement
- Acknowledgement of impacts
- Influence
- Impact of nature on business (that is, seasons, times, weather events)
- Partnerships
- Images of natural beauty
- Wider effects
- Life cycle analysis
- Communication with stakeholders
- Scope 3 GHG emissions

Humans as part of Nature

- Weather effects
- Climate change

Two aspects of the interconnectivity theme are predominantly represented in the corporate environmental reports analysed in this book: *connections between subjects* and *humans as part of nature*. While other subgroupings are also included as part of this theme, it is these two aspects which are most repeated in the texts. The repetition of words or motifs represent to Alexander (2009) an attempt to normalise a particular approach.

Connections between subjects are repeatedly represented in the environmental reports through reference to recycling, particularly where some context is given (in contrast to mentions of recycling without context, which is commonly presented in a table format, and considered a dualistic mechanism). Similarly, links and relationships between subjects such as stakeholders, employees, industry and other partners recur throughout the reports analysed.

Other links between various aspects of corporate actions which are commonly referred to in the reports include discussions of the supply chain, procurement, communication and scope 3 greenhouse gas emissions. Scope 3 greenhouse gas emissions are included here since they represent what is considered *indirect emissions*. Their discussion therefore represents an acknowledgement of the wider effects of corporate actions.

While a dualistic or transcendent approach draws the focus away from the actual physical effects of corporate actions, the interconnectivity approach openly acknowledges these effects. As such, inclusion of specific geographical characteristics, biodiversity, particular case studies, the impact of nature on the business and acknowledgment of corporate impacts on the natural environment all represent an interconnective approach. These motifs are discussed in more detail below.

Recycling

Embedded into the idea of recycling is the awareness of the wider impacts of waste disposal as well as resource consumption. Since the awareness of the connected nature of environmental effects and decisions reflects an expression of interconnectivity, recycling reflects the interconnective theme. Recycling rates are commonly reported in the environmental reports analysed for this book. Below are some examples of this frequently reported aspect of environmental reporting (Figures 6.16 and 6.17, an excerpt from Kappa's 2014 environmental report, Beta's 2014 report, and two excerpts from Sigma's 2014 and 2013 environmental reports).

Waste to landfill and recycling*					
Tonnes (estimate)	2014	2013	2012	2011	2010
Paper collected and recycled	4,585	4,455	3,797	4,084	4,502
Other waste recycled	1,464	1,111	1,013	626	414
Sub-total materials recycled/diverted from landfill	6,049	5,566	4,810	4,710	4,916
Waste to landfill	3,530	3,367	3,528	3,786	3,514
Total waste generated	9,579	8,933	8,338	8,496	8,430
Total waste to landfill per FTE (kg/FTE)	83	78	80	84	86
% waste diverted from landfill (estimate)	63	62	58	55	58

Figure 6.16 Extract from Zeta's 2014 environmental report.

END-OF-LIFE
> End-of-life packaging collection/recovery
> Packaging reuse, re-filling, composting
    anaerobic digestion
> Packaging recycling
> Energy recovery
> Landfill

Figure 6.17 Extract from Alpha's 2012 environmental report.

Extract from Kappa's 2014 environmental report:

Key achievements in 2014 included:
- Recycling rates improved from 29% to 47% since 2005
- $1.8 million of avoided landfill costs
- 6,342 tonnes of waste to landfill avoided
- [Kappa] developed and trialled more accurate waste reporting
                                                        (Kappa, 2014)

Extract from Beta's 2014 environmental report:

[recycling symbol]   Recycling rate
                        (% waster recycled)
                        FY2014: 57%
                        FY2013: 55%

Implemented a new Waste Management Strategy, improving [Sigma's] recycling rate by 14%.
                                                        (Sigma, 2014)

Some of the environmental and sustainability design features of the Event Centre include…Glass recycling systems for the bar and restaurant areas….
                                                        (Sigma, 2013)

These examples range from a predominantly quantitative reporting of recycling rates (as demonstrated in the three examples, from Kappa, Beta and Zeta), to more narrative type of reporting (as in the two quotes from Sigma's 2014 and 2013 environmental reports, and Figure 6.17).

As discussed earlier in this chapter, the predominant use of quantitative communication is considered a dualistic mechanism. As such, the reporting of recycling information in quantitative terms represents both a dualistic and interconnective approach. As discussed in Chapter 4 (Operationalising Critique), critical discourse analysis is flexible enough to allow for these crossovers and overlapping themes.

Specific Geographies

Reflecting an interconnective approach to the natural world is the ontology of specificity. Specificity is highlighted in feminist philosophy, through a focus on particularities, in contrast to Enlightenment thought which favours a universal outlook (Irigaray, 2004). A growing area in environmental philosophy is that of the phenomenology of place. This movement acknowledges the specific virtues of place, in a push against the 'averaging' tendencies of a lot of environmental discourse. By valuing specific places intrinsically, as well as for their position in the wider environment, phenomenology of place is closely linked to ecofeminism (Morrison, 2017; Plumwood, 2006, 2009). By acknowledging the specific geographical conditions of place, this approach reflects the interconnectivity theme. Interconnectivity also acknowledges specific values and particularities rather than abstract averages, which in contrast, represent distance from place, and therefore a dualistic approach. Some examples of the ways companies have communicated the specific geographical conditions of place follow.

> ...to gain more current information in relation to the marine environment surrounding [Phi] Torrens, [Phi] completed a review of marine environmental data. In FY2014, [Phi] will undertake biological surveys around Torrens Island.
>
> (Phi, 2013)

> Other agencies including Parks Victoria and the North East Catchment Management Authority also carried out willow removal upstream and downstream of [Phi]'s regulating pondage. It is anticipated that the willow removal will produce a material benefit for the biodiversity values of the pondage and the Kiewa River.
>
> (Phi, 2013)

> ... no detectable impacts on the ecology of the river system, as indicated by longterm monitoring of macro-invertebrates and blackfish undertaken by the Freshwater Ecology section of the Arthur Rylah Institute for Environmental Research....
>
> (Phi, 2013)

Water conservation is a critical issue for sites in the water-stressed areas of Australia, parts of the southern USA, Mexico and some areas of South America.

(Alpha, 2012)

To ensure a co-ordinated and effective approach to land management in the area around the Middleback Ranges, [Gamma] is an active participant in a co-operation agreement known as the Middleback Landholders Alliance. In this alliance, local land managers and the SA Department of Environment, Water and Natural Resources work co-operatively to achieve effective control of pest plants and animals at a landscape level.

(Gamma, 2012)

The Tasman region has experienced a marked increase in seal numbers during the reporting year. Re-established breeding colonies on Tasman Island and Cape Hauy mean that a proportion of seals are not travelling to Bass Strait for the breeding season. This, coupled with a successful breeding season, has resulted in an increased number of sub-adult seals frequenting the Nubeena leases.

(Psi, 2014)

Case Studies

In a similar vein to, and for the same reasons as the discussion of specific geographies, case studies which discuss specific events, species or places also reflect an interconnective approach to the environment. The four examples provided on the following two pages illustrate the ways in which environmental impacts and decision-making is communicated through case studies in the environmental reports analysed for this book. The first example (Figure 6.18), which appears in Gamma's 2012 environmental report describes how Gamma delivered an environmental benefit to the thick-billed grasswren. The case study provided in their report describes the relationship between the company, the bird and its habitat.

The second example (Figure 6.19) outlines the reduction in Zeta's energy use in narrative form. While quantitative information is supplied, the case study also explains some of the context around the energy savings, and thus reflects a more interconnective approach to environmental issues.

The third example (Figure 6.20) explains how a subsidiary of Gamma has contributed to the production of a book which aims to promote tree-planting in the Arequipa area.

CASE STUDY

THICK-BILLED GRASSWREN

The Thick-billed Grasswren is a small bird that was once widespread in arid Australia but has undergone a dramatic contraction of range since European settlement, mostly due to the introduction of feral predators and grazing animals. It is considered to be a critical indicator species of the health of Chenopod Shrublands in which it is found and is classified as vulnerable by the Commonwealth Government.

Part of the approval process for ████████ to develop the mine at Peculiar Knob was a commitment to developing a plan to deliver a significant environmental benefit to offset environmental impact. The planned offset is conservation research and a habitat management project for the Thick-billed Grasswren. This project will:

• Fund research into the basic biology of the Thick-billed Grasswren

• Initiate action to reduce predation from cats and foxes, and to reduce grazing pressure on Chenopod Shrublands by domestic and feral animals

• Increase the area and quality of Chenopod Shrubland habitat through restoration works.

above: The Thick-billed Grasswren

Figure 6.18 Case study from Gamma's 2012 environmental report.

Providing context through case studies is a method of acknowledging the relationships that exist between events, objects and subjects. In this way, related aspects of an issue are discussed together, and a fuller story is revealed; providing context also counters the dualistic tendency to reduce issues into simple, quantitative data. Other methods of acknowledging the interrelatedness of environmental issues in a corporate environmental report include discussion of the supply chain, and life cycle analyses (LCA).

Energy efficiency pays

This year, we have had two of our energy efficiency case studies independently assured by KPMG. The assurance report is available at www.▮▮▮▮▮.com/cr. These case studies illustrate examples of the types of energy efficiency opportunities that we are implementing to reduce greenhouse gas emissions from our building portfolio.

Office Building Energy Efficiency

Whilst extensive energy efficiency works have already been undertaken across the ▮▮▮commercial property portfolio, a further series of opportunities assessments was recently undertaken. This has led to the development of a further program of works across nine key sites in the commercial property portfolio. Works include a variety of control adjustments, several lighting initiatives and disconnection of surplus equipment. This is expected to result in estimated savings of 620 MWh and 680 tCO$_2$-e per annum. This is estimated to deliver annual financial savings of $86,000.

Tri-generation Heat Recovery Module

During the 2010 financial year, we completed the installation and commissioning of a tri-generation system to reduce the greenhouse gas intensity and electricity demand of our main Australian data centre. Subsequently, our National Critical Sites Operations Manager suggested an initiative to incorporate a Heat Recovery Module which was installed in November 2011. This is now estimated to harvest up to 500 kW of available waste heat to preheat hot water for the facility. This has delivered estimated savings of 6,744 GJ of energy and 343 tCO$_2$-e per annum. This is estimated to deliver annual financial savings of $30,000.

Figure 6.19 Case study from Zeta's 2012 environmental report.

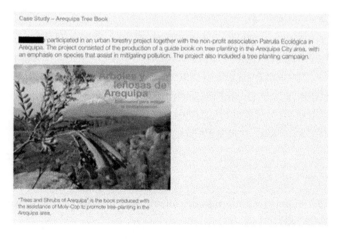

Figure 6.20 Case study in Gamma's 2014 environmental report.

Supply Chain and LCA

When supply chains are discussed, a wider view of a product or service is introduced; the product or service is usually the result of multiple preparatory events and materials, which can have an impact on the natural environment. Omitting these issues, then, tells only a partial account of the environmental impacts of business. Similarly, life cycle analysis considers the after effects of the product or service, beyond that time it is under the direct control of the company.

Many of the environmental reports analysed in this book demonstrate an awareness of these before and after effects of the products or services provided by the company. For instance, the following examples (A quote from Theta's 2013 environmental report, Figures 6.21 and 6.22 and an excerpt from Psi's 2013 environmental report) demonstrate an awareness of the environmental impacts of life cycles and supply chains.

> The Group is committed to establishing a framework for the effective life cycle management of consumer packaging through an educational approach with our team, our trade partners and our customers.
>
> (Theta, 2013)

████s goal is to invest in cleaner energy forms to reduce the greenhouse gas intensity of energy across the supply chain.

(AGL Energy Ltd., 2013, p. 64)

Figure 6.21 Supply chain effects in Phi's 2013 environmental report.

Energy Supply Footprint

The Energy Supply Footprint is an estimate of the total supply chain greenhouse gas emissions associated with the electricity and gas supplied by ████ to its customers. The Energy Supply Footprint covers greenhouse gas emissions resulting from the production, transportation, distribution and consumption of electricity and gas.

(AGL Energy Ltd., 2012, p. 71)

Figure 6.22 Supply chain emissions mentioned in Phi's 2012 environmental report.

Life cycle assessment in Psi's 2013 environmental report:

Life Cycle Assessment
A detailed 'cradle to grave' Life Cycle Assessment (LCA) of [Psi]'s supply chain was undertaken in the reporting year to better understand the environmental impacts of producing [Psi] product and to highlight areas for improvement. LCA is a comprehensive, methodological framework that quantifies the environmental impacts that occur over the lifecycle of a product.
The LCA incorporated upstream and downstream impacts associated with the production of [Psi] product.
Included in the LCA were greenhouse gas emissions, fuel use, water use and eutrophication potential.

The examples provided above establish that for many of the company's analysed in this book, the wider effects of their environmental choices have been considered. This demonstrates an interconnective approach to the natural world which acknowledges the connections between subjects within the environment. The interconnectivity theme is also expressed in the environmental reports and interviews through discussion about influence, as outlined next.

Influence

Influence is defined as the capacity to have an effect on something. The effects of things and events on others is a key aspect of interconnectivity. Influence is discussed in various ways in the environmental reports and interviews which were analysed in this book. For instance, influence was discussed in terms of the influence the company has on customers, as in the first quote from Alpha's 2012 environmental report; on suppliers and contractors, as in the second quote from the Delta interview, and Sigma and Zeta reports and on stakeholders more generally, as in the fifth quote (from Kappa's 2014 environmental report).

We work closely with our customers to influence how our packaging products are disposed of at the end of their life.

(Alpha, 2012)

...the indirect impact of our activities on the environment, so we're trying to influence our suppliers and our contractors as well to try and take that into consideration.

(Delta interview)

> Additionally, we have the ability to influence suppliers and the sustainability credentials of the products and services we procure.
>
> (Sigma, 2013)

> We also influenced the sustainable supply chain industry in Australia by speaking at a number of events.
>
> (Zeta, 2014)

> The Group is also committed to supporting and encouraging its stakeholders to reduce greenhouse gas emissions and energy use in areas within its influence.
>
> (Kappa, 2014)

As these extracts demonstrate, the companies' influence plays a large part in how the company views itself. These extracts illustrate the importance the companies place on influence, whether the influence is directed at suppliers, customers, operations or elsewhere. While the companies generally considered the influence they had on others, the interconnectivity theme also incorporates impacts on the company, such as the impact of nature.

Impact of Nature on Business

Another key way that corporations discuss the interconnected nature of their relationships with the natural world is through the impact of weather on their operations. Most references to weather refer to the effect of climate change on operations, as in the following quotes.

> ...so regardless of whether you accept the science of climate change, you have to accept the fact that you are likely to be impacted by the changes that come out of it.
>
> (Phi interview)

> We are developing innovative financial products and services to help our customers adapt to, and manage, the risks associated with climate policy and impacts....
>
> (Zeta, 2012)

> We anticipate that the physical impacts of climate change and climate-related policy will have a growing impact on our business.
>
> (Zeta, 2014)

> The Energy Services business unit provides strategic consulting advice on climate change risks and opportunities to customers,

implements projects that reduce a customer's carbon footprint, and assists in managing exposure to increased costs related to climate change policy responses.

(Phi, 2012)

Other references to the impact of nature concern the impact of operations – particularly CO_2e emissions – on nature. This concern is demonstrated in the following quotes.

As a consequence, the mitigation of climate change through reductions in GHG emissions remains a key challenge for the business community.

(Delta, 2012)

...whereas energy and emissions, climate change yes we do have a part to play in that, particularly around product stewardship issues....

(Beta interview)

While addressing climate change continues to be a priority for [Zeta], we recognise that our environmental impact is broader than just climate change....

(Zeta, 2012)

The relationship between weather and business is further discussed in terms of broader impacts of climate change, such as the impact on food security and wider social changes. This concern is reflected in the following quotes.

...and now it goes beyond a local scale, then we have the broader climate change discussion, and what will business and food production, food security, what's that going to look like into the future?

(Psi interview)

This type of work adds to our understanding of how our sites behave during different seasons. Nutrients, algae, dissolved oxygen, salinity and a range of other important parameters that influence both fish....

(Psi, 2013)

Other references to the relationship between weather and operations concern more physical references to weather, such as rain, drought and seasonal variances. Some passages which demonstrate this type of discourse follow.

There have been no brolga collisions with turbines and brolgas have successfully bred on the wind farm and continue to return to the site each year for the breeding season.

(Phi, 2014)

Dry summers and extreme temperatures: Dry summers can affect the supply of fresh water used in our hatcheries. Fresh water is also used for bathing fish at marine sites in order to combat the effects of amoebic gill disease (AGD). On extremely hot days there is a risk that water temperature can increase which could lead to an increased chance of thermal stress in our Salmon by the decreased availability of oxygen in the water.

(Psi, 2014)

Much of Australia may become drier in coming decades: Compared to the period 1981–2000, rainfall may decrease in southern areas of Australia during winter, in southern and eastern areas during spring, and in south-west Western Australia during autumn. An increase in the number of dry days is expected across the country, but it is likely that there will be an increase in intense rainfall events in many areas.

(Phi, 2012)

By communicating about the bilateral impacts of climate change, weather events and seasonal changes, the companies are illustrating their awareness that they are in fact an integral part of a wider natural system, which they both impact, and are impacted by. This approach underpins an interconnective environmental philosophy.

Leadership

Leadership involves the action of leading groups and is therefore fundamentally about relationships, and the impacts of subjects on others. As such, discussion about leadership necessarily implies an interconnective approach. The following excerpts demonstrate how leadership is referred to in the environmental reports analysed in this book.

...provide leadership and actively participate in the policy debate on energy and environmental matters.

(Phi, 2012)

The opportunities for [Phi] in cementing a leadership position in low greenhouse gas emitting energy generation and supply are significant. [Phi] continues to be Australia's leading investor in renewable energy....

(Phi, 2012)

[Outlet of Sigma] continues to be an industry leader in the use of recycled water.

(Sigma, 2012)

During the year, [subsidiary of Zeta] also took an active thought leadership role related to New Zealand's rural water quality.

(Zeta, 2014)

As the industry leader in Australian aquaculture, [Psi]'s commitments will have a far-reaching impact on the seafood supply chain in Australia.

(Psi, 2014)

The approach to leadership was supported by the perspectives of interviewees. The following three passages exemplify this reinforcement.

...corporate responsibility, being seen to be a good corporate player, so reputation – a lot of it's to do with reputation – and not wanting to be falling behind our competitors.

(Gamma interview)

...but they were quite exceptional leaders in sustainability reporting and sustainability in general....

(Gamma interview)

We need to be careful; it's a little bit like a herd, unfortunately. If you're too far out the front or the back, you're going to get picked off. You kind of want to be at the front, but kind of the front of the herd, not out on your own. Look there's no problem with being at the very front, but you don't want clear air between you and everybody else. You know what I mean? There's that whole thing – you need to be a little bit careful, because at the end of the day if you're out there, you're not necessarily bringing people with you either, that type of scenario. So you know and that's part of the challenge – people want you to be a leader, everyone wants to be a leader, it's like yes but generally speaking, there can only ever be one real leader.

(Phi interview)

Accordingly, the three philosophical themes which are applied in this book are reflected in a myriad of discursive mechanisms in the reports as well as through the interviews. Outlined above are some of the more frequently used discursive techniques.

Summary

As outlined above, the text analysed in this book is peppered with discursive techniques which implicitly express the three primary philosophical approaches towards the natural environment: dualism, transcendence and interconnectivity. These techniques involve graphical communications such as pictures, graphs and tables; written communications such as wording and topic choices, and numerical expressions. All of these mechanisms carry with them a particular message about how the corporation relates to the natural environment. This chapter has discussed these mechanisms at depth and as such forms a link between the previous results chapter and the analysis which follows.

Note

1 Direct emissions are also known as scope 1 or 2 emissions in carbon accounting. Scope 1 emissions are those emitted from sources that are either owned or controlled by the reporting entity; Scope 2 emissions are all emissions for which the entity is responsible, but do not occur at sources either owned or controlled by the entity, for example emissions from purchased electricity. Scope 3 emissions include other indirect emissions which occur as a result of the entity's purchased materials, and are not directly controlled by the entity, for example outsourced activities, taxi fuel etc. (The Greenhouse Gas Protocol, 2012).

References

AGL Energy Ltd. (2012). *2012 Sustainability Performance Report*. Melbourne, VIC.

AGL Energy Ltd. (2013). *2013 Sustainability Performance Report*. NSW.

Alexander, R. (2009). *Framing Discourse on the Environment*. New York: Routledge.

Archel, P., Husillos, J., & Spence, C. (2011). The Institutionalisation of Unaccountability: Loading the Dice of Corporate Social Responsibility Discourse. *Accounting, Organizations and Society, 36*(6), 327–343.

Ascui, F., & Lovell, H. (2011). As Frames Collide: Making Sense of Carbon Accounting. *Accounting, Auditing & Accountability Journal, 24*(8), 978–999.

Australian Conservation Foundation. (2016). *Australia's 10 Biggest Climate Polluters*. Carlton, VIC.

Australian Government. (2016). *National Greenhouse and Energy Reporting*. Retrieved September 28, 2016, from www.cleanenergyregulator.gov.au

Badiou, A. (2008). *Number and Numbers*. Cambridge: Polity Press.

Beattie, V., & Jones, M. J. (2008). Corporate Reporting Using Graphs: A Review and Synthesis. *Journal of Accounting Literature, 27*, 71–110.

Benschop, Y., & Meihuizen, H. E. (2002). Keeping Up Gendered Appearances: Representations of Gender in Financial Annual Reports. *Accounting, Organizations and Society, 27*(7), 611–636.

Bloomfield, B. P., & Vurdubakis, T. (1997). Visions of Organization and Organizations of Vision: The Representational Practices of Information Systems Development. *Accounting, Organizations and Society, 22*(7), 639–668.

Cacho, O. J., Hean, R. L., & Wise, R. M. (2003). Carbon-Accounting Methods and Reforestation Incentives. *Australian Journal of Agricultural & Resource Economics, 47*(2), 153–179.

Cañón-de-Francia, J., & Garcés-Ayerbe, C. (2009). ISO 14001 Environmental Certification: A Sign Valued by the Market? *Environmental and Resource Economics, 44*(2), 245–262.

Chua, W. F. (1995). Experts, Networks and Inscriptions in the Fabrication of Accounting Images: A Story of the Representation of Three Public Hospitals. *Accounting, Organizations and Society, 20*(2–3), 111–145.

Cooper, C., & Senkl, D. (2016). An(other) Truth: A Feminist Perspective on KPMG's True Value. *Sustainability Accounting, Management and Policy Journal, 7*(4), 494–516.

Dambrin, C., & Robson, K. (2011). Tracing Performance in the Pharmaceutical Industry: Ambivalence, Opacity and the Performativity of Flawed Measures. *Accounting, Organizations and Society, 36*(7), 428–455.

David, C. (2001). Mythmaking in Annual Reports. *Journal of Business and Technical Communication, 15*(2), 195–222.

Davison, J. (2002). Communication and Antithesis in Corporate Annual Reports: A Research Note. *Accounting, Auditing, & Accountability, 15*(4), 594–608.

Davison, J. (2010). [In]visible [in]tangibles: Visual Portraits of the Business élite. *Accounting, Organizations and Society, 35*(2), 165–183.

Davison, J. (2014). Visual Rhetoric and the Case of Intellectual Capital. *Accounting, Organizations and Society, 39*(1), 20–37.

Davison, J., McLean, C., & Warren, S. (2012). Exploring the Visual in Organizations and Management. *Qualitative Research in Organizations and Management, 7*(1), 5–15.

Deegan, C., & Gordon, B. (1996). A Study of the Environmental Disclosure Practices of Australian Corporations. *Accounting & Business Research, 26*(3), 187–199.

Dryzek, J. (2013). *The Politics of the Earth: Environmental Discourses* (3rd ed.). Oxford: Oxford University Press.

Giddens, A. (2008). *The Politics of Climate Change: National Responses to the Challenge of Global Warming.* London: Policy Network.

Global Reporting Initiative. (2015). *G4 Sustainability Reporting Guidelines.* Amsterdam.

Gray, R. (2010). Is Accounting for Sustainability Actually Accounting for Sustainability...and How Would We Know? An Exploration of Narratives of Organisations and the Planet. *Accounting, Organizations and Society, 35*(1), 47–62.

Greenfield, K. (2008). *The Failure of Corporate Law: Fundamental Flaws and Progressive Possibilities.* Chicago, IL: University of Chicago Press.

Hansen, A., & Machin, D. (2008). Visually Branding the Environment: Climate Change as a Marketing Opportunity. *Discourse Studies, 10*(6), 777–794.

Hawken, P. (1993). *The Ecology of Commerce: A Declaration of Sustainability.* New York: Harper Business.

Herzig, C., & Moon, J. (2013). Discourses on Corporate Social Ir/responsibility in the Financial Sector. *Journal of Business Research, 66*(10), 1870–1880.

Hines, R. D. (1992). Accounting: Filling the Negative Space. *Accounting, Organizations and Society, 17*(3–4), 313–341.

Hopwood, A. G. (2009). Accounting and the Environment. *Accounting, Organizations and Society, 34*(3–4), 433–439.

Hrasky, S. (2012). Visual Disclosure Strategies adopted by More and Less Sustainability-driven Companies. *Accounting Forum, 36*(3), 154–165.

Hurteau, M. D. (2008). Carbon Protection and Fire Risk Reduction: Toward a Full Accounting of Forest Carbon Offsets. *Frontiers in Ecology and the Environment, 6*(9), 493–498.

IPCC. (2013). *Climate Change 2013: The Physical Science Basis.* Cambridge: Cambridge University Press.

Irigaray, L. (2004). The Power of Discourse and the Subordination of the Feminine. In J. Rivkin & M. Ryan (Eds.), *Literary Theory: An Anthology* (2nd ed., pp. 795–811). Malden, MA: Blackwell Publishing.

ISO. (2015). *ISO 14001:2015.* Retrieved August 9, 2016, from https://www.iso.org/obp/ui/#iso:std:iso:14001:ed-3:v1:en

Koteyko, N., Thelwall, M., & Nerlich, B. (2010). From Carbon Markets to Carbon Morality: Creative Compounds as Framing Devices in Online Discourses on Climate Change Mitigation. *Science Communication, 32*(1), 25–54.

KPMG. (2013). *The KPMG Survey of Corporate Responsibility Reporting 2013.* Netherlands.

Kress, G., & Van Leeuwen, T. (2002). Colour as a Semiotic Mode: Notes for a Grammar of Colour. *Visual Communication, 1*(3), 343–368.

Kress, G., & Van Leeuwen, T. (2006). *Reading Images: The Grammar of Visual Design* (2nd ed.). London: Routledge.

Latour, B. (2004). *Politics of Nature.* Cambridge, MA: Harvard University Press.

Latour, B. (2014). *The Affects of Capitalism.* Copenhagen: Royal Academy.

Ledin, P., & Machin, D. (2016). A Discourse–design Approach to Multimodality: The Visual Communication of Neoliberal Management Discourse. *Social Semiotics, 26*(1), 1–18.

Mathews, F. (1991). *The Ecological Self.* London: Routledge.

Mathews, F. (2001). Deep Ecology. In D. Jamieson (Ed.), *A Companion to Environmental Philosophy* (pp. 218–232). Cambridge, MA: Blackwell.

Miller, P. (2001). Governing by Numbers: Why Calculative Practices Matter. *Social Research, 68*(2), 379–396.

Morrison, L. (2017). Heading South. *PAN Philosophy Activism Nature, 13*, 101–104.

Morrison, L., Wilmshurst, T., & Shimeld, S. (2018). Environmental Reporting Through an Ethical Looking Glass. *Journal of Business Ethics, 150*(4), 903–918.

Nerlich, B. (2010). Theory and Language of Climate Change Communication. *Wiley Interdisciplinary Reviews. Climate Change, 1*(1), 97–110.

Nerlich, B., & Koteyko, N. (2009). Compounds, Creativity and Complexity in Climate Change Communication: The Case of 'Carbon Indulgences'. *Global Environmental Change, 19*(3), 345–353.

Oxford Dictionary. (2016). *Oxford Living Dictionaries.* Oxford University Press, viewed 3rd October. Retrieved from https://en.oxforddictionaries.com.

Plumwood, V. (1993a). *Feminism and the Mastery of Nature.* London: Routledge.

Plumwood, V. (1993b). The Politics of Reason: Towards a Feminist Logic. *Australasian Journal of Philosophy, 71*(4), 436–462.

Plumwood, V. (2002). Decolonising Relationships with Nature. *PAN: Philosophy Activism Nature, 2*, 7–30.

Plumwood, V. (2006). The Concept of a Cultural Landscape: Nature, Culture and Agency in the Land. *Ethics & the Environment, 11*(2), 115–150.

Plumwood, V. (2009). Nature in the Active Voice. *Australian Humanities Review, 46*, 113–129.

Pollock, N., & D'Adderio, L. (2012). Give Me a Two-by-Two Matrix and I Will Create the Market: Rankings, Graphic Visualisations and Sociomateriality. *Accounting, Organizations and Society, 37*(8), 565–586.

Poole, S. (2006). Essay. *New Statesman, 135*(4780), 34.

Preston, A. M., Wright, C., & Young, J. J. (1996). Imag[in]ing Annual Reports. *Accounting, Organizations and Society, 21*(1), 113–137.

Qu, S. Q., & Cooper, D. J. (2011). The Role of Inscriptions in Producing a Balanced Scorecard. *Accounting, Organizations and Society, 36*(6), 344–362.

Robson, K. (1992). Accounting Numbers as "Inscription": Action at a Distance and the Development of Accounting. *Accounting, Organizations and Society, 17*(7), 685–708.

Rose, N. (1991). Governing by Numbers: Figuring Out Democracy. *Accounting, Organizations and Society, 16*(7), 673–692.

Singer, P. (1990/1975). *Animal Liberation: A New Ethics for Our Treatment of Animals* (2nd ed.). New York: Avon Books.

Spence, C. (2007). Social and Environmental Reporting and Hegemonic Discourse. *Accounting, Auditing & Accountability Journal, 20*(6), 855.

Spence, C. (2009). Social Accounting's Emancipatory Potential: A Gramscian Critique. *Critical Perspectives on Accounting, 20*, 205–227.

Steffen, W., Grinevald, J., Crutzen, P., & McNeill, J. (2011). The Anthropocene: Conceptual and Historical Perspectives. *Philosophical Transactions of the Royal Society, 369*, 842–867.

Stiles, D. (2004). Pictorial Representation. In C. Cassell & G. Symon (Eds.), *Essential Guide to Qualitative Methods in Organizational Research* (pp. 127–139). London: Sage.

The Greenhouse Gas Protocol. (2012). *Calculation Tools*. Retrieved January 30, 2017, from http://www.ghgprotocol.org/

Ummel, K. (2012). *CARMA Revisited: An Updated Database of Carbon Dioxide Emissions from Power Plants Worldwide*. Washington, DC.

Zillmann, D., Gibson, R., & Sargent, S. L. (1999). Effects of Photographs in News-Magazine Reports on Issue Perception. *Media Psychology, 1*(3), 207–228.

7   Unravelling the Discourse

Introduction

The previous two chapters established how corporate environmental reporting implicitly draws from western environmental philosophies by communicating the relationship between the corporation and the natural world discursively. This chapter moves from reporting the findings of the research, to providing an in-depth analysis of what these findings mean. First, it outlines the major findings of the research, highlighting the ways in which the philosophical themes have been woven into the corporate environmental reports analysed in this book. These findings are then linked to the prior research, demonstrating how the thesis of this book grows from, and extends the existing literature. Next, alternative explanations for the findings are provided, along with an explication of the importance and relevance of the research undertaken in this book. The analytic themes which have aided in this analysis are further explicated in this chapter. Following this is a discussion on the meaning of these findings in terms of corporate environmental reporting, and western attitudes towards nature more broadly.

Major Findings

The findings reported in the previous two chapters reveal an important aspect of how corporations communicate about and relate to the natural environment. Despite *what* the organisations are reporting about their interactions with the natural world, this research points towards *how* they are reporting it; it finds that organisations predominantly view the natural world as something from which they are distinct and separate – as an arbitrary extra, but certainly not something of which they are an integral part.

The first layer of results – articulated in Chapter 5 – revealed that most of the environmental reports analysed in this book used a predominantly dualistic approach in their communications about the natural environment. This was demonstrated through the discourse in the reports themselves, and supporting evidence was garnered through the interviews with the sustainability managers of those companies. Two outliers were companies which communicated environmental information through a predominantly interconnected approach, however the interviews for these companies indicated that their sustainability managers adopted a more dualistic approach.

The second layer of results – explicated in Chapter 6 – demonstrated some of the discursive mechanisms which were commonly used in the environmental reports and interviews analysed in this book. These common discursive techniques utilised techniques such as quantitative communication, graphs, images and discursive elements that were predominantly underpinned by a dualistic approach towards the natural world. The relationship between these philosophical themes and the context in which they are placed are discussed below.

Analytical Themes

In order to further explain the findings, the three primary analytic themes are explored in terms of how they were expressed in the corporate environmental reports analysed in this book. While all three philosophical themes were found to varying degrees, dualism was the most evident, through the text as well as through other discursive mechanisms such as graphic design, images and contextual placement.

Dualism

Dualism is an approach to nature which makes a distinction between subjects; particularly between humans and the rest of the natural world. Plumwood (1993) outlines dualism as a logic which not only separates the human experience from the experiences of other subjects within nature, but also creates a hierarchy between the two, where one value (usually human) is valorised at the expense of a second value. This second value is then *backgrounded*, meaning that it is only marginally recognised. To explain *backgrounding*, Plumwood (1993) uses the example of what is traditionally considered the occupation of women (that is, housework, meal preparation, raising children). This work is rarely included in the calculation of GDP, or output of societies, even though the wider, or more masculine occupations traditionally rely upon this work being done (often for little or no recompense) (Waring, 1988). Similarly, the support of the natural environment is rarely recognised in corporate accounts or GDP calculations and is thereby also *backgrounded*.

While dualism has been a foundational aspect of western culture since Plato, its effect was particularly magnified during the Enlightenment, when Descartes philosophically severed the relationship between human reason and the rest of the world. Dualism has come to represent not just the distinction between humans and nature, but also the distinction between subjects and objects within nature. This mechanistic aspect of dualism was illustrated by Mathews (2001) who explained the relationship between Newtonian science which is reflected in the view that parts of nature are interchangeable, much like parts of a machine.

Dualism was found to be the most prevalent approach used in the corporate environmental reports analysed for this book, both in terms of text and context. Since this is one of the driving environmental approaches in contemporary western culture, this alone is not surprising, however the research undertaken in this book contributes to the knowledge that corporations are reinforcing this approach. This finding concurs with earlier research which has found that corporate reports not only construct, but maintain particular socially constructed views (Cooper & Senkl, 2016; Neimark, 1992). The research in this book extends from such prior research by finding that corporations are doing so through the use of dualistic mechanisms to obfuscate, create distance (and thus reduce responsibility) and control perceptions about the environment.

On its own, dualism is a harmful approach towards the natural environment (Hamilton, 2002; Plumwood, 1993). By considering nature as something which is distinct from human life, the normative restraints to its exploitation are removed, thereby reducing the motivations for protecting it (Merchant, 1989; Plumwood, 1993). The use of discourse which supports the view that the natural world is distinct and separate from human life further erodes the normative restrictions to its harm. Such a narrative discursively removes the sense of responsibility by reinforcing the boundaries between humans and nature. A corporate environmental report which draws primarily from a dualistic philosophy is communicating that they are not responsible for the health of the environment, and therefore only reporting arbitrarily, for reasons other than a direct connection or response to the interests of the environment.

In addition to communicating that the company itself implicitly views the environment in this way, the predominance of dualism in the corporate environmental reports also contributes to the construction and maintenance of a dualistic view of reality in broader western culture. The role of corporate reporting in this maintenance is well established (Neimark, 1992), and as corporate power expands in western society, the power to promote the dualistic ideology is also magnified (Raza, Banerjee, & Mir, 2008).

Dualism in Context

In the context of the environmental reports analysed in this book, dualism is found to be part of a system which obfuscates corporate responsibility, creates distance between the company and nature, and attempts to control the natural world. Dualism constitutes this obfuscation by attempting to establish a false sense of authority and objectivity; creating boundaries between the natural world and the corporation and through the use of discursive mechanisms with ambiguous meaning. These techniques point towards the corporate *stepping away* from their responsibility towards nature, even though they appear in a report purporting to establish the corporate response, and therefore implicitly *stepping towards* the natural environment.

For most of the environmental reports analysed in this book, dualism was the predominant theme, as well as the theme which most drew from the common discursive mechanisms. Since dualism is also a predominant philosophical approach in wider western societies, in many respects this finding reflects wider western values. However, the ways in which this approach is expressed in the corporate reports illuminate the extent to which corporate interests have aligned with the view that they should be constructing barriers between their responsibilities and the natural environment.

Creating the illusion of distance between the company and the natural world is also an outcome of the dualistic approach in the environmental reports. By the reduction of environmental values to numerical values, the wide-ranging effects of the environmental decisions made by the companies analysed in this book are rendered invisible; part of a different world to the one occupied by corporate decisions. While environmental reporting seems *prima facie* to be drawing natural values into the corporate realm, what the research in this book has found is that natural values are instead distanced by discursive mechanisms such as numerical communication and the reduction of nature into objective and dislocated values.

Drawing from earlier literature, it was expected that there may be industry specific findings, in which companies within environmentally sensitive industries would report differently to those in other industries. In terms of the research in this book, it was expected that the tendency to separate the company from environmental responsibilities would be more prevalent in those industries which are perceived to be controversial in terms of environmental impacts, however this was not found to be the case. Nor did company size play a role in the reporting approach, as suggested by Gray, Kouhy and Lavers (1995). As shown in the diagram below (Figure 7.1), those companies which are found to be drawing most from dualism are from mixed industries (financial, materials, consumer discretionary, utilities and industrials), and mixed sizes (ranging from the largest company within the multiple case study to the second smallest).

This finding indicates that philosophical barriers towards the natural environment are constructed by companies more generally, and not necessarily in response to the industry to which they belong. However, looking specifically at the companies themselves rather than more generally at the industries to which they belong, there is a tendency for the more controversial companies to more intensively express a dualistic approach.

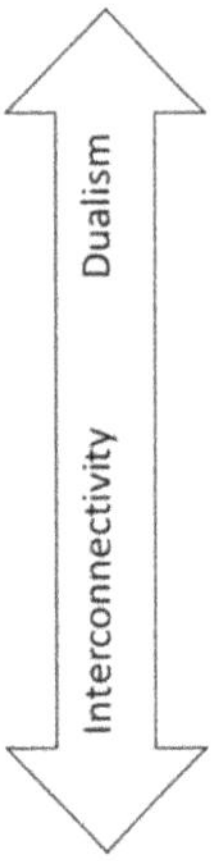

Industries	Pseudonym	Size ranking
Financial	Zeta*	1
Materials	Gamma*	9
Consumer discretionary	Beta	8
Utilities	Phi*	3
Industrials	Delta*	6
Materials	Alpha	2
Real Estate	Kappa	4
Consumer staples	Psi*	10
Consumer discretionary	Theta	7
Consumer discretionary	Sigma	5

Figure 7.1 Philosophical themes compared with industry.

In terms of controversy, Gamma, the materials company (in the mining industry) which is placed towards the dualistic end of this spectrum in the diagram is considered controversial, with the former Prime Minister making an often quoted comment in defence of this company in the face of public criticism regarding its environmental impact (Kenny, 2016; Owen & Kelly, 2011). Similarly, the banking and finance industries are considered controversial in the Australian context (Gluyas, 2016; Verrender, 2016), and the utilities company (Phi) is also facing public criticism regarding its CO_2e emissions (Australian Conservation Foundation, 2016; Hinman, 2016; Robins, 2016). The second controversial materials company (Delta) is closely linked to the mining industry and in particular some contentious mining sites (Dujon Pereira, 2015) and companies (Wiggins, 2016). As such, it has also been associated with the environmental controversies involved.

Viewed in this light, companies which are controversial have tended to report their environmental issues through the lens of dualism in an attempt to construct a barrier between their operations and environmental responsibilities. Of the five companies that are most dualistic in their approach, four have experienced recent controversy in regards to their environmental decisions and impacts (Phi, Gamma, Delta and Zeta). Of the five companies that are least dualistic in their approach, only one is considered controversial (Psi). This finding reflects earlier research which found that companies which had attracted higher levels of negative media attention tended to report on environmental issues more (Brown & Deegan, 1998). In particular, these companies tend to report using more positive language (Islam & Deegan, 2010); a finding which reflects a dualistic approach according to the conceptual framework adopted in this book.

This company (Psi) has been controversial in a localised context. Its operations are centred in a small, relatively sparsely populated area, where local discontent with its environmental impact has been building (Environment Tasmania, 2016). This company has recently been the subject of a highly impactful current affairs programme (Meldrum-Hanna, Balendra, & McDonald, 2016). In the weeks following the programme's airing, shares had dropped by 2.7% (Pash, 2016) and major shareholders had withdrawn their investments (Australian Associated Press, 2016). Since the level of controversy has so recently expanded from a local to a national concern, it would be interesting to note whether this company's environmental reporting approach changes in response to these controversies.

Dualism also expresses an attempt to control the natural world (Cooper & Senkl, 2016). Through the use of tables, charts and numerical expression, the environmental reports analysed in this book convey a message that environmental issues are easily controlled and unable to significantly impact on corporate operations. This analysis is supported by Cooper and Senkl (2016), who arrive at a similar conclusion in their analysis of corporate attempts to reduce environmental values into the logic of accounting.

Overall, dualism is considered a philosophical approach which creates a distance between subjects. In the context of environmental reporting, these subjects are the reporting company and the natural environment. Implications include that the company is attempting to influence readers' perceptions of the level of their responsibility towards the natural world. The research in this book finds that in circumstances where the company is perceived to be excessively impacting on the natural world, one response is to create distance between the company and the environment through discursive mechanisms within the environmental report. These discursive mechanisms construct a barrier which is dualistic in its underpinnings.

Transcendence

Like dualism, transcendence is a philosophical approach which creates a distance between the human and the natural. An approach which underpins the major western religions, transcendence values the abstract over the concrete. In doing so, values such as profit, spirituality and human intelligence are prized above the physical world. This approach is inherent in much of western culture's discourses, however it is less explicitly expressed in the corporate environmental reports analysed in this book.

Since transcendence is as pervasive as dualism in contemporary western culture and discourse (Berman, 1994/2001; Dodson Gray, 1981), its relative absence in the environmental reports analysed in this book sheds light on the use of dualism in such reports. If corporations are expressing their environmental issues in terms of dualism because they are innocuously reflecting the dominant discourse of wider society, then it is expected that transcendence will also play a large role. Since it does not, the question arises – why only dualism?

Since transcendence has the potential for connection, it therefore provides more of a normative restriction to the exploitation of nature than dualism. The use of dualistic expression in the near absence of a transcendent approach, then, points towards a more purposeful use of dualism. This moves the findings of this research beyond corporate reporting as an innocuous reflection of current world views about the environment (Kahn, 1992/2001), and into the realm of the calculative use of an approach which serves the purpose of reducing responsibilities of care towards the natural world.

Transcendence in Context

In the context of the research undertaken in this book, transcendence is often represented through imagery, for example, through images of stairs and pictures with a perspective which faces the sky. Transcendence was also reflected in the reports through a focus on profit an abstract goal which, much like Plato's *forms*, has been given superiority to the terrestrial world by western cultural practice (Latour, 2004). Overall, while transcendence played a part in most of the environmental reports analysed in this book, its role was fractional compared with dualism and interconnectivity.

While transcendence appears in the environmental reports to a much lesser extent than either dualism or interconnectivity, its absence is also telling. At the outset of the research undertaken in this book, it was expected that transcendence and dualism would be found in the environmental reports in greater proportions than interconnectivity. This expectation was based on the observation that dualism and transcendence are philosophies which are predominant in western culture and have profoundly informed the western relationship with nature (Berman, 1994/2001; Dodson Gray, 1981). It is therefore an unexpected finding of this research that transcendence has such a small role in the communication of the corporate relationship with nature.

The relative absence of transcendence in the corporate environmental reports speaks to the tendency to construct barriers through dualism. A message underpinned by transcendence portrays the hierarchical concept that the corporation is of higher value than nature. Since the 1960s though, corporate communications have tended towards the portrayal of an alignment with nature (Howlett & Raglon, 1992/2001). Prior to this, corporate images such as advertisements were predominantly transcendent attempts to perpetuate the idea that corporations could overcome and manipulate nature for the benefit of humans (Howlett &

Raglon, 1992/2001). It seems that the contemporary corporate image prefers to reduce the relationship to nature through a dualistic approach, rather than revert to either transcendence or interconnectivity.

Interconnectivity

Interconnectivity is a philosophical approach to the environment which is at once ancient and contemporary. First articulated by Heraclitus in Ancient Greece (Hadot, 2006), the interconnected nature of the natural world has been at the foundation of numerous indigenous cultures, but most recently has found its way back into western discourse about nature in contemporary environmental philosophy (Brennan & Lo, 2011).

The foundational aspects of interconnectivity in terms of environmental philosophy are the relationships between subjects within the natural world; the valorisation of the specific rather than the universal and the tendency to perceive the world through a feminine lens. An interconnective approach views the world as a series of related subjects; each impacting on the whole. Humans are considered a material aspect of the natural world; but no more or less valued than other subjects (Baird Callicot, 1998, 2001; Leopold, 1998; Mathews, 2001).

Interconnectivity in Context

Interconnectivity represents an approach which acknowledges the relationship between the corporation and the natural environment. In the context of the environmental reports analysed in this book, this approach is found where reference is made to the interrelations of impacts and aspects of the environment. One example is the reference to life cycle analysis, which explicitly recognises that the actions of the company will have an impact for the life of the product or service that it provides. Rather than creating a boundary between the company and its responsibilities to the natural environment, an interconnected approach expands this net of responsibility and acknowledges that the effects of the company's actions will reverberate through natural and social systems for some time and distance.

Interconnectivity is a philosophical approach which is associated with a high degree of sensitivity and empathy towards the natural world. It was not expected that any significant measure of interconnectivity would be found in the corporate environmental reports analysed. Despite this expectation, it was found that interconnectivity plays an important role in the corporate expression of environmental issues. While often portrayed as part of an obfuscating mechanism – particularly in the case of images which express interconnectivity, which are associated with a dualistic textual expression, this approach is frequently drawn from in the environmental reports which were analysed in this book.

In the environmental reports analysed as part of this book, interconnectivity is reflected through discussion of supply chains, through recycling, and when the context of issues is included in discussion.

Meaning and Importance of Findings

While interconnectivity is commonly associated with a healthy relationship to the natural environment, the research undertaken in this book finds that the way corporate reports are currently expressing interconnectivity is far from an authentic acknowledgement of the interrelated nature of the world, and their place in it. Conversely, while dualism is commonly considered to be an unhealthy philosophy in the context of the natural environment, the research in this book found that an element of dualistic discourse might in fact be a necessary way to express environmental issues.

Rather than the expected finding that dualism would represent an unhealthy relationship with the environment, and that interconnectivity should perhaps replace this philosophical approach, a more nuanced approach is found. This approach reflects the environmental reports which demonstrated a more authentic expression of environmental relationships; one which uses a combination of all three approaches.

In the reports analysed in this book, those that used a predominantly interconnective approach were perceived to be from companies which were expressing a less authentic, 'watered down' version of what stakeholders have come to expect from corporate environmental reports. This interpretation is supported by the interview data, which indicated that the sustainability managers of these companies themselves expressed a distant relationship from the environmental impacts of their companies.

Some of the same attributes which make a dualistic approach unhelpful in corporate reporting, such as control and distance (Latour, 2004) are conversely helpful to the stakeholder in keeping the organisation under control from a distance. Numerical expression, while reinforcing distance and control if predominantly used, can be helpful when used in moderation. The stakeholder can understand carbon emissions, recycling rates and energy intensity through the use of numbers, however these quantitative values were found to mislead and obfuscate in many of the reports analysed. To balance this tendency, narrative context provides background and authenticity. Thus, a mix of dualism, transcendence and interconnectivity may be the ideal 'golden mean' for the guiding philosophies of corporate environmental reporting.

Since corporations are perceived to have played a significant role in current environmental problems, it is useful to investigate their relationship towards the natural world. To find that corporations view the environment in a way that is adverse to the wellbeing of the natural world is significant not only because it problematises the way corporations relate to the natural world, but also identifies one way that such a relationship might improve. Re-writing the discourse into what Plumwood describes as "new, less destructive guiding stories" (1993 p. 196) to guide the corporate relationship with nature, is one way to ameliorate the forecasted corrosion of the natural environment (Raupach, McMichael, Finnigan, Manderson, & Walker, 2012; Steffen, Grinevald, Crutzen, & McNeill, 2011).

Meaning of Other Findings

Along with results which point towards a more nuanced use of the philosophical approaches outlined in this book, it was also found that companies which face a higher level of public controversy tend to use a more dualistic approach to construct the illusion of distance between the company and nature. Of the five companies which used the most dualism in their environmental reports, four were considered to have faced a relatively high level of controversy around their environmental impact. Of the five companies which were found to demonstrate less dualism in their environmental reports, only one company was deemed controversial. This controversy was identified through environmental NGO websites and reports as well as media reports online, in newspapers and current affairs programmes, which in the Australian context have a high level of impact.

It was also found that the personal approaches of those who oversee the environmental reporting process tend to 'balance' the reports themselves, by taking on a different philosophical approach. For instance, excepting those two companies who represent the most dualistic view in both reports and interviews, sustainability managers whose company's reports were dualistic, tended to express their views in an interconnective theme. Likewise, the companies whose environmental reports tended to be expressed in a more interconnective way, had environmental managers who expressed their views about the company as well as their own personal views, through a dualistic lens. Reasons for this may include an innate knowledge that the reports are not balanced, and the managers are expressing their views in an opposing way in an attempt to 'balance' the approaches. Alternatively, the managers were able to freely to express their views during the interviews unhindered by the regulatory and corporate pressures imposed on the reporting process.

It was also found that the philosophical themes were expressed through a series of discursive techniques such as tables, graphs, images, placement and context. That these mechanisms express implicit messages in corporate reports is not a new finding, however, the ways that they express underpinning environmental philosophies have not previously been explicated.

Overall, the findings of this research indicate that the way corporations communicate their relationship with the natural world is predominantly dualistic in approach. This dualistic approach attempts to construct a barrier between the company and the natural world, particularly through minimising the appearance of their responsibility towards nature. Companies which are perceived as more environmentally controversial have a tendency to magnify this barrier, perhaps as a mechanism for reducing their connections to such controversy.

The research in this book also found that although a predominant use of dualism contributes to the construction of these barriers, a predominantly interconnective approach has its own set of problems, namely that this approach loses a sense of authenticity and gravitas.

Practical Implications

Practical implications of the findings in this book centre around the claim by participants that environmental reporting has a direct impact on internal corporate decision-making and management. This claim is highlighted in the following passages which are drawn from interviews with the sustainability managers of Psi, Delta, Beta and Sigma, but was also a theme which ran through all of the interviews.

> ...we use energy and waste reporting on the store level, internally to – across 68 stores, to drive competition basically. So we do a leader board every month for who saved the most energy, compared to the same time last year, or who's sending out what levels of waste and recycling and, just to drive behaviours, it's been – it has quite an impact.
>
> (Beta interview)

> ... it's on the ground action, but then people see stuff reported out. I should tell you another really important thing is the transparency piece – for the guys on the farms because if they find a dolphin tangled in the net which we did a couple of years ago, I think 5, 6, 7 years ago people would say shit, we'll keep that quiet, right? ... But now they talk about it, and they'll say, its ok, we'll report it, call DPIPWE, put it in our report, and now what are we going to do to make sure it doesn't happen again?
>
> (Psi interview)

> Honestly I believe that the external stakeholders are a small part of it, I believe it's something that we do, when I joined the business we were always doing a number of retrofit projects, and energy saving projects, but we didn't have anything to wrap them up together, and to transparently to record our achievements, a really key thing is about employee engagement. So we have over eight and a half thousand staff... it's tricky around how to engage them... we're

using sustainability and environment as a key thing to keep our team members informed about what we're doing, to get their ideas, to try and improve the business and we find that it links right into our HR programmes as well.

(Sigma interview)

... also important to get traction internally because you need the – for example you need the site people behind you to identify opportunities and implement different programmes to achieve it, so it needs internal and external management.... I think too internally, because people are more and more aware of environmental issues and they want to be working for a company that I guess is in line with their values, it's important, not just for, not just getting the internal stakeholders behind it to make achievements, but also for talent retention, so that they feel like the company they're working for is doing good things.

(Alpha interview)

Since the reports are clearly perceived to have an impact as tools for internal management and behaviour shaping, the same discursive shaping of values that occurs externally is considered to impact internally. As the contemporary corporation has played a significant role in current environmental conditions, this capacity to change management decision-making makes corporate environmental reporting a powerful tool to affect change both in the wider cultural context, and the narrower context of the company itself. The discursive tools which have been procured by the findings of this research have the capacity to effect behavioural change within the corporation, and are therefore an important contribution.

How These Findings Relate to Prior Literature

These findings build upon previous research which established the socially construct*ing* nature of corporate communications (Hines, 1988; Neimark, 1992); and prior research which delves into the associated meanings and messages which are communicated through this medium (Alexander, 2009; Milne, Kearins, & Walton, 2006; Tregidga, Milne, & Kearins, 2014). In particular, the findings of the research in this book contribute to the literature which argues that the natural environment is impacted by the dominant philosophies of western culture (Merchant, 1989; Plumwood, 1993, 2002), and that corporations are responsible for much of this impact (de Vries, Terwel, Ellemers, & Daamen, 2015; Gray, 2010; Hawken, 1993; Nyilasy, Gangadharbatla, & Paladino, 2014).

Synthesising these literatures, this book brings together the often-disparate disciplines of accounting and environmental philosophy, and expands on the literature which has established the importance of this synthesis

(Alexander & Stibbe, 2014; Milne, Tregidga, & Walton, 2009; Tregidga, Milne, & Lehman, 2012). After all, if philosophy guides behaviour, then the study of the philosophies of corporations towards the natural world is critical.

Social Constructionism

This research project was founded on the idea that the way we view the natural environment is socially constructed. This means that the way we relate to and consider nature is guided by the social rules, shared beliefs and the language we use about nature (Dryzek, 2013). The way we relate to nature is in fact only one of a multitude of possible relationships we might forge with the natural world. We do not forge this relationship alone, but guided by the multitude of directives received through social relationships, through the media and through the reinforcement of particular approaches that are demonstrated around us. One of these 'directives' is through corporate communications. Corporations communicate their values through a myriad of media, one aspect of which is their environmental reporting. In doing so, they not only construct their own reality, but influence the perceptions of wider society as well. Such reports not only influence, but are influenced *by* wider social constructs.

Explorations into the ways in which the western relationship with nature has changed according to various social influences since the Renaissance (Merchant, 1989) and earlier (Hadot, 2006) demonstrate the socially constructed quality of the contemporary western view of the natural environment. This relationship not only involves the view that nature is passive and senseless, but guides the way we interact, impact and use our natural environment. The normative guidance that this relationship places on our actions towards nature is profound (Merchant, 1989; Plumwood, 1993).

Corporate reports are acknowledged in the literature to be vessels for corporate values, and active participants in the social construction of values (Neimark, 1992; Tregidga et al., 2012). By exploring the philosophical underpinnings of corporate environmental reports, these findings have uncovered one of the underpinning guides to the corporate relationship to nature. As with the wider social constructions of nature, this construction governs the actions of the corporation towards nature – either restricting or reinforcing the inclination to exploit.

Western Environmental Philosophy

In order to identify some of the overarching themes in western environmental philosophy, a historical approach was adopted. Following Haraway (2004) and Foucault (1972; Foucault, Rabinow, & Rose, 2003), the present has been considered as a manifestation of the past in this book. As such, the understanding of history as a fundamental guide to understanding contemporary approaches to nature has been supported.

Current environmental problems are commonly blamed on the affluence, practices and ideology of western culture (Figuero & Mills, 2001; Merchant, 2006). This book provides a way to discern and analyse the western approaches towards nature which are in large part responsible for these problems. In particular, this book has expanded on the prior environmental philosophy literature which outlines and discusses the narratives of dualism (Kheel, 2008; Plumwood, 1991, 1993), transcendence (Dodson Gray, 1981; Latour, 2004, 2014; Nash, 1973) and interconnectivity (Mathews, 2001, 2003, 2008; Naess, 1973). By applying these themes to corporate environmental reports, topics which are at times at risk of becoming relegated to abstract theoretical approaches, are grounded in the real-world impacts of corporate interactions with the natural environment.

Corporate Environmental Reporting

Corporate environmental reporting, as an instrument for expressing the relationship between the company and the natural environment, is an ideal location for analysis of this relationship. Fundamentally linked to the social construction of social values (Neimark, 1992; Tregidga et al., 2014), corporate reporting is an important discourse to investigate. In identifying the philosophical underpinnings of such reports, this book extends earlier literature which has explored corporate reporting from the perspective of the construction of the concept of sustainability (Tregidga et al., 2014). It also builds on earlier literature through highlighting the ways in which philosophy can be used to understand the antagonism towards meaningful changes which has been identified by Gray, Adams, and Owen (2014) and others (Milne, Kearins & Walton, 2006; Milne, Tregidga & Walton, 2009; Shafer, 2006).

Link to Theory

Numerous theories have been used to explain corporate environmental reporting. For example, stakeholder and legitimacy theories are two of the more commonly adopted approaches. More recently, institutional theory has become a more commonly adopted perspective used in accounting literature to help understand some of the issues surrounding corporate environmental reporting (Archel, Husillos, & Spence, 2011; Justesen & Mouritsen, 2011). However, the underpinning approach of this book is that of critical theory. Critical theory aims to highlight inequities in the distribution of social power, and draws from social science theorists in the early twentieth century such as Adorno and Horkheimer (Brennan & Lo, 2011).

Horkheimer's approach to critical theory was to build a way to "liberate human beings from the circumstances that enslave them" (1982, p. 244). Through this critical theorist lens, discourse is a powerful mechanism for the 'enslavement' of human beings. Discourse undertakes this role through the implicit messages which are imparted through our social communications in small and subtle, as well as grand and compelling ways. The role of critical discourse analysis in this landscape is to deconstruct the edifice of discourse; to expose the ways discourse has informed our world views. This is also the essential function of critical theory.

The research undertaken in this book enriches the critical theory landscape by expanding the critique of discourse. While the initial intention of critical theory was to liberate people, this project has since been expanded to encompass the dual emancipations of humans and others. The critical theory lens has been used to explore various facets of the human to nature relationship, particularly through critical discourse (Alexander & Stibbe, 2014; van Dijk, 1998). This book builds from this work through the findings which relate to the discourse of corporate environmental reporting, as well as by contributing to the understanding of environmental philosophy's impact on the western view of nature.

Alternative Explanations

It could be argued that these findings relate to western culture at large, and should not be laid exclusively on the shoulders of the corporate world. While it is true that these findings could be generalised to include western culture more broadly, the role of corporate reports in not only maintaining but also in constructing our cultural understandings has been firmly established (Broadbent, 1998; Hines, 1988; Neimark, 1992). So while western culture more generally might share the approaches of the companies analysed in this book, companies are in the privileged position of being able to either reinforce these cultural understandings, or to make fundamental changes towards a healthier relationship with the natural world. The role of corporations in current ecological conditions due to the emissions, the destruction of habitat and the environmental impact of business (Birkin & Polesie, 2011; de Vries et al., 2015) calls for a corporate response to change the way they respond to the natural world (Birkin, 1996; Birkin & Polesie, 2011, 2012). In communicating a version of reality which considers nature as a separate and arbitrary aspect of corporate decision-making, they construct this reality (Hines, 1988). Pointing out some of the ways they construct a reality of the status quo, this book provides a method with which they could make these fundamental changes to integrate considerations of the natural world into the structure of their decision-making processes.

Despite the narratives of innovation and environmental responsibility ostensibly expressed by many large corporations, the findings of the research undertaken in this book indicate that corporations are culturally restricted from stepping out of the crowd. The power and influence of business though, dictates that they are perfectly placed to lead our culture on these fundamental changes (Gray, 2010; Hawken, 1993). The tensions between profit margins, shareholder interests and environmental interests are the primary limitation of these changes being carried out by corporations (Ciepley, 2013; Greenfield, 2008; Strine & Walter, 2015).

Relevance of Findings

The findings discussed in this book contribute to the deconstruction of the dominant hegemonies which inform the western perception of nature. By critiquing the ways in which corporations relate to nature through their environmental reports, western approaches to nature more broadly are also critiqued.

Corporate environmental reporting provides corporations with a means to communicate their relationship with the natural environment. Current practices of environmental reporting perpetuate a 'business as usual' approach to this relationship which maintains dangerous practices (Lehman, 1999). This perspective is reinforced by others who claim that the focus of corporate environmental reporting masks an underlying antagonism towards making meaningful changes that could reduce environmental damage (Gray et al., 2014; Shafer, 2006; Spence, 2009).

If these reports are potentially masking an antagonism towards the natural environment, their scrutiny and critique becomes fundamentally important to the health of the natural world. By investigating the relationships between corporations and the natural world, this book brings to light some of the approaches which are ubiquitous – and therefore largely unquestioned – in western culture. Such a critique opens up a space to deconstruct and reconsider their use.

This book has focused on western environmental philosophy, since the contemporary corporation is characterised by its heritage in western culture. The modern corporate world is a complex structure which collectively controls more of the global economy than many national economies (CorpWatch, 2001; Vitali, Glattfelder, & Battiston, 2011). Along with this immense economic power, modern corporations and the neoliberal model they are founded on have been placed at the heart of the blame for the current degraded condition of the natural environment (Bebbington & Gray, 2001; Gleeson-White, 2014; Hamilton, 2002; Hawken, 1993). By investigating western environmental philosophy, this book sheds light on an important force which influences the relationship between the modern corporation and the natural environment.

Shedding light on the environmental philosophies which guide the actions of corporations exposes some of the approaches which perpetuate the normalisation of dangerous environmental treatment. The first step in solving a problem is to identify it; this book highlights some of the problems inherent in the current environmental harm. Once the philosophical underpinnings of corporate relationship with nature are better understood, the necessary steps towards healing this relationship become possible.

Summary

In this chapter I used the results outlined in the previous two chapters to delve into a deeper analysis by locating and exploring the themes found, and also what these mean to corporate environmental reporting and to the natural environment more widely. I found that the dominant environmental philosophy utilised in the corporate environmental reports analysed was dualism, followed by interconnectivity, with only a fraction of the reports drawing from a transcendent approach. The lack of transcendence in the reports points towards the calculative use of dualism in order to obfuscate and control the perception of environmental damage caused by the company, in part through creating an illusion of distance between the company and nature.

These findings build on prior literature which explores the topics informing the writing of this book, such as that which has established the socially constructed nature of both organisations (Hines, 1988) and our understanding of nature (Dryzek, 2013). Exploring the ways in which corporate reporting interacts with the three primary environmental philosophies extends prior philosophical literature (Brennan & Lo, 2011; Mathews, 2006; Plumwood, 1993), and also contributes to the small but growing field which considers the meanings inherent in corporate reporting (Cooper & Senkl, 2016; Milne et al., 2006; Tregidga et al., 2014).

In particular, this chapter has outlined the ways in which the ideas in this book contribute to not only the literature, but to practice, and more broadly, to current cultural understandings of western relationships with nature. It has explained the link with theory, its relevance, and the implications for wider cultural issues, as well as those related to corporate reporting practice.

References

Alexander, R. (2009). *Framing Discourse on the Environment*. New York: Routledge.
Alexander, R., & Stibbe, A. (2014). From the Analysis of Ecological Discourse to the Ecological Analysis of Discourse. *Language Sciences, 41*(Part A), 104–110. doi:10.1016/j.langsci.2013.08.011

Archel, P., Husillos, J., & Spence, C. (2011). The Institutionalisation of Unaccountability: Loading the Dice of Corporate Social Responsibility Discourse. *Accounting, Organizations and Society, 36*(6), 327–343.

Australian Associated Press. (2016, November 1). Tassal Criticises TV Report as Shares Fall. *news.com.au*. Retrieved from http://www.news.com.au/finance/business/breaking-news/salmon-farmer-tassal-rejects-abc-report/news-story/5331e7162e3146f28b1e0493dfce2c31

Australian Conservation Foundation. (2016). *Australia's 10 Biggest Climate Polluters*. VIC: ACF.

Baird Callicot, J. (1998). The Conceptual Foundations of the Land Ethic. In M. Zimmerman, J. Baird Callicot, G. Sessions, K. J. Warren, & J. Clark (Eds.), *Environmental Philosophy* (pp. 101–123). Upper Saddle River, NJ: Prentice Hall.

Baird Callicot, J. (2001). The Land Ethic. In D. Jamieson (Ed.), *A Companion to Environmental Philosophy* (pp. 204–217). Cambridge, MA: Blackwell.

Bebbington, J., & Gray, R. (2001). An Account of Sustainability: Failure, Success and a Reconceptualization. *Critical Perspectives on Accounting, 12*(5), 557–588. doi:10.1006/cpac.2000.0450

Berman, T. (1994/2001). The Rape of Mother Nature? In A. Fill & P. Muhlhausler (Eds.), *The Ecolinguistics Reader: Language, Ecology and Environment* (pp. 258–269). London: Continuum.

Birkin, F. (1996). The Ecological Accountant: From the Cogito to Thinking Like a Mountain. *Critical Perspectives on Accounting, 7*(3), 231–257. doi:10.1006/cpac.1996.0031

Birkin, F., & Polesie, T. (2011). An Epistemic Analysis of (Un)Sustainable Business. *Journal of Business Ethics, 103*(2), 239–253. doi:10.1007/s10551-011-0863-4

Birkin, F., & Polesie, T. (2012). *Intrinsic Sustainable Development: Epistemes, Science, Business and Sustainability*. Singapore: World Scientific Publishing Company.

Brennan, A., & Lo, Y. (2011). Environmental Ethics. *The Stanford Encyclopedia of Philosophy*. Retrieved from http://plato.stanford.edu/entries/ethics-environmental/

Broadbent, J. (1998). The Gendered Nature of "Accounting Logic": Pointers to an Accounting that Encompasses Multiple Values. *Critical Perspectives on Accounting, 9*(3), 267–297. doi:10.1006/cpac.1997.0158

Brown, N., & Deegan, C. (1998). The Public Disclosure of Environmental Performance Information – A Dual Test of Media Agenda Setting Theory and Legitimacy Theory. *Accounting & Business Research, 29*(1), 21–41.

Ciepley, D. (2013). Beyond Public and Private: Toward a Political Theory of the Corporation. *American Political Science Review, 107*(01), 139–158.

Cooper, C., & Senkl, D. (2016). An(Other) Truth: A Feminist Perspective on KPMG's True Value. *Sustainability Accounting, Management and Policy Journal, 7*(4), 494–516.

CorpWatch. (2001). *Corporate Globalization*. Retrieved from San Francisco: www.corpwatch.org

de Vries, G., Terwel, B., Ellemers, N., & Daamen, D. (2015). Sustainability or Profitability? How Communicated Motives for Environmental Policy Affect Public Perceptions of Corporate Greenwashing. *Corporate Social Responsibility and Environmental Management, 22*(3), 142–154.

Dodson Gray, E. (1981). *Green Paradise Lost.* Wellesley, MA: Roundtable Press.

Dryzek, J. (2013). *The Politics of the Earth: Environmental Discourses* (3rd ed.). Oxford: Oxford University Press.

Dujon Pereira, J. (Writer). (2015). *Black Hole.* Melbourne, VIC.

Environment Tasmania. (2016). Our Marine Campaign. *Environment Tasmania.* Retrieved from http://www.et.org.au/marine

Figuero, R., & Mills, C. (2001). Environmental Justice. In D. Jamieson (Ed.), *A Companion to Environmental Philosophy* (pp. 426–438). Cambridge, MA: Blackwell Publishing.

Foucault, M. (1972). *The Archaeology of Knowledge* (S. Smith, Trans.). New York: Pantheon Books.

Foucault, M., Rabinow, P., & Rose, N. S. (2003). *The Essential Foucault: Selections from The Essential Works of Foucault, 1954–1984.* New York: New Press.

Gleeson-White, J. (2014). *Six Capitals: The Revolution Capitalism Has to Have; or Can Accountants Save the Planet?* Sydney: Allen & Unwin.

Gluyas, R. (2016, October 15). ASIC Chairman Says Australian Banking Industry Is 'an Oligopoly'. *The Australian.* Retrieved from http://www.theaustralian.com.au/business/financial-services/asic-chairman-says-australian-banking-industry-is-an-oligopoly/news-story/e6e279150832b005cb8153553d28e6b3

Gray, R. (2010). Is Accounting for Sustainability Actually Accounting for Sustainability...and How Would We Know? An Exploration of Narratives of Organisations and the Planet. *Accounting, Organizations and Society, 35*(1), 47–62. doi:10.1016/j.aos.2009.04.006

Gray, R., Adams, C., & Owen, D. (2014). *Accountability, Social Responsibility and Sustainability: Accounting for Society and the Environment.* Harlow: Pearson Education.

Gray, R., Kouhy, R., & Lavers, S. (1995). Constructing a Research Database of Social and Environmental Reporting by UK Companies. *Accounting, Auditing & Accountability Journal, 8*(2), 78–101. doi:10.1108/09513579510086812

Greenfield, K. (2008). *The Failure of Corporate Law: Fundamental Flaws and Progressive Possibilities.* Chicago: University of Chicago Press.

Hadot, P. (2006). *The Veil of Isis: An Essay on the History of the Idea of Nature* (M. Chase, Trans.). Cambridge: The Belknap Press of Harvard University Press.

Hamilton, C. (2002). Dualism and Sustainability. *Ecological Economics, 42*(1–2), 89–99. doi:10.1016/S0921-8009(02)00051-4

Haraway, D. J. (2004). *The Haraway Reader.* New York: Routledge.

Hawken, P. (1993). *The Ecology of Commerce: A Declaration of Sustainability.* New York: HarperBusiness.

Hines, R. D. (1988). Financial Accounting: In Communicating Reality, We Construct Reality. *Accounting, Organizations and Society, 13*(3), 251–261.

Hinman, P. (2016, October 7). AGL's Dirty Carbon Emissions — Not So Secret. *Green Left Weekly.* Retrieved from https://www.greenleft.org.au/content/agl%E2%80%99s-dirty-carbon-emissions-%E2%80%94-not-so-secret

Horkheimer, M. (1982). *Critical Theory.* New York: Seabury Press.

Howlett, M., & Raglon, R. (1992/2001). Constructing the Environmental Spectacle. In A. Fill & P. Muhlhausler (Eds.), *The Ecolinguistics Reader: Language, Ecology and Environment* (pp. 245–257). London: Continuum.

Islam, M. A., & Deegan, C. (2010). Media Pressures and Corporate Disclosure of Social Responsibility Performance Information: A Study of Two Global Clothing and Sports Retail Companies. *Accounting and Business Research, 40*(2), 131–148. doi:10.1080/00014788.2010.9663388

Justesen, L., & Mouritsen, J. (2011). Effects of Actor-Network Theory in Accounting Research. *Accounting, Auditing & Accountability Journal, 24*(2), 161–193. doi:10.1108/09513571111100672

Kahn, M. (1992/2001). The Passive Voice of Science. In A. Fill & P. Muhlhausler (Eds.), *The Ecolinguistics Reader: Language, Ecology and Environment* (pp. 241–244). London: Continuum.

Kenny, M. (2016, April 7). Whyalla Wipeout Looms but Carbon Tax Not to Blame, News. *The Sydney Morning Herald*. Retrieved from http://www.smh.com.au/federal-politics/political-news/whyalla-wipeout-looms-but-carbon-tax-not-to-blame-20160407-go0s27.html

Kheel, M. (2008). *Nature Ethics*. London: Rowman & Littlefield.

Latour, B. (2004). *Politics of Nature* (C. Porter, Trans.). Cambridge, MA: Harvard University Press.

Latour, B. (2014). *The Affects of Capitalism*. Paper presented at the the Royal Academy Lecture in the Humanities and Social Sciences, Copenhagen.

Lehman, G. (1999). Disclosing New Worlds: A Role for Social and Environmental Accounting and Auditing. *Accounting, Organizations and Society, 24*(3), 217–241. doi:10.1016/S0361-3682(98)00044-0

Leopold, A. (1998). The Land Ethic. In M. Zimmerman, J. Baird Callicot, G. Sessions, K. J. Warren, & J. Clark (Eds.), *Environmental Philosophy* (pp. 87–100). Upper Saddle River, NJ: Prentice-Hall.

Mathews, F. (2001). Deep Ecology. In D. Jamieson (Ed.), *A Companion to Environmental Philosophy* (pp. 218–232). Cambridge, MA: Blackwell.

Mathews, F. (2003). Becoming Native to the City. In J. Cameron (Ed.), *Changing Places: Re-Imagining Australia* (pp. 197–205). Double Bay, NSW: Longueville Books.

Mathews, F. (2006). Beyond Modernity and Tradition: A Third Way for Development. *Ethics and the Environment, 11*(2), 85–113.

Mathews, F. (2008). Thinking from Within the Calyx of Nature. *Environmental Values, 17*(1), 41–65.

Meldrum-Hanna, C., Balendra, J., & McDonald, A. (Writers). (2016). Big Fish [Television]. In *Four Corners*. Australia: ABC Television.

Merchant, C. (1989). *The Death of Nature: Women, Ecology, and the Scientific Revolution*. New York: Harper & Row.

Merchant, C. (2006). The Scientific Revolution and the Death of Nature. *Isis, 97*(3), 513–533. doi:10.1086/508090

Milne, M. J., Kearins, K., & Walton, S. (2006). Creating Adventures in Wonderland: The Journey Metaphor and Environmental Sustainability. *Organization, 13*(6), 801–839.

Milne, M. J., Tregidga, H., & Walton, S. (2009). Words Not Actions! The Ideological Role of Sustainable Development Reporting. *Accounting, Auditing & Accountability Journal, 22*(8), 1211–1257. doi:10.1108/09513570910999292

Naess, A. (1973). The Shallow and the Deep, Long-Range Ecology Movement. A Summary. *Inquiry, 16*(1–4), 95–100.

Nash, R. (1973). *Wilderness and the American Mind*. New Haven: Yale University Press.

Neimark, M. (1992). *The Hidden Dimensions of Annual Reports: Sixty Years of Conflict at General Motors*. New York: Wiener.

Nyilasy, G., Gangadharbatla, H., & Paladino, A. (2014). Perceived Greenwashing: The Interactive Effects of Green Advertising and Corporate Environmental Performance on Consumer Reactions. *Journal of Business Ethics, 125*(4), 693–707.

Owen, M., & Kelly, J. (2011, April 27). Tony Abbott Presses Carbon Tax Message in Steel City. *The Australian*. Retrieved from http://www.theaustralian.com.au/national-affairs/climate/tony-abbott-presses-carbon-tax-message-in-steel-city/story-e6frg6xf-1226045602963

Pash, C. (2016, November 1). Tassal Shares Drop after Salmon Industry Sustainability Is Questioned. *Business Insider*. Retrieved from http://www.businessinsider.com.au/tassal-shares-drop-after-salmon-industry-sustainability-is-questioned-2016-11

Plumwood, V. (1991). Nature, Self, and Gender: Feminism, Environmental Philosophy, and the Critique of Rationalism. *Hypatia, 6*(1), 3–27.

Plumwood, V. (1993). *Feminism and the Mastery of Nature*. London: Routledge.

Plumwood, V. (2002). Decolonising Relationships with Nature. *PAN: Philosophy Activism Nature, 2*, 7–30.

Raupach, M., McMichael, A., Finnigan, J., Manderson, L., & Walker, B. (2012). *Negotiating Our Future: Living Scenarios for Australia to 2050*. ACT: Australian Academy of Science.

Raza, M., Banerjee, S. B., & Mir, A. (2008). Hegemony and Its Discontents: A Critical Analysis of Organizational Knowledge Transfer. *Critical Perspectives on International Business, 4*(2/3), 203–227. doi:10.1108/17422040810869990

Robins, B. (2016, September 28). AGL Hit by Backlash on Carbon Emissions and Executive Pay. *The Sydney Morning Herald*. Retrieved from http://www.smh.com.au/business/agl-announces-600m-buyback-and-dividend-payout-hike-20160927-grpe9m.html

Shafer, W. (2006). Social Paradigms and Attitudes toward Environmental Accountability. *Journal of Business Ethics, 65*(2), 121–147. doi:10.1007/s10551-005-4606-2

Spence, C. (2009). Social Accounting's Emancipatory Potential: A Gramscian Critique. *Critical Perspectives on Accounting, 20*, 205–227.

Steffen, W., Grinevald, J., Crutzen, P., & McNeill, J. (2011). The Anthropocene: Conceptual and Historical Perspectives. *Philosophical Transactions of the Royal Society, 369*, 842–867.

Strine, L. E., & Walter, N. (2015). Conservative Collision Course?: The Tension between Conservative Corporate Law Theory and Citizens United. *Cornell Law Review, 100*(2), 335–390.

Tregidga, H., Milne, M., & Kearins, K. (2014). (Re)Presenting 'Sustainable Organizations'. *Accounting, Organizations and Society, 39*(6), 477–494. doi:10.1016/j.aos.2013.10.006

Tregidga, H., Milne, M., & Lehman, G. (2012). Analyzing the Quality, Meaning and Accountability of Organizational Reporting and Communication: Directions for Future Research. *Accounting Forum, 36*(3), 223–230. doi:10.1016/j.accfor.2012.07.001

van Dijk, T. (1998). *Ideology: A Multidisiplinary Approach*. London: Sage.

Verrender, I. (2016, 10 October). Distrust in Government, Banking Industry Needs Urgent Attention for Sake of Economy, Analysis. *ABC News.* Retrieved from http://www.abc.net.au/news/2016-10-10/distrust-in-government,-banking-industry-needs-urgent-attention/7916788

Vitali, S., Glattfelder, J., & Battiston, S. (2011). The Network of Global Corporate Control. *PLoS One,* 6(10), e25995.

Waring, M. (1988). *Counting for Nothing: What Men Value and What Women Are Worth.* New Zealand: Allen and Unwin.

Wiggins, J. (2016, 6 July). Downer Does New Deal with Adani to Develop Indian Coalmines. *Financial Review.* Retrieved from http://www.afr.com/business/construction/downer-does-new-deal-with-adani-to-develop-indian-coal-mines-20160706-gpztaj

8 Reflecting on the Discourse of the Corporate Report

Introduction

Western environmental philosophies underpin and inform the western relationship with the natural world. In doing so, they provide a lens through which to observe and analyse the range of ways those in the West consider, interact with and approach nature. This research has explored the ways in which western environmental philosophy is conveyed through contemporary corporate environmental reports, and what this reveals about the corporate relationship with the natural world. Understanding corporate reporting from this perspective strengthens the existing knowledge of such practices.

This chapter concludes the book by underlining the narrative which has grown from the literature reviews, the methodology, the major findings, and the analysis undertaken in addressing questions about how western environmental philosophy is communicated through corporate environmental reporting, and what this means about the corporate relationship with nature.

This will lead to a discussion of the original contributions and significance of this research. Also acknowledged are the limitations involved in this research project, and suggestions for further research which could extend, challenge or supplement the findings in this book, and the extant knowledge of corporate environmental reporting practices, particularly through the lens of environmental philosophy.

Background

The motivation for this research project stemmed from the apparent disconnect between the cultural environmental discourse, and the parallel stagnation in terms of *actual* care for the environment. Such care would be evident through a reduction in CO_2e emissions (Baskin, 2015; IPCC, 2013), a pause and reversal in the rate of flora and fauna extinctions (Baskin, 2015; Gregory, 2009), expansion of natural habitat, reduction of pollution (Moore, 2012; Ryan, Moore, van Franeker, & Moloney, 2009) and a cessation (or at least a reduction) in the consumption of non-renewable resources, leading to the stabilisation of, and decrease in global temperatures (Raupach, McMichael, Finnigan, Manderson, & Walker, 2012; Steffen, Grinevald, Crutzen, & McNeill, 2011). In other words, if the public discourse was realised, an improvement in the well-being of the natural environment would be evident. Despite the apparent intention underpinning the cultural discourse, these changes are not evident, and the rise in global temperatures (IPCC, 2013), extinction rates (Steffen et al., 2011), pollution and the consumption of non-renewable resources continue to be observed (Raupach et al., 2012).

While the corporate world is not responsible for all of this damage, it has been argued that corporate acts of commerce are implicated in many of the environmental problems that the world now experiences (Birkin & Polesie, 2011; Birkin & Polesie, 2012; Hawken, 1993). As such, the relationship between nature and corporate reporting is an important narrative to examine. One way to explore the corporate relationship with the natural world is through the lens of western environmental philosophy.

Bringing these issues together, corporate environmental reporting sits at the junction between western environmental philosophy, cultural discourse and the environmental interactions of large corporations. Drawing from a history of western attitudes towards nature, this book has demonstrated how corporate environmental reporting elucidates the relationship between the corporation and nature. In exploring this relationship, and to unravel the problem of the apparent dissimilitude between cultural discourse and ongoing multiple environmental problems, the philosophies which underpin such practice have been investigated in this book.

Environmental Philosophies

Three prominent philosophical themes were highlighted and explored: dualism, transcendence and interconnectivity. How these themes have been integrated into our cultural understanding of nature, and the corporate relationship with the natural world was explored.

Ranging from the pre-Socratic era to contemporary times, the three approaches are woven through the fabric of western culture. The historical view which was taken in Chapter 2 followed a nonlinear thread which reflects Haraway's *amodern* account of the role of history (2004), and Foucault's *genealogy* (1972), both of which hold that the present and the past interweave to form a constantly negotiated *now*.

Haraway's (2004) *amodern* historical approach was applied through a social constructionist lens. This means that historical philosophical approaches to nature have been embedded into the contemporary western world view through social practices such as the production and consumption of discourse (Alexander, 2009). In this way, environmental philosophy influences not only cultural attitudes, but also guides actions towards the natural world (Hay, 2002); structuring the normative ethical restraints to its exploitation (Merchant, 1989; Plumwood, 1993). The intimate relationship between environmental philosophy and the treatment of the natural world was explored through the multiple lenses of dualism, transcendence, and interconnectivity, each of which sanctions different treatments of nature.

Of these three philosophical themes, dualism and transcendence are the most prevalent in western culture. Chapter 2 illustrated how the roots of contemporary dualism and transcendence can be traced to the Platonian philosophy of Ancient Greece (Plumwood, 1993), and are now reflected in powerful western conventions such as Christianity, neoliberal economics, Newtonian science and Cartesian philosophy (Abram, 1996). The beginnings of the philosophical separation of humans and nature have continued to be woven through western philosophies and world views through time (Wiman, 1990). The argument was established here that these traditions in thought support the rationalisation of economic benefit at the expense of the natural environment (Kheel, 2008; Warren, 1998).

In contrast to both dualism and transcendence, interconnectivity is a philosophical approach which promotes a respect for and relationship with the natural world; placing humans within – as opposed to separate from – nature (Naess, 1973). Interconnectivity's branches connect contemporary environmental philosophies such as ecofeminism (Kheel, 2008) and deep ecology (Fox, 2000), with Ancient Greek philosophers such as Heraclitus (Hadot, 2006) and Aristotle (Ackrill, 1981) in a holistic view of the world.

The ways in which changes in western environmental philosophy have reflected similar changes in corporate reporting highlights the ways in which accounting – and corporate environmental reporting in particular – constructs barriers which reinforce dualistic approaches towards the natural world. Dualism in this sense is expressed through other parallel ideologies such as neoliberal economics (Hamilton, 2002) and post-Enlightenment thought, and through mechanisms such as quantitative expression and positivist language (Plumwood, 1993). These cultural discourses construct and maintain an attitude towards nature which is embedded in the shared language which is used in corporate environmental reports.

While the increasing production of environmental reports represents a potential step towards diminishing the metaphorical distance between organisational understanding and nature, it is yet to realise this capacity (Spence, 2009). In an attempt to realise this potential, I have in this book, deconstructed and critiqued the philosophies which underpin accounting and the approaches of corporations in their relationships with the natural world.

In order to identify and analyse the underpinning philosophical approaches of contemporary corporate environmental reporting, I adopted a multiple case study approach, in a search for multiple perspectives. To recap, ten ASX 200 listed companies were selected, and from each of these ten companies, three years of environmental reporting was collected. In addition, semi-structured interviewing techniques allowed for the in-depth discussion of values, ethics, ambiguities and some of the intangible perspectives of the managers overseeing this corporate reporting process (Peräkylä & Ruusuvuori, 2011). Critical discourse analysis was applied to the reports and interviews to unmask implicit meanings (Fairclough, 1992/2003). This analysis was undertaken through the lens of the three philosophical themes which have informed western environmental philosophy since at least the Ancient Greek era: dualism, transcendence and interconnectivity.

The Verdict?

The research in this book unveiled some important aspects regarding how corporations communicate about and relate to the natural environment. While organisations may be reporting on the topics required, *how* they are communicating in their environmental reports is problematic, in that it is masking an antagonism towards the natural world which constructs a dualistic barrier separating the natural world from corporate activities. Western environmental philosophies are being implicitly communicated in corporate environmental reporting through a series of discursive motifs and mechanisms which convey a perception of the natural world as distinct and separate. In doing so, these companies are reducing the sense of responsibility they are perceived to have towards the well-being of the natural world.

While this could be understood as an innocuous reflection of wider cultural values (since dualism is one of western culture's dominant worldviews), the lack of transcendent approaches in the corporate reports points towards a more strategic attempt to communicate this implicit perception. This is because both dualism *and* transcendence are the dominant cultural philosophies of the West (Dodson Gray, 1981; Plumwood, 1993). If the reports were innocuously reflecting cultural values, then it is reasonable to expect a significant expression of *both* of these sets of philosophies.

Conversely, the findings indicate that while a predominantly dualistic approach constructs an unhelpful barrier, an absence of dualism is also problematic. The corporate reports which were most interconnective in their approach to the natural world were found to lack gravity. While the corporate bias towards dualism found in many of these reports tended towards a control *of the natural world*, dualism might also be useful in the control *of the company* in its environmental interactions. In this way, a combination of philosophical approaches may provide the ideal way to construct and communicate a convincingly authentic and reliable corporate relationship with the natural world.

Other findings which support this analysis include the more predominant use of a dualistic approach found in the reports of the five companies which are considered to be the most environmentally controversial companies of the case studies analysed in this book. That these companies would hope to decrease the perception of their environmental responsibilities reflects the level of public scrutiny that they have undergone. These findings concur with and extend the extant accounting literature which claims that corporate environmental and sustainability reporting masks an underlying indifference towards the natural world (Gray, 2010; Gray & Milne, 2002).

Contribution of Research

In responding to the motivations which have guided the research undertaken in this book, a number of important contributions have been made. First, it has made a significant contribution to our understanding of cultural discourse about the natural world. This is an important contribution because the discourse used in relation to nature not only describes the approaches used in the treatment of nature, but also constructs the ethical boundaries within which the treatment of nature is either accepted or not (Alexander, 2009; Alexander & Stibbe, 2014). In exploring cultural discourse, the normative restraints which guide the western relationship with the natural world are also exposed for critique. An increase in the awareness of how these normative guides are constructed and maintained offers western culture a way to *re*construct and maintain a healthier set of cultural guides with which to inform our treatment of nature.

Focusing on this broader contribution towards the corporate relationship with nature, the research outlined in this book offers corporations a way to foster a more authentic and robust relationship with nature, through making a shift in the discourse provided in their environmental reports. The importance of such discourse has been highlighted as more than 'just talk' about the environment, but as a tool to shape (or *re*shape) and maintain not only the corporate, but also the cultural relationship with nature (Spence, 2007, 2009). These contributions advance understandings of the cultural (and corporate) relationship with nature, building on earlier research which has pointed towards this perception within the accounting literature, for instance that which has critiqued corporate environmental and sustainability reporting as inauthentic (Gray, 2010), misleading (Livesey, 2001, 2002), or antagonistic towards the health of the natural world (Gray, 2010; Lehman, 1999). Other bodies of accounting literature to which this book contributes include those which have explored the socially constructing nature of the corporate report (Hines, 1988; Neimark, 1992), and those which explore the underpinning meanings which are communicated through such reporting processes (Bebbington & Gray, 2000; Cooper & Senkl, 2016; Milne, Kearins, & Walton, 2006; Milne, Tregidga, & Walton, 2009; Spence, 2007; Tregidga, Milne, & Kearins, 2014; Tregidga, Milne, & Lehman, 2012).

Practical implications centre around many of the interviewees' claims that that their companies' environmental reporting has a direct impact on internal corporate decision-making and management. The capacity to drive management decision-making makes corporate environmental reporting a powerful tool to effect change both in the wider cultural context, and the specific context of the company itself. The discursive and philosophical mechanisms which have been identified in this book have the capacity to effect behavioural change within the corporation, and therefore comprise an important contribution.

This book contributes to critical theory by expanding the critique of discourse. While the initial intention of critical theory was to liberate people, it has since been expanded to encompass the freedoms of others – such as nature – as well. A critical lens has previously been used to explore the human-nature relationship, particularly through discourse (Alexander & Stibbe, 2014; van Dijk, 1998). By exploring the discourse of corporate environmental reporting, the research undertaken in this book has built from previous literature, as well as contributing to the understanding of environmental philosophy's impact on the western view of nature through corporate reporting.

This book also contributes to the bodies of literature which have explored the discursive impact of corporate reporting (Alexander, 2009; Alexander & Stibbe, 2014; Archel, Husillos, & Spence, 2011; Milne et al., 2009), and of environmental discourse more broadly (Alexander, 2009; Butteriss, Wolfenden, & Goodridge, 2001; Clare, Krogman, & Caine, 2013; Dick, 2004; Dryzek, 2013; Fairclough, 2013). In this way, the thesis presented here advances not only theoretical understanding, but also provides an interpretation of methods with which future researchers might arm themselves on similar explorations.

Limitations

The research undertaken in this book has been guided by an interpretive and somewhat subjective process of analysis. This means that although the research is governed by the confines of academic rigour, it is also informed by my own values. While some may consider this a limitation, many regard the acknowledgment of subjectivity, and the inclusion of researcher values as a strength (Berman, 1994/2001). Accordingly, this project might have been undertaken with any number of analytical themes and was restricted to dualism, transcendence and interconnectivity based on my own understanding and interpretation of the philosophical literature. Similarly, the application of these themes to the environmental reports of the sample companies was based on my interpretation of the text. Since this type of research is a growing area, there was scant prior literature to guide this part of the analysis. Despite this limitation, I have consistently justified and explained my interpretations, adding to the credibility of the research.

Suggestions for Further Research

Suggested research for the future which could grow from this book includes research which replicates this analysis in a larger sample. This might include an expanded number of reports and interviews, or reports only. Similarly, an expanded longitudinal aspect is likely to uncover the changing corporate relationship with nature, in a similar way to Neimark's (1992) longitudinal study of corporate attitudes towards gender and class. Rather than restricting this sample to companies listed only in Australia, such research could also include companies listed in other western countries. This would strengthen the claim that these findings relate to western culture more generally, instead of an exclusively Australian context. Alternatively, an interesting study would compare the philosophical underpinnings of environmental reports which have been informed by different cultures.

Research which could extend the findings in this book that companies which are considered more controversial provided environmental reports with a higher level of dualism would be beneficial. The question of whether different types of controversies engender different disclosures could be answered in future suggested research. This research could build from earlier findings, such as those in Islam and Deegan (2010), and Brown and Deegan (1998), which view environmental reporting through the lenses of legitimacy and media agenda setting theories.

Other suggested research for the future includes using different conceptual frameworks. One example of this is in Morrison, Wilmshurst and Shimeld (2018), where the framework for analysis is built from environmental ethics. Accordingly, utilitarianism, deontology and virtue ethics were used in the analysis, however there are numerous other frameworks which could contribute to current understandings of corporate environmental reporting.

Including an analysis of shadow accounts would also contribute to the extant literature about corporate environmental reporting. Dey (2003, 2007) outlines the potential uses for shadow accounts, which draw from sources outside of the corporate boundary, including online forums, NGO reports, blogs, and the wider public discourse which informs stakeholder views about particular corporations. Future research could expand on this intertextuality by exploring the role of other perspectives such as those presented in shadow accounts (Dey, 2003, 2007). This would underpin any claims regarding the authenticity (or otherwise) of corporate reports; since if other media and groups are reporting information which conflicts with the corporate narrative, the corporate reports become less credible (Adams, 2004).

During the undertaking of this research, I was acutely aware of the possible accusation of Eurocentrism which might arise from the focus on western environmental philosophies. As explained in Chapter 2, the focus on western philosophies arose from an awareness of the damage caused by western corporations, affluence and lifestyle, and not from any bias against other environmental perspectives. On the contrary, research exploring environmental philosophies which reflect indigenous and other cultural views towards nature would highlight many alternatives to the current western focus, many of which would likely produce a much healthier approach to the natural world (Plumwood, 1993, 2002).

Summary

The findings of this book indicate that corporate environmental reporting expresses a level of antagonism towards the natural world through a heavy bias towards a dualistic approach to nature. This approach constructs a barrier which separates the corporation (and its environmental responsibilities) from the physical impact of its decision-making. Such a separation was more intentional than expected, as indicated by the proportions of other philosophical approaches found.

Conversely, while a predominantly dualistic approach constructs an unhelpful barrier, an absence of dualism is also problematic. In response, a combination of philosophical approaches may be the ideal way to construct and express an authentic and felicitous relationship with the natural world.

The aim of this book was to explore the disparity between the social discourse which purported to care for the environment, and the actual outcome of such discourse, which seemed to be pointing in the opposite direction. In exploring this gap, corporate environmental reporting provided the material and, examined through the lens of western environmental philosophy, the gap was identified and further analysed. At the end of this book, the claim can now be made that the object which impedes the apparent intentions behind the corporate environmental discourse is the predominantly dualistic philosophical approach. Steps towards the repair of such discourse have been suggested, and fields of further research in this direction are now possible.

References

Abram, D. (1996). *The Spell of the Sensuous: Perception and Language in a More-than-Human World.* New York: Vintage Books.

Ackrill, J. L. (1981). *Aristotle the Philosopher.* Oxford: Clarendon Press. cat02831a database.

Adams, C. (2004). The Ethical, Social and Environmental Reporting-Performance Portrayal Gap. *Accounting, Auditing & Accountability Journal, 17*(5), 731–757.

Alexander, R. (2009). *Framing Discourse on the Environment.* New York: Routledge.

Alexander, R., & Stibbe, A. (2014). From the Analysis of Ecological Discourse to the Ecological Analysis of Discourse. *Language Sciences, 41*(Part A), 104–110.

Archel, P., Husillos, J., & Spence, C. (2011). The Institutionalisation of Unaccountability: Loading the Dice of Corporate Social Responsibility Discourse. *Accounting, Organizations and Society, 36*(6), 327–343.

Baskin, J. (2015). Paradigm Dressed as Epoch: The Ideology of the Anthropocene. *Environmental Values, 24*(1), 9–29.

Bebbington, J., & Gray, R. (2000). Accounts of Sustainable Development: The Construction of Meaning within Environmental Reporting. *Aberdeen Papers in Accountancy, Finance & Management*, Working Paper No. 00-18.

Berman, T. (1994/2001). The Rape of Mother Nature? In A. Fill & P. Muhlhausler (Eds.), *The Ecolinguistics Reader: Language, Ecology and Environment* (pp. 258–269). London: Continuum.

Birkin, F., & Polesie, T. (2011). An Epistemic Analysis of (Un)Sustainable Business. *Journal of Business Ethics, 103*(2), 239–253.

Birkin, F., & Polesie, T. (2012). *Intrinsic Sustainable Development: Epistemes, Science, Business and Sustainability.* Singapore: World Scientific Publishing Company.

Brown, N., & Deegan, C. (1998). The Public Disclosure of Environmental Performance Information – A Dual Test of Media Agenda Setting Theory and Legitimacy Theory. *Accounting & Business Research, 29*(1), 21–41.

Butteriss, C., Wolfenden, J. A. J., & Goodridge, A. P. (2001). Discourse Analysis: A Technique to Assist Conflict Management in Environmental Policy Development. *Australian Journal of Environmental Management, 8*(1), 48–58.

Clare, S., Krogman, N., & Caine, K. J. (2013). The "Balance Discourse": A Case Study of Power and Wetland Management. *Geoforum, 49*(0), 40–49.

Cooper, C., & Senkl, D. (2016). An(other) Truth: A Feminist Perspective on KPMG's True Value. *Sustainability Accounting, Management and Policy Journal, 7*(4), 494–516.

Dey, C. (2003). Corporate 'Silent' and 'Shadow' Social Accounting. *Social and Environmental Accountability Journal, 23*(2), 6–9.

Dey, C. (2007). Developing Silent and Shadow Accounts. In J. Unerman, J. Bebbington, & B. O'Dwyer (Eds.), *Sustainability Accounting and Accountability* (pp. 307–326). Oxon: Routledge.

Dick, P. (2004). Discourse Analysis. In C. Cassell, & G. Symon (Eds.), *Essential Guide to Qualitative Methods in Organizational Research* (pp. 204–213). London: Sage.

Dodson Gray, E. (1981). *Green Paradise Lost.* Wellesley, MA: Roundtable Press.

Dryzek, J. (2013). *The Politics of the Earth: Environmental Discourses* (3rd ed.). Oxford: Oxford University Press.

Fairclough, N. (1992/2003). *Discourse and Social Change.* Cambridge: Polity Press.

Fairclough, N. (2013). *Analysing Discourse: Textual Analysis for Social Research* (2nd ed.). Abingdon: Routledge.

Foucault, M. (1972). *The Archaeology of Knowledge.* New York: World of Man, Pantheon Books.

Fox, W. (2000). Deep Ecology and Virtue Ethics. *Philosophy Now, 26*(April/May), 21–23.

Gray, R. (2010). Is Accounting for Sustainability Actually Accounting for Sustainability...and How Would We Know? An Exploration of Narratives of Organisations and the Planet. *Accounting, Organizations and Society, 35*(1), 47–62.

Gray, R., & Milne, M. (2002). Sustainability Reporting: Who's Kidding Whom?. *Chartered Accountants Journal, 81*(6), 66–70.

Gregory, M. R. (2009). Environmental Implications of Plastic Debris in Marine Settings—Entanglement, Ingestion, Smothering, Hangers-On, Hitch-Hiking and Alien Invasions. *Philosophical Transactions: Biological Sciences, 364*(1526), 2013–2025.

Hadot, P. (2006). *The Veil of Isis: An Essay on the History of the Idea of Nature.* Cambridge: The Belknap Press of Harvard University Press.

Hamilton, C. (2002). Dualism and Sustainability. *Ecological Economics, 42*(1–2), 89–99.

Haraway, D. J. (2004). *The Haraway Reader.* New York: Routledge.

Hawken, P. (1993). *The Ecology of Commerce: A Declaration of Sustainability.* New York: HarperBusiness, cat02831a database.

Hay, P. (2002). *Main Currents in Western Environmental Thought.* Sydney: University of New South Wales Press.

Hines, R. D. (1988). Financial Accounting: In Communicating Reality, We Construct Reality. *Accounting, Organizations and Society, 13*(3), 251–261.

IPCC. (2013). *Climate Change 2013: The Physical Science Basis.* Cambridge: Cambridge University Press.

Islam, M. A., & Deegan, C. (2010). Media Pressures and Corporate Disclosure of Social Responsibility Performance Information: A Study of Two Global Clothing and Sports Retail Companies. *Accounting and Business Research, 40*(2), 131–148.

Kheel, M. (2008). *Nature Ethics.* London: Rowman & Littlefield.

Lehman, G. (1999). Disclosing New Worlds: A Role for Social and Environmental Accounting and Auditing. *Accounting, Organizations and Society, 24*(3), 217–241.

Livesey, S. M. (2001). Eco-Identity as Discursive Struggle: Royal Dutch/Shell, Brent Spar, and Nigeria. *Journal of Business Communication, 38*(1), 58–91.

Livesey, S. M. (2002). Global Warming Wars: Rhetorical and Discourse Analytic Approaches to Exxonmobil's Corporate Public Discourse. *Journal of Business Communication, 39*(1), 117–146.

Merchant, C. (1989). *The Death of Nature: Women, Ecology, and the Scientific Revolution.* New York: Harper & Row, cat02831a database.

Milne, M. J., Kearins, K., & Walton, S. (2006). Creating Adventures in Wonderland: The Journey Metaphor and Environmental Sustainability. *Organization, 13*(6), 801–839.

Milne, M. J., Tregidga, H., & Walton, S. (2009). Words Not Actions! The Ideological Role of Sustainable Development Reporting. *Accounting, Auditing &
Accountability Journal, 22*(8), 1211–1257.

Moore, C. (2012). *Plastic Ocean.* New York: Penguin.

Morrison, L., Wilmshurst, T., & Shimeld, S. (2018). Environmental Reporting Through an Ethical Looking Glass. *Journal of Business Ethics, 150*(4),
903–918.

Naess, A. (1973). The Shallow and the Deep, Long-Range Ecology Movement.
A Summary. *Inquiry, 16*(1–4), 95–100.

Neimark, M. (1992). *The Hidden Dimensions of Annual Reports: Sixty Years
of Conflict at General Motors.* Wiener New York: Critical Accounting Theories, cat02831a database.

Peräkylä, A., & Ruusuvuori, J. (2011). Analyzing Talk and Text. In N. K.
Denzin & Y. S. Lincoln (Eds.), *The Sage Handbook of Qualitative Research*
(4th ed., pp. 529–543). Thousand Oaks: Sage.

Plumwood, V. (1993). *Feminism and the Mastery of Nature.* London: Routledge.

Plumwood, V. (2002). Decolonising Relationships with Nature. *PAN: Philosophy Activism Nature, 2*, 7–30.

Raupach, M., McMichael, A., Finnigan, J., Manderson, L., & Walker, B.
(2012). *Negotiating Our Future: Living Scenarios for Australia to 2050.*
Canberra: ACT, AAo Science.

Ryan, P. G., Moore, C. J., van Franeker, J. A., & Moloney, C. L. (2009).
Monitoring the Abundance of Plastic Debris in the Marine Environment.
Philosophical Transactions: Biological Sciences, 364(1526), 1999–2012.

Spence, C. (2007). Social and Environmental Reporting and Hegemonic
Discourse. *Accounting, Auditing & Accountability Journal, 20*(6), 855.

Spence, C. (2009). Social Accounting's Emancipatory Potential: A Gramscian
Critique. *Critical Perspectives on Accounting, 20*, 205–227.

Steffen, W., Grinevald, J., Crutzen, P., & McNeill, J. (2011). The Anthropocene: Conceptual and Historical Perspectives. *Philosophical Transactions of
the Royal Society, 369*, 842–867.

Tregidga, H., Milne, M., & Kearins, K. (2014). (Re)presenting 'Sustainable
Organizations'. *Accounting, Organizations and Society, 39*(6), 477–494.

Tregidga, H., Milne, M., & Lehman, G. (2012). Analyzing the Quality, Meaning and Accountability of Organizational Reporting and Communication:
Directions for Future Research. *Accounting Forum, 36*(3), 223–230.

van Dijk, T. (1998). *Ideology: A Multidisiplinary Approach.* London: Sage.

Warren, K. J. (1998). The Legacy of Carolyn Merchant's The Death of Nature.
Organization & Environment, 11(2), 186–188.

Wiman, I. M. B. (1990). Expecting the Unexpected: Some Ancient Roots to
Current Perceptions of Nature. *AMBIO, 19*(2), 62–69.

Index

Note: *Italic* page numbers refer to figures

For Product Safety Concerns and Information please contact our EU
representative GPSR@taylorandfrancis.com
Taylor & Francis Verlag GmbH, Kaufingerstraße 24, 80331 München, Germany

www.ingramcontent.com/pod-product-compliance
Ingram Content Group UK Ltd.
Pitfield, Milton Keynes, MK11 3LW, UK
UKHW020940180425

457613UK00019B/484